Education, Indigenous Knowledges, and Development in the Global South

The book's focus is the hegemonic role of so-called modernist, Western epistemology that spread in the wake of colonialism and the capitalist economic system, and its exclusion and Othering of other epistemologies.

Through a series of case studies the book discusses how the domination of Western epistemology has had a major impact on the epistemological foundation of the education systems across the globe. The book queries the sustainability of hegemonic epistemology both in the classrooms in the global South as well as in the face of the imminent ecological challenges of our common earth, and discusses whether indigenous knowledge systems would better serve the pupils in the global South and help promote sustainable development.

Anders Breidlid is Professor of International Education and Development at Oslo University College.

Routledge Research in Education

For a full list of titles in this series, please visit www.routledge.com.

Education, Indigenous Knowledges, and Development in the Global South

Contesting Knowledges for a Sustainable Future

Anders Breidlid

Routledge
Taylor & Francis Group
NEW YORK   LONDON

First published 2013
by Routledge
711 Third Avenue, New York, NY 10017

Simultaneously published in the UK
by Routledge
2 Park Square, Milton Park, Abingdon, Oxon OX14 4RN

*Routledge is an imprint of the Taylor & Francis Group,
an informa business*

Library of Congress Cataloging-in-Publication Data
Breidlid, Anders, 1947–
    Education, indigenous knowledges, and development in the global
south : contesting knowledges for a sustainable future / Anders Breidlid.
        pages cm. — (Routledge research in education)
    Includes bibliographical references and index.
    1. Education—Southern Hemisphere.   2. Education—Southern
Hemisphere—Case studies.   3. Indigenous peoples—Education—
Southern Hemisphere.   4. Indigenous peoples—Education—Southern
Hemisphere—Case studies.   I. Title.
    LC2605.B74 2012
    370.9181'4—dc23
    2012008398.

ISBN13: 978-0-415-89589-7 (hbk)
ISBN13: 978-0-415-62988-1 (pbk)
ISBN13: 978-0-203-09792-2 (ebk)

Typeset in Sabon
by IBT Global.

Contents

Figures

Acknowledgments

This book could not have been written without the assistance and support of many people and institutions. Many of the ideas in this book have benefited from discussions with colleagues and students from many parts of the world. The ideas expressed in the case studies of this book have been tried out at a number of international conferences, and I am grateful for the feedback I received from various colleagues at these conferences.

While chapters 1, 2, 3, 7, and 8 are written specifically for this book, parts of the chapters on South Africa, Sudan, and Cuba are drawn from conference contributions and articles published in various academic journals. However, the chapters are thoroughly revised, particularly my discussions on sustainability and sustainable development.

I am grateful to the numerous principals, teachers, and students in the various schools in South Africa, Sudan and South Sudan, Cuba, and Chile who were willing to let us into their schools, interview them, and observe classes. It was during these visits that I came to realize in earnest how what Jones calls the 'global architecture of education' (Jones 2007) was an impediment to learning in many of the schools visited.

My thanks go to my research assistants during the field-work in Africa and Latin America, who did a wonderful job collecting data often under very difficult conditions. In Sudan, Avelino Androga Said, Ezra Remo Weleya, Joshua Paul Maya, Thomas Eri, Ingunn K. Mork Bjørndal, Ingrid Marie Breidlid, and Astrid Kristine Breidlid. In South Africa, Ragnhild Meisfjord, Jorun Nossum, and Neill Matthee.

In Cuba, Professor Alejandro Torres was of great help in identifying informants and discussing current political and educational issues. We also received much assistance from the Instituto Pedagógico Latinoamericano y Caribeño.

In Temuco, Chile, Alejandro Manquepi was our interpreter when our competence in Spanish was insufficient, and he accompanied us throughout our field-work in the Temuco region. Thanks also to Maximiliano Novoa who helped us in Coñaripe during our investigation of the the planned power plants on Mapuche territory.

I also want to thank Professor Vanensio Mulediang Tombe from the University of Juba, Sudan (whose main campus was in Khartoum during the war) who helped us to open doors to the various ministries in the capital. It meant that we got research permits much more quickly than was anticipated. The assistance of Norwegian Church Aid for transportation in the Khartoum area and in the South facilitated our field-work immensely. I am also grateful to Norwegian People's Aid, which provided us with cheap accommodation in Yei.

In South Africa, Dr. Abner Nyamende at the University of Cape Town, a Xhosa, friend, colleague, has been the best informant you could dream of when trying to get an insider's view of the Xhosa universe. Abner also read through the chapter on the Xhosa in this book and came up with useful suggestions.

In Cuba, our discussions with Miriam Leiva Chepe and Oscar Espinosa Chepe conveyed alternative, non-hegemonic views on the political and economic situation in Cuba, both in 2005 and 2012. In Chile, both Dr. Alejandro Herrera at the Institute of Aboriginal Studies at the Universidad de la Frontera in Temuco and human rights lawyer, Jose Aylwin, gave us valuable information about the situation of the Mapuche in the Araucanía region. Moreover, the staff at the Universidad Católica in Villarica was of the utmost help and provided us with free accommodation during the time we did fieldwork in the region. Throughout the fieldwork in Chile and Cuba, my wife, Halldis, was my companion and field researcher; without her diligence and perseverance, we would have covered far less territory and acquired far less information than we actually did.

Closer to home in Oslo, my erstwhile colleagues, Dr. Bob Smith and Professor David Stephens, were inspiring discussion partners on issues of education and development. I am also thankful to Harald Michelsen for reading through and commenting on the section on science.

At the Department of International Studies and Interpreting, I am particularly grateful to Dr. Louis Botha for reading sections of the manuscript and for giving useful comments in his area of expertise—indigenous knowledges. I would also like to pay thanks to PhD student, Thomas Eri, for providing important and useful information and knowledge about the CHAT theory, and to my graduate students who over the years have been eager to discuss my ideas on education, epistemologies, and development in the global South.

Finally, I am very grateful to Dr. Tom G. Griffiths, University of Newcastle, Australia, for his competent and useful comments on the more theoretical part of this book, particularly on Immanuel Wallerstein, and to Professor Lene Buchert, University of Oslo, and Dr. Yusuf Sayed, University of Sussex, for having read more or less the whole draft manuscript and offered helpful ideas and suggestions for improving the manuscript. Thanks also to Routledge editor Max Novick for showing patience during the writing process, and to Eleanor Chan for guiding me through the proof reading process.

The research in Sudan and South Africa was funded by the Norwegian Research Council.

Oslo, May 2012
Anders Breidlid

Excerpts from the following materials have been used in this book:

Breidlid, A. 2003. Ideology, cultural values and education: The case of Curriculum 2005 in South Africa. *Perspectives in Education* 21(2; June), 83–103.

Breidlid, A. 2005. Sudanese migrants in the Khartoum area: fighting for educational space. *International Journal of Educational Development*, 25, 253–268.

Breidlid, A. 2005. Education in the Sudan: The privileging of an Islamic discourse. *Compare*, 35 (3), 247–263.

Breidlid, A. 2006. Resistance and education—counter-hegemonic struggle in Southern Sudan. *Nordisk Pedagogik*, 26, 16–29.

Breidlid, A. 2007. Education in Cuba—an alternative educational discourse: lessons to be learned? *Compare*, 37(5), October, 617–634.

Breidlid, A. 2009. Indigenous knowledge systems, sustainable development and education. *International Journal of Educational Development*, 29(2), 140–149.

Breidlid, A. (2010). Sudanese Images of the Other: Education and Conflict in Sudan. *Comparative Education Review*, 54(4; November), 555–579.

1 Introduction

One cannot expect positive results from an educational or political action program that fails to respect the particular view of the world held by the people. Such a program constitutes cultural invasion, good intentions notwithstanding.

—Paulo Freire, *Pedagogy of the Oppressed* (1970, p. 84)

I do not see a delegation
For the four-legged.
I see no seat for the eagles.
We forget and we consider
Ourselves superior.
However, we are after all
A mere part of Creation.
And we must consider
To understand where we are.
And we stand somewhere between
The mountain and the Ant
Somewhere and only there
As part and parcel
Of the Creation.

—Chief Oren Lyons, from an address to the Non-Governmental Organizations of the United Nations, Geneva, Switzerland, 1977. (*Source*, Wall and Arden, 1990, p. 71)

The focus of this book is the hegemonic role of so-called modernist, Western epistemology that spread in the wake of colonialism and the capitalist economic system, and its exclusion and Othering of other epistemologies. The book's concern is how the domination of Western epistemology has had a major impact on the identity construction of the Other, and how the people in the South have been marginalized and subalternized due to the imposition of Western epistemology.

The term Western is here used to identify the hegemonic Eurocentric knowledge system, which originated in 16th-century Europe and together with industrial capitalism produced a specific kind of knowledge that is embodied in modern science. Modern science with its mechanistic view of the world is founded on the Cartesian-Newtonian version of science as something universal and objective. It is related to the so-called logical and empirical way in which science examines information (Merton 1973).

Western and Eurocentric are used interchangeably in the book. 'Episte-mology' refers to the traditional meaning of the word, that is, the 'theory of knowledge.' Epistemology deals with questions of what knowledges are and how they are acquired—in other words, the nature, scope, and sources of knowledges. This is in line with Bateson (1979) who defines epistemology as "the way people view and make sense of the world according to what they have learned and what they believe. This implies interaction and recursiveness between what we know and what we see, which can further influence what we know" (in van Rooyen, 2010, p. 6). I use epistemology and knowledge in the singular when referring to Western hegemonic epistemology/knowledge because the focus is on a particular version of that epistemology and knowledge, which assumes a hegemonic role globally.[1] Epistemologies and knowledges in the plural are used to denote the multiplicity of indigenous epistemologies/knowledges.

The book discusses how the domination of Western epistemology has had a major impact on the epistemological foundation of the education systems across the globe—in the South as well as in the North.[2] In other words: what are the consequences of this epistemological hegemony, which permeates the global architecture of education and its presumed universality? The "global architecture of education"[3] is defined as a common epistemological discourse,[4] which dominates most educational systems in the South and the North, even though there are, as I show in this book, Islamist and (although more debatable) socialist exceptions to this rule (Jones, 2007, p. 325).

In addition to interrogating the impact of Western epistemology on nation building, education systems, and the citizens in the South, the book queries the sustainability of hegemonic epistemology in the face of the imminent ecological challenges of our common earth.

The book seeks the points of view, the insights, and sensitivities of primarily marginalized and dominated groups, and it explores indigenous knowledges as alternatives or supplements to the hegemonic Western knowledge system both educationally and in terms of the sustainability of the globe.

1.1   THE REASONS FOR WRITING THIS BOOK

The reasons for writing this book are multiple, but it was my many visits to schools and classrooms in the South that convinced me that there is something fundamentally problematic with the educational discourses in many of the countries visited. This, I felt, had to be interrogated.

There is a sense of alienation when entering a primary school classroom where a colonial language is spoken (often rudimentarily by the teacher and even more so by the students) and where the contents of the teaching are minor adaptations of what is being taught in the West/North. Students not only battle to understand what is actually being taught because of the language barrier, but they are located in a space where their own cultures and worldviews are seldom, if ever, taken into account beyond their folkloristic aspects. While the cognitive and learning problems of not being taught in the students' mother tongue during formative years are well researched, less attention has been paid to the alien epistemological universe that many students encounter in the classroom. It is my contention that this affects the learning of these students and impairs identity construction. One reason for writing the book is to highlight these cognitive and epistemological issues, which, I argue, are at least partly due to the gap between curricula content, the students' home environment, and epistemological orientation. In other words, I query the hegemonic Western knowledge system that is pervasive in the education systems across the globe (the global architecture of education) and discuss the ways in which indigenous knowledges have been marginalized and subalternized over the centuries.

In the current economic and ecological crisis that the world is facing, the cognitive issues discussed above transcend the challenges on the individual, micro level. The dislocation of indigenous knowledges in the curriculum and in the classrooms seems to signal that Western knowledge/epistemology is the only game in town, and that indigenous knowledges are more or less irrelevant in addressing the critical global issues of our time. In this book I attempt to join those scholars and activists who want to resurrect indigenous knowledges from oblivion, both on the micro and macro level, by claiming that indigenous knowledges have important assets that need to be seriously considered in a world that is completely dominated by Western epistemology and knowledge production.

1.2 THE STRUCTURE OF THE BOOK

Chapter 2 (after this introduction) first outlines the trajectory of Western hegemonic knowledge production and its Othering of alternative knowledges. It then sets out to discuss issues revolving around the co-existence of hegemonic Western knowledge, colonialism, and capitalism, as well as the impact and consequences of modernity, modernization, and globalization. The chapter briefly analyses the relativity of Western science's truth claims, as well as the merits and demerits of modern science. In particular, ecological challenges as a consequence of the exploitation of the earth's finite resources are reviewed. By way of conclusion, the chapter examines the critique of Western knowledge production from within its own ranks.

The next chapter (Chapter 3) examines the debates about who is indigenous and what are indigenous knowledges/epistemologies. The chapter proceeds to discuss the assets and the problematic aspects of indigenous knowledges. It further examines the potential for co-existence between Western and indigenous knowledge systems, the potential for a third space, and the application of cultural-historical activity theory to accommodate negotiations between Western and indigenous knowledge systems.

The chapter goes on to discuss the global architecture of education and its alienating effects on students with an alternative epistemological background. By discussing the potential of a decolonized curriculum, the chapter exposes the debate between modern science and ethno-science in order to situate science in its cultural context. The chapter's concluding section analyses the interventions of, for example, the World Bank and UNESCO in education in the South and queries to what extent alternative epistemologies are taken on board when strategies and interventions are being implemented.

The book's next chapters (Chapters 4, 5, 6, and 7) represent case studies from four (now five) countries, South Africa, South Sudan and Sudan (one country prior to July 9, 2011[5]), Cuba, and Chile. The discussion in the four chapters is based on field-work of varying lengths during the first decade of the 21st century. The focus in all the case studies is the relationship between educational discourses and epistemological orientation, and it centers in different ways around the students' learning in the various epistemological settings. Moreover, the chapters discuss issues related to indigenous knowledges and sustainable development in the schools and beyond. Sustainable development refers to 'development at a level which can be maintained, within the limits imposed by the carrying capacity of the planet, indefinitely' (Towards Sustainability, 2011). Sustainability as a notion in an ecological context has emerged as a result of major concerns about the social, economic, and environmental consequences of the unbridled exploitation of the earth.

The selection of these four (five) countries is due to the fact that the countries, besides representing two continents in the South, illustrate different trajectories of the global architecture of education with the Islamist government in Khartoum (and to a lesser extent Cuba) as interesting contrasts. Even though the thematic focus is similar in all of the cases, the chapters are not neatly patterned in the same way for a variety of reasons linked to, for example, historical, political, ethnic, and epistemological factors, and the fact that the field-work took place at different periods of time. While the case studies focus on what I have termed indigenous populations (with the exception of Cuba), only the chapter on Chile is entirely devoted to a minority people, that is, the Mapuche. The chapter on South Africa also focuses on an indigenous ethnic group, the Xhosa, but I consider the Xhosa as part of the majority black population in the country. The chapter on Cuba is included because the country is reputed both to have one of the best education systems in the South (see UNESCO, EFA Global Monitoring Reports), as well as offering an alternative educational discourse unlike the majority of discourses in the South. Moreover, the country's focus on sustainable development is reviewed both in the classroom and in the society at large.

Since the focus of the book is the dislocation of indigenous knowledges, the case studies *do not highlight* how indigenous knowledges are applied and represent sustainable development in all the cases. It is the purpose of the book and the case studies to explore to what extent the global architecture of education is hegemonic and to what extent the cultures, values, and epistemological orientation of indigenous peoples are included in educational and political discourses in the South. The cases try, in varying degrees, to explore the worldviews and knowledge production of indigenous peoples and how their role, if any, in the educational discourses impacts indigenous identity construction, learning, sustainability, and sustainable development.

The complexity of issues related to both knowledge production and change and sustainable development should not be underrated, but the book suggests that the faith in "solutions" based solely on Western epistemology continues to be overvalued. Since the book addresses "the big issues" both related to epistemologies and sustainability there are obviously many areas of relevance that can only be briefly touched on within the scope of this book.

As a privileged scholar from the North I do not pretend to speak on behalf of indigenous peoples and their struggle for epistemic recognition. Such a pretension is reminiscent of Spivak's rhetorical question: can the Subaltern Speak? The underlying assumption is that someone has to speak on their behalf. The problem is that the West speaks on behalf of the subaltern without, as it were, taking their epistemological basis into consideration. The Mapuche fight for epistemic, cognitive, and territorial autonomy in Chile; they network and seek alliances between indigenous and non-indigenous peoples in Chile, the rest of Latin America, and the world. Indigenous and non-indigenous alliances cut across localities, nations, and continents and signal a need for reassertion of epistemologies that were drowned in the wake of Western colonization and imperialism. Such a struggle for reassertion is urgent in terms of recovering indigenous peoples' identities and in terms of global sustainability, and it knows no borders.

2 The Hegemonic Role of Western Epistemology

2.1 INTRODUCTION

> People were always getting ready for tomorrow.
> I didn't believe in that.
> Tomorrow wasn't getting ready for them.
> It didn't even know they were there.
> —Cormac McCarthy *The Road* (2006), p.168

> For purposes of world history, the margins sometimes demand more attention than the metropolis. Part of the mission . . . is to rehabilitate the overlooked, including places often ignored as peripheral, peoples marginalized as inferior and individuals relegated to bit-parts and footnotes.
> —Felipe Fernandez-Armesto *Millennium* (1995), p. 8

An important concern in this book is the hegemonic role of Western epistemology and knowledge production. This chapter explores the genesis and trajectory of Western hegemonic epistemology in the wake of colonialism and capitalist expansion and how it has excluded or "Othered" non-hegemonic epistemologies in world history with dire consequences.

Boaventura de Sousa Santos, João Arriscado Nunes, and Maria Paula Meneses's description of the trajectory of Western epistemology is noteworthy:

> From the fifteenth century onwards, the constitution of the modern/colonial world-system . . . rested upon multiple "creative destructions," often carried out on behalf of "civilizing," liberating, or emancipatory projects, which aimed at reducing the understandings of the world to the logic of Western epistemology. Examples of this were the conversion of the knowledges of colonized peoples and of the diversity of their cultures and cosmologies to expressions of irrationality, of superstition . . . (2008, p. xxxiii)

It is one of the characteristic traits of colonialism that it denied diversity, epistemic diversity, and created instead inferiority. The production of the hegemonic epistemology necessitated the Other, which was characterized as uncivilized, irrational, superstitious.

This inferiorization or Othering was done in terms of race, gender, knowledges, and education systems, whereas hegemonic epistemology was, in the wake of modernity, hailed as the savior and the only means with which to achieve progress and development. The Othering not only alienated students in school but also defined what kind of development to pursue in the reconstruction of the South after the demise of colonialism. Therefore, there are reasons to question the hegemonic development paradigm, which according to Vincent Tucker can be defined as "the process whereby other peoples are dominated and their destinies are shaped according to an essentially Western way of conceiving and perceiving the world" (1999, p. 1). Such a hegemonic perception of the world is also problematic in light of the pending ecological crisis, so the chapter queries to what extent a Western epistemology, with its attendant view of nature, is sustainable. It is one of the normative assumptions of this chapter and the book as a whole that the dominant epistemology is incapable of resolving key crises confronting the globe in its own terms, that the concepts of "green development" and the belief in technological innovations and breakthroughs are insufficient to break with the hegemonic paradigm; therefore, a more fundamental critique and reconstruction is needed. This is one reason why it is important to explore indigenous knowledges, that is, when considered in a non-romanticized and critical spirit as supplements to the hegemonic knowledge system.

2.2   THE EPISTEMIC AND ECONOMIC MARGINALIZATION OF THE SOUTH

The Hegemonic Role of Western Knowledge and Science

The hegemonic role of Western knowledge and science from the 15th and 16th centuries and the Othering that was briefly discussed above are further examined in the subsections below. The perception of Europe (the West) as the superior entity in the world contributed to paving the way for imperialism, the colonial discourse, colonialism, and the military, political, economic, and epistemic conquest of the South.

Although the Spanish invasion, conquest, and subsequent colonization of America was in many ways a controversial endeavor that caused debate about political, ethical, and theological issues, the hegemonic view and rationale for the conquest was the civilizing mission (the superiority of Western civilization) and the conversion of the natives. Despite the fact that the Catholic Church was an important accomplice of Spanish colonialism, the conquest took place at a time when the Catholic Church also was influenced by humanist theologians such as Thomas Aquinas. Some of the Spanish missionaries in America, particularly members of the Dominican order, were inspired by Thomas Aquinas and began to doubt the justification for the civilizing mission. Bartolomé de Las Casas (1484–1566) and Franciscus de Victoria (1492–1546) were two of the most influential critics of Spanish colonialism. Their criticism of the barbaric behavior of the conquistadors could not, however, stop the horrors and abuses of colonialism in the Americas.

In England and France the "intellectual" foundation of the Othering of non-dominant knowledges and people was laid from the 16th century onwards. The famous philosophical statement by French philosopher René Descartes (1596–1650), "I think therefore I am," signified central ideas of the Enlightenment that helped to shape European thinking and thus European colonial conquest. Descartes underlined the autonomous individual who behaves on the basis of reason and rationality to make sense of the world as well as the individual as the source of all knowledge and experience. John Locke (1634–1704), often called the father of the Enlightenment movement, supported the colonial policies of the British and defended slavery (see Arneil, 1996). David Hume (1711–1776), well known for his skepticism, did not question all the prejudices of his life time, declaring that "I am apt to suspect that the Negroes to be naturally inferior to the Whites. There scarcely ever was a civilized nation of that complexion, nor even any individual, eminent either in action or speculation. No indigenous manufactures among them, no arts, no sciences" (Hume, 1753–54).[1]

Other Enlightenment philosophers such as Immanuel Kant (1724–1804) and Denis Diderot (1713–1784) were, however, critical of the consequences of colonialism and challenged the idea of the West's civilizing mission, but to no avail.

Epistemic Marginalization: Orientalism

A systematic analysis of European perceptions of superiority about the East was conducted by Edward Said in his seminal book *Orientalism* (1978). In the book, Said explored the literary and textual production of the Orient in the 19th century, linking the texts and their social and political meaning and significance.

According to Said, it was not capitalists that primarily influenced the construction of the Orientalist discourse, but narratives/discourses about the Orient by Western intellectuals, academics, artists (visual and literary artists), teachers, scientists, travelers, and journalists. One of Said's (1978) epigraphs in *Orientalism*, from Karl Marx's *The 18th Brumaire of Louis Napoleon*, tells of the derogatory attitude of Western thinkers with regard to the Other: "They cannot represent themselves; they must be represented" (p. 3). The

Orientalist representation of the Other was filtered through the lenses of a European bias. Said is right when contending that:

> A representation is *eo ipso* implicated, intertwined, embedded, interwoven with a great many other things besides "truth," which is itself a representation. What this must lead us to methodologically is to view representation (or misrepresentation—the distinction is at best a matter of degree) as inhabiting a common field of play defined for them not by some inherent common subject matter alone, but by some common history, tradition, universe of discourse (pp. 272–273).

According to Said, the Orientalist discourse examined in *Orientalism* makes a particular way of interpreting and getting knowledge about the world hegemonic. As Hayden White states about discourse, it constitutes "the ground whereon to decide what shall count as a fact in the matters under consideration and to determine what mode of comprehension is best suited to the understanding of the facts thus constituted." (1987, p. 3). Thus, the discursive expressions have two functions that are important in Said's *Orientalism*: they shape people's social and personal reality and they are shaped by this reality. The discourse produces an understanding and knowledge of "reality" and "truth," which is fictitious but is still "reality." The Orientalist discourse is based on an ontological and epistemological dichotomy between the West and the East, between the Occident and the Orient, between Christianity and Islam, between the Self and the Other. Orientalism produces knowledge about the Orient as the West's subordinate Other, based on stereotypes of the Orient and the Oriental people. By essentializing the Other with regard to identity, difference, and knowledge production, the rigid dichotomy between Self and the Other is perpetuated. Orientalism is based on the West's conception of the Orient by "making statements about it, authorizing views of it, describing it, settling it, ruling over it, in short Orientalism as a Western style for dominating, restructuring, and having authority over the Orient" (Said, 1978, p. 3). This implies a comprehensive political and epistemological control based on domination vs. subordination. The Self/Other dichotomy between the West and the East was described in Manichean (good vs. evil) absolute terms. The Self (the West) was characterized as rational, dynamic, civilized, scientific, and progressive, whereas the Other (the East) was seen as irrational, voiceless, feminine, superstitious, underdeveloped, uncivilized, barbaric, and static. The dichotomy between the West and the East was considered to be more or less unbridgeable. As Rudyard Kipling stated: "Oh, East is East, and West is West, and never the twain shall meet " (1889).

Conquest and domination followed in the wake of the Orientalist discourse due to the close relationship between Western knowledge production, epistemology, and cultural utterances and the material and political power of the West. The concept and underlying principles of

Orientalism were later extended to other areas of Western domination (Africa, Latin America).

Accordingly, what were perceived as European values, knowledge, and science, that is, the Orientalist or colonial discourse, were all used to legitimatize colonization and imperialism.

The Kenyan author Ngũgĩ wa Thiong'o (1981) is adamant about the real aim of colonialism:

> [It] was to control the people's wealth . . . through military conquest and subsequent political dictatorship. However, its most important area of domination was the mental universe of the colonized, the control, through culture, of how people perceived themselves and their relationship to the world. Economic and political control can never be complete or effective without mental control. To control a people's culture is to control their tools of self-definition in relationship to others (p. 16).

Like other seminal books, Said's *Orientalism* has both been hailed as ground-breaking as well as criticized for being stereotypical, unnuanced, and unbalanced. Particularly, Said's focus on textual dichotomies and their ideological consequences has been critiqued as being too narrow and having too little emphasis on institutional and material realities (Ahmad, 1992). Moreover, Western texts about the East are not all as biased and negative towards the East as Said postulates in *Orientalism*. Said seems to ignore that texts can be colonial and anti-colonial, hegemonic and counter-hegemonic at the same time (Irwin, 2006; Lewis, 1993). Particularly his exclusion of texts from German, Dutch, and Italian scholars has been critiqued, since they often presented a more positive picture of the East. While the flaws and omissions in *Orientalism* should be acknowledged, the Western *hegemonic* discourse about non-Western peoples (in Said's case the people in the East) and cultures has been, and still is, marked by condescension and presumed epistemological superiority and has justified colonialism and its aftermath. The historian John M. Hobson (2004) uses Orientalism and Eurocentrism interchangeably, calling the Self/Other dichotomy "intellectual apartheid." Epistemic apartheid is an equally appropriate term.

Franz Fanon's Manicheism and Ngũgĩ wa Thiong'o's *Decolonising the Mind*

In many ways, Fanon pre-empted Said's *Orientalism* with his books *Black Skin, White Masks* (1967) and *The Wretched of the Earth* (1963). In contrast to Said, Fanon focuses on colonization in Africa by analyzing the state of the colonized based on his own clinical studies from Algeria. Using the term Manichean to describe the colonial relationship as understood by the colonizer, Fanon analyses the dichotomy between the colonizer and the colonized in terms of good vs. evil, rational vs. irrational. According to Fanon, the identity of the colonized is destroyed after the encounter with the colonizer—he is no longer a man. "At the risk of arousing the sentiment of my coloured brothers, I will say that black man is not a man" (1967, p. 8). His analysis of the colonizer's perception of the colonized is indeed bleak:

> The settler paints the native as a sort of quintessence of evil . . . The native is declared insensitive to ethics, he represents not only the absence of values, but also the negation of values. He is, let us dare to admit, the enemy of values, and in this sense he is the absolute evil (1963, p. 32).

Writing within the same ideological paradigm, Ngũgĩ (particularly in *Decolonising the Mind*, 1981) is concerned with how the Self/Other dichotomy has created a colonized mind as the perception of the West is adopted by the global South. It is therefore necessary to decolonize the mind. Ngũgĩ describes how he experienced an epistemic genocide in school where he was not allowed to speak his own language (Gĩkũyũ), and was even punished if he spoke Gĩkũyũ in the schoolyard.

It is this epistemological deprivation and the hegemonizing of the Western discourse that is the focus of this book. Said may be right in contending that it was not the capitalists who primarily influenced the construction of the Orientalist discourse, but narratives/discourses about the Orient. The discourse provided the intellectual, epistemological, and political basis and justification for colonialism and the global capitalist system.

It is to a discussion of the symbiotic relationship between the Eurocentric and Orientalist discourse, and colonialism and capitalism that I now turn. Immanuel Wallerstein's world-systems analysis is an appropriate point of departure for the discussion of this interrelationship.

Economic Marginalization:
Immanuel Wallerstein's World-Systems Analysis

The hegemonic role of Western epistemology from the 15th and 16th centuries has been interpreted as a bedfellow to the systematic expansion of capitalism into a world economy, which resulted in subalternization, marginalization, and Othering.

Wallerstein developed world-systems analysis in order to correct what he thought were the flaws of the modernization school of the 1960s and 1970s (Skocpol, 1982, p. 1075). While modernization theory focused on nation-states as a separate unit of analysis, Wallerstein made the various states' position in the global system the major explanatory factor, even though national factors also were included.

According to Wallerstein, the "successive expansions (of capitalism) have transformed the capitalist world-economy from a system primarily located in

Europe to one that covers the entire globe" (1990, p. 36). Wallerstein argues that the "incorporation into the capitalist world-economy was never at the initiation of those being incorporated. The process derived rather from the need of the world-economy to expand its boundaries" (1989, p. 129). The incorporation of the colonies as peripheral members of the world-economy served the economic interests of the core nation-states. Due to this colonial incorporation, Wallerstein rejects the concepts of the Third World and the Fourth World, since his main thesis is that there is only *one* world of complex economic networks, that is, a world-system. The West's political and economic hegemony by means of colonialism facilitated this incorporation.

Wallerstein's main preoccupation has been how the present system of global hierarchy operates and how the structural differences between countries can be understood on the basis of what he terms a unified world-system. According to Wallerstein, the capitalist world-system is very diverse and consists of a core (the most developed nations in the North) with semi-periphery and periphery (the so-called developing nations). The core countries dominate the periphery and often the semi-periphery, while the semi-periphery often dominates the periphery as well. There is a division of labor between the core and the periphery where the periphery, marginalized from the core, provides raw material, agricultural products, and cheap labor for the core. Moreover, there is an unequal economic exchange between the core and the periphery where the periphery sells its unprocessed products at a cheap price to the core, but is forced to buy the processed products from the core at a very high price. The semi-periphery is in a liminal situation where it works as the periphery to the core, but as the core to the periphery. This division of labor has created huge differences in terms of social and economic development and in the accumulation of capital, the central value in capitalism, between the core and the periphery. Wallerstein has repeatedly underlined the structural crisis in the capitalist world system, which will not be rectified through modifications of the system (Wallerstein, 2010). On the contrary Wallerstein predicts the collapse of the present economic world system, opening up for revolutionary change. Wallerstein is clearly influenced by André Gunder Frank (1969) and his dependency theory, where the underlying idea is the prevention of development in the periphery by the center (core) as a necessary condition for the functioning of the global system. However, as Tucker correctly states, dependency theory never questioned the ecological implications of the growth-oriented model (the evolutionary model of progress) and did not include indigenous peoples nor gender issues in the theory (Tucker, 1999). Nor did dependency theory interrogate the epistemological foundations of the development paradigm.

Wallerstein's Critics

Wallerstein has received harsh criticism from various academic circles, not only from neo-liberal and conservative scholars. One criticism against the world-systems analysis is that it is economically deterministic (Levy, 1981;

Rapkin, 1981; Skocpol, 1982), whereas others have criticized it for paying too much attention to the external global context in which nations develop and disregarding internal, national factors. This is one of Ian Roxborough's objections:

> Some radical dependency theorists have at times inclined toward a one-sided emphasis on the determining role of the world-market, and have seen developments within Third World countries as mere reflections of, or responses to, exogenous changes (1979, p. 25).

Despite harsh criticism, Wallerstein's analyses have made a major impact in academic institutions around the world; his influence on macro-historical sociology is undisputed, and he has been an important contributor to the anti-globalization movement. The strength of his world system analysis is dual: (1) the development of a nation-state is decisively determined by the world economic order, and (2) world -systems analysis focuses on the fundamental explanations for exploitation between the core and the periphery.

Based on the discussion above, the link between Said and Wallerstein, their differences notwithstanding, is rooted in their analyses of the marginalization of the South by the North over the centuries in terms of epistemic or economic marginalization and how the nation-state can no longer function as the dominant unit of analysis. The latter point is underlined by Meyer's world society approach, which adopts an institutional rather than a political-economic approach to world system analysis.

Meyer's World Society Models

John W. Meyer, John Boli, George M. Thomas, and Francisco O. Ramiriez claim that "world society models shape nation-state identities, structures, and behaviour via worldwide cultural and associational models" (1997, p. 173). While Wallerstein makes an apparently similar point regarding the world economy, Meyer et al. focus on cultural factors globally. Referring, for example, to educational development they claim that the implementation of standard scripts occur "in countries of all sorts, without regard to their particular circumstances [and] produces results that often seem quite bizarre . . ." (Meyer et al., 1997, p. 149). Moreover, they note that that basic "functional justifications of schooling are rarely questioned" (Meyer et al., 1997, p. 149), regardless of the evidence contradicting them. This world culture perspective is similar to what I referred to earlier as the global architecture of education, and it presents the increase of mass school education as a part of the global spread and institutionalization of modern state forms and state institutions. As Tom G. Griffiths and Lisa Knezevic claim, these "models in turn include a core role for schooling in creating members or citizens of the modern state" (2009, p.70).

While Meyer et al.'s thesis about the global spread of mass schooling with the same implicit epistemic foundation is correct, Meyer and Wallerstein separate on the sustainability of such a development. Meyer et al. "argue for the utility of recognizing that rationalized modernity is a universalistic and inordinately successful form of the earlier Western religious and postreligious system" (1997, p. 149). Meyer et al. moreover advocate for the success of world society by stating that events "like political torture, waste dumping, or corruption, which not so long ago were either overlooked entirely or considered routine, local, specific aberrations or tragedies, are now of world-societal significance" (1997, p. 175). Ignoring, as it were, the inequalities within and between nation-states, Meyer et al. differ from Wallerstein in the sense that they applaud the penetration of a universalized culture and rationalized modernity (Meyer et al., 1997, p. 174).

Interestingly, Wallerstein argues "if social science is to make any progress in the twenty-first century, it must overcome the Eurocentric heritage that has distorted its analyses and its capacity to deal with the problems of the contemporary world" (1999, pp. 168–169). To do this, Wallerstein maintains that we must understand what constitutes Eurocentrism and its "many avatars" (1999, p. 169). While Wallerstein is a fierce critic of global capitalism and the dominant structures of knowledge within capitalism, it is difficult, however, to see that he has gone beyond Eurocentrism himself in his critique of the world economic system. He hardly critiques Eurocentrism's embedded epistemic limitations and he seems never, to my knowledge, to refer to indigenous peoples and epistemologies as alternatives or supplements to the Eurocentric epistemic monopoly. What he suggests is an epistemologically reunified world of knowledge, being concerned with bridging the gap between natural science, humanities, and social sciences (Wallerstein, 1999, p. 220).

Admittedly, Wallerstein critiques Marxism's perception of progress as an accomplice of capitalism:

> The Marxists' embrace of an evolutionary model of progress has been an enormous trap, which socialists have begun to suspect only recently, as one element in the ideological crisis that has been part of the overall structural crisis of the capitalist world economy (1995, p. 98).

However, as Gregor McLennan (1998) states:

> Wallerstein's own position, in spite of its crusading tone, as one which has insufficiently broken with Eurocentric thought patterns . . . [Accordingly] it is the motif of rational progress, and the obsession with it, rather than any particular content it is given, that defines the Western imaginary (p. 154).

McLennan's critique of Wallerstein underlines the profound and comprehensive penetration of the West's epistemic hegemony even in one of capitalism and colonialism's fiercest critics.

It has been noted that hegemonic Western epistemology has not developed in a political or economic vacuum. The trajectory of Western epistemic hegemony is rather inextricably linked to the spread of colonialism and capitalism and to the dislocation of other epistemologies. Similarly, modernity and modernization has often been associated with the rise and expansion of capitalism.

It is modernity and modernization and its link to capitalist expansion and penetration that is interrogated in the next subsection.

Modernity, Modernization, and Westernization

It was through the development of capitalism, and through the transformation and incorporation process of semi-periphery and periphery, that these zones outside the core were exposed to modernity/modernization or Westernization/Europeanization. As Tucker states, "Under the rubric of modernization, Westernization gained the status of a universal goal and destiny" (1999, p. 7). Clearly the European societies as they have emerged since the 15th and 16th centuries were very much linked to the concept of modernity, starting with the voyages of "discovery." The scientific inventions of the 17th century, the Reformation—which spearheaded the Protestant work ethic and the line of demarcation between the secular and the spiritual—and the technological revolution of the 18th century, are perceived as watershed events in the history of modernity. This is in clear contrast to the spiritualism and holism of indigenous cultures. However, more than just a distinct historical period, modernity can be seen as a cultural code. Key concepts here are the individual, rationality, and "progress." The emphasis on individualism, on the individual's right to be creative, on the individual's right to be free and critical, and to be able to exercise individual capabilities is of paramount importance. The emphasis on individual autonomy had far-reaching consequences because it meant breaking away from place and traditional communitarian bonds and the establishment of universal values and universal discourses that transcended the discourses of place and a close-knit community.

The perception in Europe was that Europe and the West had emerged into modernity, whereas the Orient and other cultures in the South were static and could not transcend the pre-modern, traditional state.

Said's *Orientalism* underlined the perceived symbiotic link between modernization/modernity and Westernization; that is, Western culture was perceived to have exceptional internal characteristics, and as noted, was absolutely superior compared to the non-West.

Modernity is often defined in opposition to tradition.[2] Anthony Giddens, for one, distinguishes between the two terms and states that "the radical turn from tradition intrinsic to modernity's reflexivity makes a break . . . with preceding areas" (1991, pp. 175–176). Giddens sees himself as living in a post-traditional society without necessarily Orientalizing the East/South. Still, his strict dichotomization between modernity and tradition is strikingly similar to the West/East dichotomy in Orientalism, where the West's presumed superiority was perceived to be independent of any influences from the East/the South. This exclusivist perception of modernity as a European construct underlines how the hegemonic discourse manipulated the reality by not taking into account the exchange of ideas and knowledges between Europe and the rest of the world for centuries. As Hobson writes, this Eurocentric exclusivity was a complete perversion of history:

> This marginalisation of the East constitutes a highly significant silence because it conceals three major points. First, the East actively pioneered its own substantial economic development after about 500. Second, the East actively created and maintained the global economy after 500. Third, and above all, the East has significantly and actively contributed to the rise of the West by pioneering and delivering many advanced "resource portfolios" (for example, technologies, institutions, and ideas) to Europe. Accordingly, we need to resuscitate both the history of economic dynamism in the East and the vital role of the East in the rise of the West. (2004, p. 5).

In the same vein, Dipesh Chakrabarty de-territorializes Europe by stating that Europe is not a name of a continent but is" reified and celebrated in the phenomenal world of everyday relationships of power as the scene of the birth of the modern, continues to dominate the discourse of history" (1992, p. 2). Modernity is thus, according to Chakrabarty, not something exclusively invented in isolation in North-Western Europe, but has been assimilated, incorporated, molded, and universalized to fit European colonial expansion.

Globalization New and Old

What is important for the purpose of this book is the exposure of the West's epistemological colonization and how it has impacted knowledge production across the globe. Globalization has become the new buzzword and is often defined as "a process of interaction and integration among the people, companies, and governments of different nations, a process driven by international trade and investment and aided by information technology" (The Levin Institute, 2011). Jürgen Habermas (2001) claims that globalization is in its emergent phase and identifies globalization as "the increasing scope and intensity of commercial, communicative, and exchange relations beyond national borders" (p. 66).

Wallerstein, however, is very dismissive of the term because of its failure to describe something new or novel:

> The processes that are usually meant when we speak of globalization are not in fact new at all. They have existed for some 500 years . . . One would think, reading most accounts, that "globalization" is something that came into existence in the 1990s—perhaps only upon the collapse of the Soviet Union, perhaps a few years earlier. The 1990s are not however a significant time marker to use if one wants to analyze what is going on. Rather, we can most fruitfully look at the present situation in two other time frameworks, the one going from 1945 to today, and the one going from circa 1450 to today (2000b, p. 250).

While one aspect of globalization is indeed old, with the spread of capitalism and colonialism,[3] Wallerstein seems to ignore that globalization has taken qualitative new forms through the rapid expansion of electronic technologies like mobile phones and the Internet. Information and Communications Technology (ICT) and social media have changed the daily lives of millions of people, not only in the North, but also for millions of people in the South. Even in remote towns like Malakal in one of our case study countries, South Sudan, the ICT revolution is visible at every street corner, with hundreds of cell phones waiting to be charged at the local shopkeepers. In the concluding chapter, I discuss briefly the potentially crucial role of ICT in discussions of a sustainable future.

However, what is the implication of the new aspects of globalization for knowledge production and hegemonic epistemology? The question is whether such globalization means the end of localized knowledge production. While the new globalization can accelerate the erosion of people's languages and indigenous knowledges and solidify hegemonic knowledge production, globalization has also, as H. S. Bhola states optimistically, "brought about its dialectical opposite; the desire for localization, the search for community, indigenous values, mother tongues; and the wish to preserve cultural heritage and indigenous knowledge" (2003, p. 6). Despite the hegemonic knowledge monopoly and its universality claims, knowledge production occurs in diverse cultural sites also outside the core since knowledges are legitimized and delimited through cultural processes.

The question is, however, if this desire for localized knowledges is a sufficient buffer against the forces of globalization which hegemonize a Western epistemic discourse. Clearly the struggle for non-hegemonic knowledge systems has, up to now, been an uphill battle against the forces of globalization and neo-colonization.

In times of globalization and multinational capitalism there is therefore more need than ever to question the belief that the Cartesian epistemological foundation is something universal and unshakeable, and thus provide people in the South with a consciousness about this. As Ladislaus Semali and

Joe Kincheloe state: "Universality cannot escape unscathed in its encounter with socio-cultural, epistemological particularity" (1999, p. 17).

2.3 THE SUPERIORITY AND TRUTH CLAIMS OF WESTERN KNOWLEDGE

The Superiority Claims

The close relationship between Western epistemology—with its universalistic truth claims—modernity, and colonialism resulted in hegemonic control of epistemologies that did not have universalist pretensions. According to the Orientalist discourse, the Western worldview and epistemic foundations were rational, dynamic, civilized, scientific, and progressive. Since the West's truth claims were indisputable, epistemologies with no universalistic truth claims were easily colonized, Orientalized, and rubbished. As Arturo Escobar states, "the seeming triumph of Eurocentered modernity can be seen as the imposition of a global design by a particular local history, in such a way that it has dislocated other local histories and designs (2004, p. 217). The perception of non-European epistemologies and ontologies as inferior, less evolved, and primitive suggested that they were obstacles to development and modernity. Through epistemological colonization the West imposed its authority to authenticate or invalidate knowledge systems other than its own, which implied invalidation and resulted in epistemic genocide across the globe. As Griffiths and Knezevic state, "Even societies that were widely recognized for their social sophistication were deemed incapable of progress without the European universalism of modernity. . ." (2009, p. 67).

The presumed superiority of Western epistemology is not a phenomenon of the past. It is mainstream thinking in the West today. Charles Taylor, for one, argues that Western superiority in weapon technology "commands attention in a quite nontheoretical way" (1982, p. 104). Employed against both the Zulu and the Ashanti in the 19th century, the effective Gatling gun helped the British to conquer these sub-Saharan territories with their weapons designed for mass killings. The advanced weapon technology embodied in the Gatling gun was based on what Taylor terms the superiority of Western epistemology. As stated by James Maffie: Taylor's "might makes right" argument "confounds military subjugation with philosophical refutation" (2009, p. 1).

Writing in the same vein as Taylor, Ernest Gellner states: "The cognitive and technological superiority of [the scientific-industrial] form of life is so manifest, and so loaded with implications for the satisfaction of human wants and needs . . . that it simply cannot be questioned (Gellner, 1973, 71–72).

The arguments of epistemological superiority articulated by Taylor and Gellner are unmistakably written within the tradition of the hegemonic knowledge monopoly tradition, which until recently has not been seriously interrogated. Taylor openly admits that the so-called epistemic superiority belongs to the legacy of colonialism and imperialism. Other scholars, notably Zygmunt Bauman (1989), claim that the Holocaust should be seen as deeply implicated with modernity, and its focus on rationality. Following a similar line of argument, Aimé Cesaire (2000) noted, in his *Discourse on Colonialism*, that the Jewish Holocaust was not unique phenomenon in European history, but rather represented a continuation of the crimes committed by the colonial powers in the global South.

With this legacy of human suffering and misery, there is an urgent need to question the epistemological assumptions of Western science and technology. The urgency of this query is also related to the contemporary ecological degradation of the planet, where Western science is the major accomplice and culprit. Clearly global warming, paradoxically evidenced by the best Western scientists in the world, challenges the epistemological and scientific superiority claim of Taylor, implying that the same scientists who work within the Western scientific framework question some of its major consequences. The price paid for the blessings of scientific "progress" has been high in terms of ecological devastation and destruction. Nevertheless, the epistemic penetration of Western hegemony has been so successful that it seems difficult to perceive alternatives or supplements to Western epistemic domination. In the next subsection the universality and truth claims of Western scientific research and epistemology are discussed.

The Relativity of Science's Truth Claims

It is worth noting that Western epistemology is not as united and non-contradictory as one might assume, even though its hegemonic, monological version has been an important bedfellow for colonial and capitalist expansion over the last 500 years. Santos et al. refer to the discussion in the North between the internal and external plurality of knowledges. The first interrogates the presumed epistemological unity of science and "questions the monolithical character of the epistemological canon," while the second questions "the epistemological exclusivism of science and focuses on the relationships between science and other knowledges" (2008, p. xxix).

Similarly Wallerstein, working on challenges within science in relation to earlier universal truth claims, acknowledges that scientific knowledge changes and is not simply reversible. Wallerstein describes how two "major knowledge movements have arisen in the last third of the twentieth century: complexity studies in the natural sciences and cultural studies in the humanities" (2006, p. 67). The advocates of complexity studies reject the "linear time-reversible determinism" typical of classical science, insisting that natural systems are not linear and that it is "impossible to determine the future trajectories of any projection . . . since there exists an 'arrow of time' operating in all phenomena, including not only the universe as a whole but every microscopic element within it" (Wallerstein, 2006, p. 67).

Moreover, Maurizio Iaccarino (2003) claims that while the understanding of complex systems remains a major challenge for the future:

> Modern, or Western, science may not be best suited to fulfill this task, as its view of the world is too constrained by its characteristic empirical and analytical approach that, in the past, made it so successful. We should therefore remember the contributions of other civilizations to the understanding of nature . . . Such traditional or indigenous knowledge is now increasingly being used not only with the aim of finding new drugs, but also to derive new concepts that may help us to reconcile empiricism and science (p. 220).

The truth claims of Western science prove often, although not always, to be "Truth" during the period of time when the research was done and often seem to rust with the passing of time. The mantra of Western research, empiricism, is also exposed to the researcher's bias, not only in social science, but in natural science as well. The common perception in Western science that something is finally scientifically proven is not always well founded. Jonah Lehrer (2010) refers to this phenomenon as "the decline effect":

> If replication is what separates the rigor of science from the squishiness of pseudoscience, where do we put all these rigorously validated findings that can no longer be proved? Which results should we believe? Francis Bacon, the early-modern philosopher and pioneer of the scientific method, once declared that experiments were essential, because they allowed us to "put nature to the question." But, it appears that nature often gives us different answers (2010). Moreover, many of the scientific results published are prone to what is termed publication bias, that is, the inclination of scientific journals and scientists to prefer positive data over no results, that is, when no outcome is found. Additional to the publication bias is the selective reporting of data, that is, the data that scientists choose to publish.

A former academic scientist now working for a large biotech company wrote in an e-mail to Lehrer:

> When I worked in a university lab, we'd find all sorts of ways to get a significant result. We'd adjust the sample size after the fact, perhaps because some of the mice were outliers or maybe they were handled incorrectly, etc. This wasn't considered misconduct. It was just the way things were done. Of course, once these animals were thrown out [of the data] the effect of the intervention was publishable (Lehrer, 2010).

Robert Palmer, a US biologist, sums up the state of affairs, saying, "We cannot escape the troubling conclusion that some—perhaps many—cherished generalities are at best exaggerated in their biological significance and at worst a collective illusion nurtured by strong a-priori beliefs often repeated" (2000, p. 70). Palmer's assertion is reminiscent of Simon and Garfunkel's song "The Boxer": "A man hears what he wants to hear and disregards the rest." Since the picture of natural science is "much more messy and muddled" (Appiah, 1992, 128) than the "official view" often seems to postulate, the wisdom "of epistemological modesty is, surely," as Kwame Appiah states, "one of the lessons of natural science; indeed, if there is one great lesson of the failure of positivism as a methodology of the sciences, it is surely . . . that there are no a priori rules that we will guarantee us true theories (Appiah, 1992, p.117).

This does not mean that all scientific results are biased. Natural selection and climate change, to take only two examples, have been verified in thousands of different ways by thousands of scientists working in many different fields. Still, there is no guarantee that these theories will not be modified as time passes. Even Albert Einstein's relativity theory has come under new scrutiny recently.[4]

The Merits of Modern Science

The reason for interrogating the truth claims of Western science is not to undermine its importance and merits, but to put its self-proclaimed superior position globally in perspective. Scientific discoveries and technological change have in many ways been a blessing in the sense that these discoveries have made life more manageable and easier for millions of people, viz. discoveries in medicine, agriculture, transport, and information technology, to mention just a few. There is no reason to reject or de-emphasize the merits of modern science and technology. Science and technology are very important aspects of modern society and societies in the South. They permeate, in one way or another, almost every society on earth and are in many ways indispensable.

2.4   THE ECOLOGICAL CONSEQUENCES OF WESTERN HEGEMONIC EPISTEMOLOGY

Limits to Growth

There is, however, reason to also underline the limits and negative consequences of Western hegemonic knowledge—a warning was already published in 1972 with the seminal book *Limits to Growth* (Meadows et al., 1972). The book analyzed the consequences of, and the relationship between, a rapidly growing world population and the world's finite resources. It concluded that there would be a societal and economic collapse in the 21st century. This was due to the fact that the world's resources could not keep up with the increase in five crucial variables, that is, world population, industrialization, pollution, food production, and resource depletion. By analyzing these five variables they found that the variables would grow exponentially, whereas technology's ability to increase the resources available would only grow linearly; hence, the big crisis in the 21st century. The book was criticized and rubbished by many as based on insufficient scientific data and the authors' disbelief in modern technology's ability to renew itself. An update of the book three decades later, *Limits to Growth: The 30-Year Update* (Meadows et al, 2004) reiterated the results of the original book and stated "we have been steadily using up more of the Earth's resources without replenishing its supplies" (p. 16) The consequences, according to the authors, may be catastrophic. The conclusion from the *Limits to Growth Update* was reinforced by Graham Turner, who found that changes in industrial production, food production, and pollution are all in line with the book's predictions of economic and societal catastrophe in this century (Turner, 2008). This is also in line with Wallerstein's predictions referred to earlier in this chapter (1999, 2010). One of the most distinguished scientists in the UK, Martin Rees, asks in his book *Our Final Century* if globalization will survive the 21st century. Rees states: "In the twenty-first century, humanity is more at risk than ever before from misapplication of science. And the environmental pressures induced by collective human actions could trigger catastrophes more threatening than any natural hazards" (2004, p. 186).

In particular, the ecological challenges of the planet are now mainstream thinking both among politicians and scientists. The pollution of the planet, that is, the atmospheric concentration of CO_2, is a serious threat to the climate of the earth. In the same vein the availability of oil resources is about to reach its peak, at least in the next 10 to 20 years. While there is not global warming denial among many leading policy makers globally, there is still a Western technology optimism that refuses to act on the basis of the serious warnings related to the finiteness of the global resources and the imminent danger of a global disaster. As Jørgen Randers, one of the authors of *Limits to Growth*, states, "Global collapse triggered by ever growing emissions of greenhouse gases is still conceivable in the first half of the 21st century, because of the unfortunate combination of global decision delays and self-reinforcing feedback in the climate system " (2008, p. 864).

Western Epistemology and Humankind's Relation to Nature

Philipp Pattberg (2007) discusses the ideology of domination over nature that is still with us today, how it is "[d]eeply rooted in our every-day beliefs, actions, reflections and hopes, it lies at the center of any attempt to transform the world into a more loveable, friendlier, lighter and safer place" (p. 7). By discussing what he terms the enslavement of nature and the enslavement of humans by other humans, he concludes that this has led to a global state which is not sustainable. Exploring its historical trajectory, the ideology of domination over the natural environment took hold, according to Pattberg, "in the context of . . . the decline of Christianity as a total explanatory structure for human existence, the scientific turn of Cartesianism and the rise of capitalism to a self-replicating structure of rational choice" (p. 8).

Lynn White (1974) suggests that the ecological crisis is due to the orthodox Christian legacy, especially its Western branch, stating, "Christianity, in absolute contrast to ancient paganism and Asia's religions (except, perhaps Zorastrianism), not only established a dualism of man and nature but also insisted that it is God's will that man exploit nature for his proper ends" (p. 4). Moreover, White proposes that "[o]ur science and technology have grown out of Christian attitudes towards man's relation to nature which are almost universally held, not only by Christians and neo-Christians but also by those who fondly regard themselves as post-Christians" (p. 5). Interestingly, White suggests a return to unorthodox Christianity spearheaded by St. Francis, an idea I will return to later in this book.

Max Weber's thesis, *The Protestant Ethic and The Spirit of Capitalism* (1905/2001), is based on the assumption that there is a close relationship between Protestantism and capitalism, that capitalism's basis is (what was interpreted as) the Christian work ethic, particularly in Calvinism. The idea is that domination over nature through hard work and frugality will be rewarded by God.

There is therefore an important epistemological dimension to this crisis. As Kincheloe and Steinberg (2008) put it, "Some indigenous educators and philosophers put it succinctly: We want to use indigenous knowledge to counter Western's science destruction of the Earth. Indigenous knowledge can facilitate the 21st century project because of its tendency to focus on relationships of human beings to both one another and to their eco-system" (pp. 136–137).

The exclusion of alternative epistemologies and the privileging of rational science have meant the demise of ecological sustainability while the epitomization of scientific truth and rationality has excluded values that transcend the so-called rationality dogma of the West. This denial of epistemological diversity and the privileging of European epistemic mono-culture is still hegemonic and perceived as a sign of development and modernity.

Ideological Pathology

There is a naive belief among modernization theoreticians that since ecological problems are a result of the economic activities of modernization, further economic activities should cure these environmental problems. Due to the finiteness of the earth's resources, the vicious circle of repairing the consequences of progress with further progress is not sustainable. Ronald Wright (2004) argues that the 20th century was a period where unlimited growth in terms of population, consumption, and technology exploited the natural systems in an unsustainable way. Wright calls these activities of ecological unsustainability the very worst kind of "ideological pathology."

While colonialism and the capitalist world system have been beset with territorial, political, and economic conquest, Western science is based on the same idea of conquest, that is, not respecting the earth's ecological limits. Moreover, in line with world-systems analysis, there is an ecological unequal exchange here, as the core's exploitation and utilization of the world's resources is matched in the periphery with the burden of negative ecological costs imposed by the core.

As has been discussed above, the issue of Western science and knowledge production is existentially important because the Eurocentric epistemology of knowing (mastering) and dominating the world is, despite its merits, dramatically problematic in a world where the majority of the world's population not only suffers from hunger and malnutrition, illiteracy, and lack of work, but where the hegemonic epistemology upsets the relationship between man and nature as it seeks to possess the earth in the same way as a master exploits his slave.

The ecological challenges are closely intertwined with the current economic challenges in the West, and it is difficult to ignore that the aggressive ideology of exploitation and the maximizing of profits, which are so central to European hegemonic epistemology, is detrimental to the efforts to save the planet from ecological disaster. Vivas (2011) is right when contending that the difference between the present economic crisis and those of the 1970s and 1929 is "its ecological aspect. Indeed, we cannot analyze the global ecological crisis separately from the crisis in which we are immersed or the critique of the economic model that has led us into it." Even if we do not agree that the crisis is due to capitalism's inherent contradictions, the global economic crisis has long been there; the economic crises in Greece, Italy, and Spain are miniscule compared to the permanent crises in the South, where millions go hungry to bed every day and live on a dollar per day despite heavy interventions from the aid communities in the West/North.

Even though economic hegemony is shifting to Asia (China and India) and Latin America (Brazil), there is no reason to believe that the hegemonic discourse of resource exploitation and profit maximization will change. On the contrary, China's economic growth is based on the same Eurocentric discourse, and the ecological challenges in China are, as a consequence, enormous, not only for China, but for the world as a whole. Its emission of greenhouse gases is the highest (in volume) in the world. There is a shortage and pollution of water. Annual desertification of land amounts to an area of about 13000 sq km (the size of Connecticut), and economic growth and rapid development mean "increasing urbanization, consumerism, and pollution" (Council on Foreign Relations, 2011).

The failures of past climate summits in Copenhagen (December 2009), Cancun (December 2010), and Durban (December 2011) show the inertia of the governments in wealthy countries. Actually, there is no global leadership to fend off the ecological crisis, simply because the leaders of wealthy countries are entrenched in an economic system that prioritizes non-sustainable development. There seems to be no willingness or ability to find a solution that requires a comprehensive social and economic transformation, such as the necessity to decrease consumption levels in the North (given that similar consumption levels across the globe would require several planets). Here there is no difference between Communist China (a capitalist in economic matters) and the US. This is one important reason why "the critique of the epistemic foundations of Western academic discourse has triggered and nourished discussions on the possibilities of construction of an alternative to capitalism" (Santos et al., 2008, p. xxxiv).

It was the universalist claims of Europe's hegemonic epistemology (as discussed earlier in the chapter) that was employed to justify Europe's "civilizing mission," which is still hegemonic globally. As Griffiths and Knezevic (2009) state:

> This scientific universalism, the most recent manifestation of European universalism, asserts objectivity across all phenomena and time . . . Such claims of universalism, or assertions of universal truths, function as meta-narratives that encapsulate the ideology of those groups with power in the world-system . . . (pp. 67–68).

The Recognition of Non-Hegemonic Epistemologies Contested

The recognition of non-hegemonic epistemologies by the West/North is contested territory because it involves the interrogation of the basic political, economic, ecological, and epistemological basis on which the Western civilizing mission has been and still is based. The scholars who work on climate change, to take one example, have experienced the wrath of powerful interest groups who see sustainable interventions as a threat to their economic interests, even though these climate scholars do not necessarily interrogate the current capitalist system in a comprehensive way (Oreske and Conway, 2011). However, any tampering with the philosophy of unlimited growth is perceived as sacrilege in the corridors of vested capitalist interests and big international corporations. Even those with a capitalist inclination who accept global warming as a scientific fact assert the sustainability of capitalism in a recession-riddled, carbon-constrained world (Newell and Paterson, 2010). The terrain of epistemological struggle is a struggle for power, with the only superpower, the US, in a very awkward and dangerous position.

While the overall position of Western hegemonic epistemology so far does not seem to be seriously threatened (at least not in the short run), despite the pending economic and ecological crises, the unfaltering faith in two of the most important concepts of modernist epistemology, rationality and empiricism, with their positivist ramifications, have been severely critiqued, most notably by the members of the Frankfurt School. It is to this critique I now turn.

2.5   A CRITIQUE OF WESTERN HEGEMONIC KNOWLEDGE PRODUCTION FROM WITHIN

This belief in "rationality" and the rejection of "irrationality" has permeated and hegemonized the scientific knowledge production in the West. The Frankfurt school's critique of positivist thought has exposed "the specific mechanisms of ideological control that permeate the consciousness and practices of advanced capitalist societies" (Giroux, 2003a, p. 32).

Positivism, according to Herbert Marcuse (1964), encompasses:

> (1) The validation of cognitive thought by experience of facts; (2) the orientation of cognitive thought to the physical science as a model of certainty and exactness; 3) the belief that progress in knowledge depends on this orientation. Consequently, positivism is a struggle against all metaphysics, transcendentalisms, and idealisms as obscurantist and regressive modes of thought . . . and stigmatizes non-positive notions as mere speculation, dreams or fantasies (p. 172).

The Frankfurt School[5] was wary of positivism's problematic relationship to self-criticism, critical thinking, and for its lack of questioning its own normative basis. The very focus on what were considered facts and objectivity and its technocratic view of science left a terrain relatively free from ethical considerations and commitment. Portraying itself as objective, rational, and universal, positivism claims to be beyond the culturally determined criteria of assessment used by other fields of study or knowledge traditions. For the Frankfurt School, the emphasis on social change and emancipation was an essential feature of critical thinking.

While strong positivist sentiments may have waned in recent years, faith in the rationality of science is still hegemonic and permeates the dominant structures of the core nations. Under the guise of objectivity and neutrality Western hegemonic knowledge is termed "rational" but, as the Frankfurt School points out, that knowledge is a social construction deeply embedded in the structures of power and privilege and therefore is not ideologically, culturally, or epistemologically neutral. It is the dominance of this hegemonic, mono-cultural epistemology that is more or less taken for granted and seldom interrogated or evaluated.

Postmodernism

The Frankfurt School's critique of hegemonic Western modernist epistemology is similar, if not identical, to the post-modernist critique of science.

While Western hegemonic epistemology is perceived to be objective, depersonalized, and decontextualized, post-modernist epistemology is more relativist of nature, culturally embedded, and, as Paul Ernest (2007b) states, "not transferable across contexts without significant transformations and shifts in meaning" (p. 16). From a post-modern perspective there is no grand narrative, and there is a multiplicity of meanings and perspectives. In such a perspective, "knowledge is constructed, not discovered; it is contextual, not foundational" (Elliott, 1996, pp. 18–19). While the post-modernist critique of science has been important in questioning science's truth claims it sparked much controversy, particularly in the 1990s, in the so-called science wars (Gross and Lewis, 1997; A. Ross, 1996). While there is no space to discuss the controversy surrounding the post-modernist critique of science here, suffice it to say that some postmodernist critics have acknowledged that their critiques have been misinterpreted and served the interests of reactionary academics, for example, the interests of the global warming skeptics (Latour, 2004).

What is important in the context of this book is the new role of knowledges, that is, the marketability of knowledges in the world economy. In the knowledge economy "knowledge, rather than products or services . . . is treated as the primary saleable and exploitable commodity" (Ernest, 2007b, p. 2). It means that any type of knowledges, Western or indigenous, are of interest as long as they are profitable in the marketplace. In times of globalization and modern technology geographical location is of less importance. Post-modern epistemology does thus "not provide a conceptualization of knowledge that leads it away from the knowledge economy. Instead it delivers it directly to the marketplace" (Ernest, 2007b, p.17). Since governments and multi-national corporations in the North have come to realize that knowledge is money, knowledges outside the hegemonic core that previously were rubbished, have now become of prime value. The struggle over intellectual property rights in the South (discussed later) is a result of this knowledge economy.

Feminism

Like post-modernism, feminism has also been a severe critic of modernism's grand narratives and decontextualized profile. Feminism has repeatedly criticized the hegemonic mono-culture of Eurocentric epistemology because of its exclusion of the marginalized, and particularly, the subalternized women. Feminist critique has contributed to asking new questions, interrogating dominant science, identifying new themes and topics, and uncovering male chauvinism.

Undoubtedly feminism has, from a Western perspective, provided some of the most substantial and useful criticism of the hegemonic knowledge system of the West. The marginalization, inferiorization, and subalternization of women, both in the North and the South, is reminiscent of the more comprehensive global picture of subjugation and domination. The situation of women in the South has entered the global arena through international organizations like the UN and International Non-Governmental Organizations (INGOs), particularly in terms of education policies. Gender and education policies were promoted by the publication of the United Nations Millennium Development Goals (MDGs) in 2000 and through the Education for All goals that legitimized the focus on gender equality and education. The situation is, however, difficult in many countries in South in terms of gender equality; globally, little improvement seems to have taken place. Both the Global Monitoring Reports of 2003/2004 (UNESCO, 2003/2004) and of 2011 (UNESCO, 2011) found that two-thirds of the illiterate globally were girls/women. In one of our cases, South Sudan, between 1% and 2% of females finish primary school, in what is probably the worst situation globally.

There are multiple reasons for the dismal situation in many countries in the South, ranging from traditionally skewed gender roles, different household types, and abject poverty to lack of prospective employment for girls with education. As noted, feminist thinking has informed much of the debate and initiatives around women and gender. Three important initiatives, Women in Development (WID), Women and Development (WAD), and Gender and Development (GAD) have been launched, the latter focusing on gender differences due to ideological, economic, historical, religious, and ethnic factors (Arnot and Fennell, 2008).

From an alternative, non-Western perspective these initiatives have had at least two important consequences. They helped to expose the situation of the women in the South, women who are often doubly marginalized, but it also exposed the limitations of a discourse, which despite its critique of the hegemonic mono-culture, is also part of that very same hegemonic mono-culture. Feminism does not address the issue of epistemic superiority beyond its feminist perspective, and such a feminist critique, while important up to a point, may also Orientalize women in the South who are situated in a completely different socio-economic and politico-cultural context. Feminist critique does not escape the colonialism of power and knowledge as discussed in the role of women in Sudan (Chapter 5).

The Western feminist agenda has therefore been challenged by female voices from the South as yet another type of colonial imposition from the North, as various countries in the South perceive gender relations in different ways depending on their traditions and socio-economic and cultural reference points. Madeleine Arnot and Shailaja Fennell (2008) state:

> The privileging of gender relations and patriarchy above other social form of power does not translate easily across societies. Nor do the categories for example of 'woman' and 'man,' the concept of the public or notions of the family since they too are arbitrary cultural formations (p. 6)

There are also big variations in the South (as well as in parts of the North) between urban-rural, nomads, half-nomads, and non-nomads as well as economic differentials and differences related to caste and race. Interestingly the feminists in the North have not paid much attention to these differences, nor have the UN organizations and the INGOs, thus reinforcing the perception of ideological and epistemological imposition on the South (Ramphal, 2005; Amadiume, 1997).

Making global recommendations on gender across cultures and places is thus not always unproblematic (Battiste and Barman, 1995; Gruenewald and Smith, 2008; King, 2007). There is a danger here of defining the women in the South as weak, disempowered, victimized, oppressed by men and by a hostile socio-economic environment, and incapable of agency. As Kriemild Saunders (2002) states, "The figure of the poor woman in the South is well suited to victimology narrative that rationalizes the planned management and liberation of the women in the South by Westernized professionals in the development apparatus" (p. 14).

This discussion of women's rights and the liberation of women in the South exemplifies the inherent danger of transferring values and ways of thinking from the North without taking into account the cultural embeddedness in the life and behavior of females in the South. There is a sense of a superiority syndrome here as well as a civilizing or liberatory mission that can easily reproduce a Self/Other dichotomy reminiscent of previous colonial interventions in the global South.

3 Indigenous Knowledge Systems, Sustainability, and Education in the Global South

3.1 INTRODUCTION

Even though Eurocentric epistemology has hegemonized the scientific discourse globally, there are also voices in the West beyond the feminist critics and the critics of positivism who have started listening to alternative knowledge systems.

The alliances between Western and Southern scholars and activists may in the long run help to readjust the asymmetry between us and the Other.

It is to the discussion of these alternative knowledge systems that the next sections are devoted, in particular indigenous knowledges.

3.2 INDIGENOUS PEOPLES AND INDIGENOUS KNOWLEDGES

Who Is Indigenous?

In my discussion of indigenous knowledges there is a need to explore the notion indigenous (and indigenous peoples) in some detail.

Indigenous peoples in our context are not only defined as people of indigenous minorities, like the Indians in the Americas, the Lapps in the circumpolar North, or minority indigenous groups in Asia or Oceania, but also the majority population in Africa that originated on the continent before the colonization process of the 19th and 20th century. In a South African context, for example, not only are the San and the Khoi peoples defined as indigenous in this book, but also the majority black populations with their worldviews and knowledge systems. This understanding of indigenous differs from the conventional modern usage of indigenous, which seems more restricted to "those who by a variety of historical and environmental circumstances have been placed outside of the dominant state systems" (Intercontinentalcry, 2011). It also differs from the definition of "indigeneity" adopted by the Special Rapporteur of the UN Economic and Social Council Sub-Commission on Prevention of Discrimination and Protection of Minorities:

Indigenous communities, peoples and nations are those which, having a historical continuity with pre-invasion and pre-colonial societies that have developed on their territories, consider themselves distinct from other sectors of the societies now prevailing in those territories, or parts of them. They form at present non-dominant sectors of society and are determined to preserve, develop and transmit to future generations their ancestral territories, and their ethnic identity, as the basis of their continued existence as peoples, in accordance with their own cultural patterns, social institutions and legal systems (United Nations, 2004, p. 2)

With a restrictive definition like the one above, the fact is suppressed or concealed that many peoples and majority population groups in Africa, Asia, and Latin America adhere to cultures, belief systems, and epistemologies that differ from the hegemonic Western ones. Such suppression also occurs in the education systems.

My extended definition arises from the fact that I identify with those who define "indigenous" primarily in terms of a shared experience of domination (Semali and Kincheloe, 1999). For indigenous peoples this domination originates with, and is perpetuated by, their contact with Western hegemonic epistemology.

Indigenous Knowledges

Due to the alienation caused by Eurocentric epistemology in the education systems in the South—the meager result of modernist interventions in terms of sustainable development in the South and the accelerating global ecological crisis—Western science and knowledge systems have been questioned and critiqued by a number of scholars, activists, and politicians in Africa, Latin America, Asia, Oceania, and in the West. Even though indigenous knowledges are multiple we can still identify some common threads that bind them together. Indigenous knowledges are knowledges produced in specific historical and cultural contexts and are typically not "generated by a set of pre-specified procedures or rules and [are] orally passed down from one generation to the next" (Semali and Kincheloe, 1999, p. 40). Indigenous knowledges are often characterized as traditional, aboriginal, Indian, vernacular, or African. Often indigenous knowledges are called local knowledges, as T. Moodie (2004) states:

"Local" can only be understood in relation to "universal," and thus the term *indigenous knowledge* incurs a string of negative judgements: "universal" is identified with "mainstream," and hence with "progress." And so "local" comes to be understood as referring to an intellectual backwater, and whatever is indigenous is then regarded as primitive or, at best, quaintly ethnic (p. 3).

Inspired by the African Renaissance in particular, interest in and focus on worldviews and indigenous cultures and knowledge systems in Africa as a supplement to what some call reductionist science and knowledge systems that have led to a comprehensive exploration of "the role of the social and natural sciences in supporting the development of indigenous knowledge systems" (Odora Hoppers, 2002, p. vii). P. Pitika Ntuli (2002) is correct when claiming that indigenous knowledge systems are a counter-hegemonic discourse in the context of the African Renaissance. Similarly, indigenous peoples and scholars in Latin America press for alternative ways to understand and conceptualize knowledges that take into account indigenous knowledges, not only in indigenous communities, but in majority societies as well.

The discussion of indigenous knowledges in a South African context centers on the Africanization of the country's knowledge production. While some scholars propose to place indigenous knowledges at the center of learning (Dei, 1994; Mkabela, 2005), Odora Hoppers (2002), for one, calls for the renaissance of indigenous knowledges that go "beyond finding an aggregate position or middle ground" (p. 20). Kai Horsthemke (2009), on the other hand, rejects "the status of knowledge and truth to the beliefs and knowledge claims of indigenous peoples, members of small-scale communities, etc." (p. 7). According to Horsthemke, the qualification of knowledges as indigenous is therefore redundant (2004).

Like Catherine Odora Hoppers, Arun Agrawal (1995) questions the clear line of demarcation between Western and indigenous knowledges and proposes some sort of coexistence between the two epistemological positions. Although the binary divide between the two knowledge systems is based on different epistemological foundations, there is reason to question the view of two competing knowledge systems where dialogue is completely precluded. Moreover, like Western hegemonic knowledge, which did not emerge in a vacuum in Europe, indigenous knowledges have also been influenced by external actors, as very few communities have lived in complete isolation from the outer world.

W. Kyle (1999) takes this one step further by arguing that the term "Western" is in itself an indigenous system as it is rooted in European cultures and worldviews.

The concern in this book is that indigenous knowledges in the global South are dislocated knowledges, and, it is therefore argued, in line with Odora Hoppers, that the epistemological silencing of non-hegemonic, indigenous epistemologies must be reversed.

The call for re-evaluation of modern and indigenous knowledge systems referred to above is articulated in Odora Hoppers's influential book (2002) as well as by a number of scholars who have done substantial research on indigenous worldviews and knowledge systems (Ogunnyi, 1988; Jegede,

1995; Hountondji, 1997). The important contributions of philosophers and theologians like, for example, John Mbiti (1969) and E. B. Idowo (1982), have exposed the importance of metaphysics, spirituality, and religion in African epistemologies, whereas the Ghanaian philosopher Kwame Gyekye (1997) has analyzed African worldviews and cultures in terms of a traditional-modern dichotomy.

While Gyekye (1997) sees culture as socially created and nurtured meanings constituting "the greater portion of our necessary social context" (p. 44), Geert Hofstede's view is perhaps more internally oriented as "the collective programming of the mind" (1991). While social anthropologists often define culture as encompassing societal structures as well as ways of acting and thinking, sociologists often make a distinction between culture and structure where various groups have different access to power and resources. However, separating culture from the structures of cultural reproduction fails to do justice to the mutually constituting dialectic of their relations. If Michael Kearney's (1984) definition of a worldview is plausible, then the line of demarcation between culture, worldview, and epistemology is thin. He defines worldview as:

> A culturally organized micro-thought: those dynamically interrelated assumptions of a people that determine much of their behaviour and decision making as well as organizing much of their symbolic creations . . . and ethno-philosophy in general (p. 1).

Peter Crossman and René Devisch (2002) emphasize this interrelatedness in their understanding of indigenous, or as they prefer to call it, endogenous knowledge systems and worldviews, and characterize them in terms such as holistic and organic, non-dominating, non-manipulative, non-mechanical, social and people-centered, and relational. While Crossman and Devisch can be criticized for being normative and idealizing indigenous knowledge systems, Odora Hoppers and P. Makhale-Mahlangu, in their definition of indigenous knowledge systems, may seem to tone down the metaphysical aspects of such systems by referring to them as:

> The combination of knowledge systems encompassing technology, social, economic and philosophical learning, or educational, legal and governance systems. It is knowledge relating to the technological, social, institutional, scientific and developmental, including those used in the liberation struggle (Odora Hoppers and Makhale-Mahlangu, 1998; quoted in Odora Hoppers, 2002, pp. 8–9).

It is, however, imperative that indigenous knowledge systems are understood in relation to a worldview that is often realized in religious ceremonies, rituals, and other practices. My field-work among the Xhosa in South Africa and among the Mapuche in Chile confirms such a view (see Chapters

4 and 7). Even though there are aspects linked to indigenous, cultural practices other than religion, religion and religious practices are the *sine qua
non* of indigenous epistemologies.

Vimbai Chivaura's (2006) comment on development in an African setting is worth noting:

> The African worldview declares that our world has two aspects: They
> are the physical and the spiritual . . . The differences between African
> and European worldviews concerning earth and heaven relate to differ-
> ences in their attitudes towards the material and the spiritual. Africans
> regard them as compatible . . . The danger of adopting the European
> worldview to solve African problems is therefore obvious. It is hostile
> to our worldview and idea of development. African development can
> only be truly achieved through an African worldview (p. 217).

A very similar picture is painted by Mbiti (1969) and Idowu (1982) of
other ethnic groups across the African continent. In Chile, the divergent
epistemological positions encompassed by the Mapuche *Kimün* and Western worldviews have important political, philosophical, psychological, and
pedagogical consequences. The two epistemological positions clash, both
in relation to spirituality, but also in relation to the land issue, not only in
Chile, but also in other countries in Latin America. From such a perspective, Eurocentric epistemology is viewed as a violent epistemology destroy-
ing the sacred relationship between man, nature, and the supernatural.

The holistic nature of the interrelationship between nature, human
beings, and the supernatural is founded on indigenous knowledge systems.
As Patrick Chabal and Jean-Pascal Daloz (1999) state, "A crucial feature
of African belief systems is the absence of a firm boundary between the
religious and the temporary" (p. 65).

A definition of indigenous knowledges must therefore account for the
holistic, metaphysical foundation (worldviews) of indigenous knowledge systems and their various ramifications. Consequently, I argue that indigenous
knowledge systems encompass worldviews, cultural values and practices,
and knowledge systems derived from these worldviews and practices, and
they are related to metaphysical, ecological, economic, and scientific fields.

In Europe this holism was undermined by the Protestant reformation
(Delanty, 2000, p. 39), which played an important role in the rise of modern science (and the separation between the secular and the spiritual) and
thus in the advent of modernity (Breidlid, 2002).

It has been noted earlier that indigenous knowledges with their non-uni-
versalist pretensions are, contrary to Western epistemology's transcendence
of place, delimited geographically and culturally. Moreover, indigenous
knowledges are, as Paul Sillitoe (2000) argues, as "much skill as knowledge,
and its learning across generations is characterized by oral transmission
and learning through experience and repetitive practice" (p. 4). Indigenous

knowledges pose an alternative to narrowly focused scientific disciplines that neglect the interconnections of natural phenomena that could promote sustainable development. Contrary to what a Western discourse often seems to assume, indigenous knowledges are often "flexible, adaptable, and innovative" (Sillitoe, 2000, p. 4) but should not be interpreted and categorized within the realms of a Western paradigm. Within such a paradigm, "African worldviews and wisdom look like myth and superstitious metaphysics" (Chivaura, 2006, p. 219). However, post-colonial Africa and Latin America have exposed areas in which indigenous knowledge systems are relevant and useful as discussed later in the book.

There is a need here for communication between the various knowledge systems, not by opposing everything Western knowledge systems and education represent, but by creating dialogue between different concepts and practices of knowledges. Indigenous knowledges focus on the relationship " of human beings to both one another and to their ecosystem . . . an emphasis which has been notoriously absent in the knowledge produced in Western science over the last four centuries" (Semali and Kincheloe, 1999, p. 16).

The imposition of a Western secular knowledge has to a large extent isolated human beings from nature and spirituality. Since spirituality is an integral part of how indigenous peoples perceive the world, the elimination of spirituality in the Western epistemological discourse has alienated the colonized from themselves. As Isabelle Barker (2002) states, "[secularism] legitimized colonial and neo-colonial forms of domination as it was situated in opposition to the non-secular, conceived of variously in terms of religion, tribalism and the irrational" (p. 105).

It seems clear from the definitions of Western epistemology discussed earlier that spirituality does not feature strongly—if at all. In fact, the hegemonic atomistic materialism and aversion to spirituality of Western knowledges is well known by indigenous peoples who participate in academia. As Philip Walker (2001) points out, "The sacred aspects of indigenous experience are directly silenced when they are eliminated from formal research, relegated to religion or labeled as lacking rigor" (p. 19).

Kwame Appiah questions the rejection of Western hegemonic knowledge of the possibility of the reality of the spiritual. In his book *In My Father's House* (1992), Appiah discusses African spirituality and Africans' belief in spirits as real personal agents (although invisible) in comparison to Western rational epistemology. He challenges the *a priori* refusal of mainstream modern Western thought even to consider the possibility of the reality of the spiritual. According to Appiah, Western scholars perceive spirituality as symbolism or mythology at best, superstition at the very least. Simply put, Appiah states, "the symbolists are able to treat traditional believers as reassuringly rational only because they deny that traditional people mean what they say. . . . It is peculiarly unsatisfactory to treat a system of propositions as symbolic when those whose propositions they are appear to treat them literally *and* display, in other contexts, a clear grasp of the notion of symbolic representation" (p.116).[1] This exclusion or reinterpretation of spirituality does not take seriously the lived realities of traditional believers.

The importance of spirituality for indigenous peoples is stressed by Njoki Nahtani Wane (2006):

> Spirituality as an anti-colonial discourse is shaped by the lived realities of colonial subjects who question the concept of universal standard by pointing out, or recognizing, its limited scope and perspective . . . Spirituality as a discourse cannot be taught since it is a biologically built-in constituent of what it is to be human . . . Spirituality may be understood as process of struggle, a way of self-recovery and the path to follow in order to become whole and human . . . Spirituality is the vital life force that animates African peoples and connects them to the rhythms of the universe, nature, ancestors and the community. It permeates merely every domain of African lives. Historically, spirituality has served as a personal and communal source of liberation, solace, hope, meaning and forgiveness (pp. 88–89).

In *Africa Works* (1999), Chabal and Daloz claim that Africa works, but works differently from the development paradigm of the West. Even though the imposition of Western knowledge production has been massive over a long period of time there is, in fact, a re-traditionalization of society in Africa (p. 45). This is in line with my results from exploring the Xhosa in South Africa, as the Xhosa identity has not been worked over by colonial oppression. Moreover, Chabal and Daloz claim that while Africa is different, African political action can be explained in terms of rational behavior (p. xvii). Their analysis of witchcraft and religion in Africa confirms an impression of the pervasiveness of religious and spiritual belief, both traditional and modern, as the religious faith is "part of the very fabric of the African psyche" (p. 68). In contrast to many Western Africanists, Chabal and Daloz attempt to find the rationale and the rationality underlying the behavioral patterns of Africans without, as it were, imposing Western, secular standards.

For indigenous and oppressed people, reclaiming spirituality can be a way of evoking agency to fight further oppression and exclusion and to establish an identity based on authenticity. The deprivation of spirituality is therefore a blow against their selves and their autonomy as human beings. In an educational context, Kurt Alan Ver Beek (2000) points out that taking cognizance of the indigenous students' spirituality gives them "a sense of power and hope" (p. 32).

Peter Berger's (1999) theories of secularization and desecularization signal that religion does not disappear in the wake of modernization, even though Europe is different from the US and the rest of the world:

> A shift in the institutional location of religion, then, rather than secularization, would be a more accurate description of the European

situation. All the same, Europe stands out as quite different from other parts of the world, and certainly, from the United States. One of the most interesting puzzles in the sociology of religion is why Americans are so much more religious as well as more churchly than Europeans (p. 10).

The point here is, however, that such spiritual elements are, as Walker and others underline, strongly resisted within hegemonic Western knowledge-making traditions and institutions. Exceptions here are physicists like Fritjof Capra (2000) and F. David Peat (1992, 1996), who in different ways incorporate a spiritual view of reality.[2]

3.3 INDIGENOUS ECOLOGICAL KNOWLEDGES

Nature and the land are central concepts in indigenous knowledges as these concepts are related to spirituality and the supernatural. For both the Xhosa in South Africa and the Mapuche in Chile, land is important for its attachment to their ancestors and their sacred burial places. Among the Xhosa, for example, the homesteads and the cattle enclosures are sacred, and as we will see in Chapter 4, for them place and territory are important identity markers not easily eliminated by a modernist discourse. Oftentimes the sacredness of land is related to ancestral beliefs.

The struggle of indigenous peoples' territorial and epistemic rights is particularly visible in Latin America. The Mapuche resistance to land grabbing by the big international corporations and the government is, however, not only justified in terms of the sacredness of the land, but also ultimately in terms of protecting the resources on the Mapuche land.[3] Our case study from Chile shows that the activism among the Mapuche is met with anti-terrorist laws and harassment, and an unwillingness on the part of the Chilean authorities to uphold the indigenous rights written down in the ILO convention, which Chile eventually signed in 2008. The struggle for territorial and epistemic rights still goes on, however, but since the Mapuche represent a minority in the country, the leverage to effect change is not as big as in countries like Bolivia, where a majority of the population is indigenous. Moreover, the various Chilean governments, center-left or right, are not willing to acknowledge subaltern epistemologies. The Mapuche perception of the sacredness of the land and the Western hegemonic concept of nature as exploitable and for profit maximization is based on the classical conflict between contesting epistemologies. The West's taming of nature parallels the taming of the savage—the Other. Both had to be exploited to serve the interests of the West. As Santos et al. (2008) state:

The civilizing violence enacted upon the "savages" via the destruction of native knowledges and the imprinting of true, civilized knowledge is performed, in the case of nature, through its transformation into an unconditionally available natural resource . . . The savage and nature are, in fact, the two sides of the same purpose: to domesticate "savage nature," turning it into a natural resource. This unique will to domestication makes the distinction between natural and human resources as ambiguous and fragile in the sixteenth century as it is today (p. xxxvi).

In other words, the physical colonization is closely linked with epistemological colonization. The Mapuche leadership claims that there can be no social justice without cognitive justice. Since the activist Mapuche resist the exploitation of their land for hydro-electric plants or mineral extraction, they are often applauded by conservationist and ecologically conscious agents.

Growing Recognition of Indigenous Ecological Knowledges

There is a growing recognition that huge ecological knowledges are stored in the indigenous communities globally, and that indigenous knowledges, biodiversity, and sustainable development are closely linked (Claxton, 2010; Berkes, Colding, and Folke, 2000). By synthesizing findings from a variety of research projects, Fikret Berkes, Johan Colding, and Carl Folke discovered that there exists "a diversity of local or traditional practices for ecosystem management" (Berkes et al. 2000, p. 1251). Indigenous peoples' perception of the interrelationship between man and nature is vital here, and while there are exceptions, the general pattern seems to be:

> Where Indigenous peoples are living on their traditional lands, comparatively healthy ecosystems remain. The lesson here is obvious: Native peoples have performed remarkably better than industrial peoples in preserving the ecological integrity of their homelands, and in practicing sustainability (Faulstich, 2003, p. 5).

Indigenous peoples, not only in Latin America, but also globally, use a variety of strategies to conserve the environment, and this has often been ignored by the North. Some of these strategies are very local and unique to a particular environment and cannot easily be transferred to other environments whereas other approaches like mixed cropping, intercropping, and shifting cultivation (UNEP 2008, p. 33) are applied globally. Temporal restriction on harvesting is used in some indigenous management systems, for example, among African herders (Niamir-Fuller, 1998). In the semi-arid regions in Sahel, "plants' productivity oscillates seasonally and follows the rains" (Berkes et al., 2000, p. 1255). The implication is that many cattle herders undertake seasonal migrations providing "rotational management, enabling the recovery of heavily grazed rangelands" (Berkes et al., 2000, p. 1255). Moreover, the migration of the Sahel herders is adapted to the unpredictability of the environment. The Masai of Kenya, for example, migrate away from the wells as the rainy season starts in order to leave enough grazing ground closer to the wells during the dry season. African herders also establish range reserves for grazing ground in times of emergency. These reserves function to sustain the ecosystem and help the herders to recover after an emergency situation (Niamir-Fuller, 1998). In Sudan, on the fringe of the desert, many ethnic groups undertake nomadic movements throughout the year because it is the only way to use the scarce resources. According to Meine van Noordwijk (1984), "The animal owners do not have a permanent place of residence, although the movements *are far from random* and people generally move in regular cycles, modified by the rainfall pattern of that particular year (p. 143, my italics).

Given the holistic nature of indigenous knowledges, some strategies designed for one specific environmental challenge may end up impacting on other aspects of the environment as well, for example, "biodiversity, forest conservation, land use and management, and so on" (UNEP, 2008, p. 34).

What differentiates indigenous knowledges from conventional Western ecological knowledge is the situatedness of indigenous knowledges. Indigenous knowledges are local (although similar practices may be widespread) and depend upon local social mechanisms. There is some sort of hierarchical system here where indigenous knowledges as manifested in indigenous practices are anchored in social institutions that again are based on indigenous worldviews and epistemologies. The circles proceeding from indigenous knowledges via indigenous practices (related, for example, to land conservation) to worldview imply that indigenous practices do not function in a vacuum, but they are closely related to worldviews and epistemologies that are spiritual and religious of nature (Fig. 3.1 shows this interrelatedness). This is, for example, true with the Mapuche in Chile. Rituals and religious institutions help to sustain ecological sound practices and function often as a script, which is to be followed if impending doom is to be avoided.

Carriers of indigenous knowledges like elders, chiefs, or mythical figures, who are often rubbished by people from the North, may help to maintain sound ecological practices. Examples of such people in various countries who keep up sound ecological practices abound. Berkes et al. (2000) refer to the hunters' guild of the Yoruba culture that controls the maintenance of indigenous knowledges and traditions, as does the hero of the *milpa* agro-ecosystem in Latin America and the Gitksan of British Columbia.

During the 17th Conference of the Parties to the United Nations Framework Convention on Climate Change (UNFCCC) in December 2011 (COP17, 2011), regional initiatives to incorporate indigenous knowledges into fighting climate change were taken. For example, the African Young Scientists and Youth Initiative on Climate Change and Indigenous Knowledge Systems (AYSICCIKS) issued a communiqué stating that it seeks to

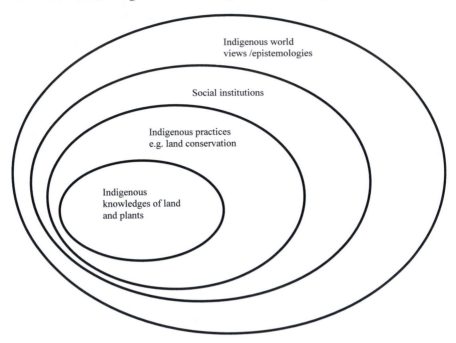

Figure 3.1   Ecological circles: indigenous knowledges (adapted from Berkes et al., 2000).

"mobilize African young scientists and youth within and outside Africa to promote the role of African indigenous knowledge systems in climate change adaptation and mitigation through research and community engagement." Moreover, the group wants to "facilitate the formulation of national, regional and continental policy and legal frameworks to protect and promote the role of IKS in climate change" (AYSICCIKS, 2011). Such bottom-up initiatives reflect the increasing uneasiness about global change in the global South and the conviction that the South has something to offer in the struggle for a sustainable future.

Indigenous Medicine

One of the definitions given for African indigenous or traditional medicine by the WHO Center for Health Development (2011) is the following:

> The sum total of all knowledge and practices, whether explicable or not, used in diagnosis, prevention and elimination of physical, mental, or societal imbalance, and relying exclusively on practical experience and observation handed down from generation to generation, whether verbal or in writing.

In South Africa, "most people associate traditional medicine with the herbs, remedies (or *muti*), and advice imparted by *sangomas* or *izinyangas*—traditional healers from African indigenous groups—and with strong spiritual components" (Richter, 2003, pp. 7–8). Indigenous medicine is primarily plant based, but animal-based medicines and medicine from minerals are also used in healing practices. Due to the extensive use of plant materials, however, traditional medicine is often associated with herbalism. Given the holistic nature of indigenous knowledges, indigenous medicine is based on the assumption that illness and diseases result from the disruption of the body's harmony with nature. Indigenous medicine is used for diagnosis, prevention, and cure and can, according to the WHO, treat various infectious and chronic conditions (WHO, 2011). The WHO estimates that up to 80% of the population in many African countries make use of indigenous or traditional medicine as their primary health care. In Sub-Saharan Africa, the ratio of traditional healers to the population is approximately 1 in 500, while medical doctors have a 1 in 40,000 ratio to the rest of the population (Richter, 2003).

Indigenous medicine is also used in Latin America. In Chile, one of our case studies, indigenous medicine is not only used among indigenous groups like the Aymara in the North and Mapuche in the South (SIT Study Abroad, 2011), but Mapuche indigenous medicine has spread throughout the country to complement Western medicine in treating more than 50 diseases (Sci Dev Net, 2011). The issue over patenting the products is, however, a growing concern. I will return to this issue in the next subsection.

Indigenous Intellectual Property Rights and Patents

According to Vandana Shiva (2007), "indigenous medical systems are based on over 7000 species of medicinal plants and on 15000 medicines of herbal formulations in different systems . . . The economic value to 100 million rural households is immeasurable (p. 273).

While indigenous medical systems are invaluable to millions of people, the new intellectual property systems and patents are a source of grave concern in the South. According to the WTO's 1994 TRIPS Agreement (Trade-Related Aspects of Intellectual Property Rights), "patents shall be available for any inventions, whether products or processes, in all fields of technology, provided that they are new, involve an inventive step, and are capable of industrial application" (WTO, TRIPS Article 27, 1994, p. 1). Patenting also means, on the other hand, the right to exclude "others from making, using, offering for sale, selling, or importing the patented product made from the patented process (Shiva, 2007, p. 275). The patent system as part of the intellectual property system is unmistakably a part of the colonial legacy and of European/American capitalism. While land and resources were important elements for extraction and exploitation in colonial times, indigenous knowledges that were dislocated for centuries have now become increasingly attractive as they can be used for ownership, investment, production, marketing, and profit maximization. The strategy of the former colonial powers and the US has not changed in the new century, where the asymmetrical relationship between the North and the South is still sustained and perpetuated.

While the major intellectual property systems protect the intellectual property and patents of the North, there is concern that the same rights and patents viz. indigenous knowledges of nature are often ignored and appropriated by multi-national corporations and nations in the North (Shiva, 2007; Mgbeoji, 2006). According to Ikechi Mgbeoji:

> The exploitative relationship and alleged theft of biodiversity and associated traditional knowledge has given rise to allegations of "biopiracy" against industrialized states and corporate institutions involved in the business of bioprospecting and the commercialization of indigenous peoples' biocultural knowledge (p. 11).

Biopiracy is, in other words, a term used to describe how the North is exploiting and stealing indigenous knowledges for profit. Theft means that this happens without the necessary permission and compensation to the indigenous communities. The consequences are alarming; the people in the South "will have to buy their seeds and medicines at high costs from the global biotechnology and pharmaceutical giants (Shiva, 2007, p. 275). Joel Bakan's (2004) characterization of a modern corporation is stinging:

> As a psychopathic creature, the corporation can neither recognise nor act upon moral reasons to refrain from harming others. Nothing in its legal makeup limits what it can do to others in pursuit of its selfish ends, and it is compelled to cause harm when the benefits of doing so outweigh the costs (p. 60).

Resistance to biopiracy has been on the agenda of the anti-globalization movement for a long time. This is ultimately a resistance against the recolonization of the South and against the theft of the indigenous knowledges of nature. While there has been some success in reducing the activities and powers of the pharmaceutical industry and agribusiness, for example, in South Africa and Brazil,[4] the struggle is by no means over. In Chapters 4 and 7, the issue of biopiracy in South Africa and Chile is discussed further.

Negative Effects of Indigenous Practices

Even though "the decline effect" of modern science referred to in the previous chapter may open up more space for other epistemologies, indigenous knowledges must be viewed critically, and the contradictions within indigenous knowledges need to be exposed. The potential rebirth of indigenous knowledges does not mean that indigenous knowledges should be essentialized, romanticized, or presented as monolithic and uncontested even by indigenous populations. First of all, it is not possible to return the indigenous to some pure, pre-colonial existence. All cultures are in a state of change. As Kincheloe and Steinberg (2008) state:

> Without such a burial indigenous cultures are discouraged from shifting and adapting and indigenous knowledges are viewed simply as sacred relics fixed in a decontextualized netherland. It is important to recognise the circulation of culture, the reality of "contamination" (p. 143)

Moreover, indigenous identities are multiple and in flux, depending on status, religion, class, and gender. Identities are diverse and do not fit into one single box or category.

> The indigenous cultural experience is not the same for everybody, indigenous knowledge is not a monolithic epistemological concept . . . Not everyone who identifies with a particular indigenous culture produces knowledge the same way, nor do different indigenous cultures produce the same knowledges (Kincehloe and Steinberg, 2008, pp. 143–144).

While there is much truth in indigenous peoples' awe for nature and thus for ecologically sound practices, the picture is more ambiguous in the real world. It is not an *a priori* fact that indigenous approaches to land management are always more sustainable, as indigenous knowledges do not always support a view of nature that is inherently benign. If such a view is sustained there is a real danger of romanticizing these knowledges unduly.

The fragile relationship between man and nature among indigenous peoples is captured in the myth of the Dinka (the biggest ethnic group in South Sudan) about the introduction of death in the world. The myth exists in several versions with a similar message, that is, the connection with God was broken because of greed, or lack of modesty in the relationship between human beings and nature:

> In the beginning of times God and man were directly connected by a rope. Death did not exist on earth, and one grain of dura was sufficient to feed the people. However, a woman who cultivated this grain decided that she could cultivate more grains, that is, more than was necessary to sustain the people. In response to this greediness, God broke the rope that gave the connection with mankind.
>
> In another version the woman was stamping dura when a small bird took away a grain. The woman got angry and killed the bird whereupon it (God) cut the rope with its bill (van Noordwijk, 1984, p. 232).

See also the story of the kujur below (Fig. 3.2).

Indigenous knowledges are therefore, as Briggs (2005) states, not a "'given' benign and consensual knowledge, simply waiting to be tapped into" (p. 18).

Jared Diamond (1993) notes, for example, that even though the New Guinea natives have comprehensive knowledge of plants and animals in the region, some groups, nevertheless, impact negatively on their native environment. Richard J. Hamilton (2001) discusses the role of indigenous knowledges in the depletion of a limited fish resource on Salomon Islands.

Moreover, ethnic conflicts and warfare had and still have adverse effects on the ecological balance, like "confrontations over rangeland and rain-fed agricultural land" in the various parts of South Sudan (UNEP, 2007).

Figure 3.2 The story of the kujur (Sudan) (from van Noordwijk, 1984).

While indigenous medicine is invaluable to many people across the globe there are reasons to warn against a complete and unconditional surrender to indigenous medicine (the same goes, of course, for Western medicine). Some herbal medicines can have negative side effects and can even be dangerous if not taken in the right way. Some adverse side effects may be kidney and liver problems, mental confusion, and heart problems. Moreover, the proven positive effects of certain types of indigenous medicine are not verified. In South Africa, some traditional healers have claimed, with no justification whatsoever, to have found a cure for AIDS, which has caused unethical behavior by the healers towards the patients in some cases (Richter, 2003).

While indigenous medicine can have positive and negative effects on health, certain indigenous cultural practices are clearly detrimental in terms of health and well-being. The HIV/AIDS pandemic has exposed the untenability of certain indigenous practices and attitudes related to sexual behavior and unequal gender roles. As Nicoli Nattrass (2004) states, "gender inequality, sexual violence, a preference for dry sex, fatalistic attitudes and pressures to prove fertility contribute to a high-risk environment" (pp. 26–27). Suzanne Leclerc-Madlala (2002) is more specific in her discussion of cultural sexual practices, referring to Zulu sexual culture, which is "underpinned by meanings which associate sex with gifts and manliness with the ability to attract and maintain multiple sex partners" (pp. 31–32).

Moreover, while spirituality is often perceived as a positive asset to indigenous knowledges, for example in terms of identity construction and land conservation, the belief in spirits (see e.g. Mbiti, 1969 and Orimoogunje, 2009) may also cause anxiety and fear among indigenous peoples and have a negative impact on the individual and the society at large.

Consequently, indigenous knowledges, while arguably a necessary supplement for a more sustainable development, are no miracle cure *per se*. As Bhola (2003) states, "In sum, indigenous knowledge is holistic at its best and inert at its worst" (p. 11).

What is at stake in this book is the dislocation of indigenous knowledges, both in the public debate as well in the education systems across the world, at a period of time when hegemonic Western knowledge alone is demonstrably unable to adequately resolve current serious social, educational, economic, and ecological challenges.

Suffice it to reiterate that the epistemological foundation of indigenous knowledges draws on knowledges that transcend the atomistic materialism of Western hegemonic knowledge and inform the lived existence of indigenous peoples in various ways. It is the exclusion of these knowledges that is my concern here, both because it deprives indigenous peoples of "their" knowledges in a very existential way, and because the indigenous knowledges' perception of the interconnectedness between man, nature, and the supernatural may challenge the aggressive exploitation of nature that guides Western epistemic hegemony. There is therefore a need for collaboration and conversation between the knowledge systems. In the next subchapter, the issue of collaboration/conversation and even co-existence is explored in some detail.

3.4 THE CO-EXISTENCE OF WESTERN AND INDIGENOUS KNOWLEDGE SYSTEMS: CHAT AND EXPANSIVE LEARNING

Such a conversation, which involves non-Western knowledge systems, requires some sort of humility as to the potential capacities of Western hegemonic knowledge to provide a way out of the deadlock in which the world finds itself; it also requires an acknowledgement of the limitations of Eurocentric epistemology in "solving" the critical issues. A key question is how we can overcome hegemonic Eurocentric modernity without throwing away everything modern that is sustainable. There is no easy answer to such a question, since it involves a discussion of which aspects of Eurocentric modernity/Western rational modernism, however labeled and defined, must be jettisoned, and which might contribute to resolving the pressing dilemmas.

Interestingly, some leading scientists steeped in the Western, Eurocentric tradition are starting to suggest that religion may play an important role in salvaging the environment in a situation where the world leaders are unable and unwilling to take the necessary steps. Edward O. Wilson, for one, a pioneer of sociobiology, and Robert, Lord May of Oxford, the former President of the Royal Society in the UK (neither of them professed religious men or Christians), have urged the establishment of an alliance between science and religion to combat the ecological crisis (see *Daily Telegraph*, 2009). The implication is that science alone cannot solve the serious global challenges and that more science and more technology are not going to get us out of the present ecological crisis. Lynn White (1974) also suggests that religion may have a role to play here; he proposes to "find a new religion. Or rethink of our old one" (p. 5). It is with such a perspective that White reminds us of St. Francis of Assisi, who preached humility not only for each individual, but for man as a species (White, 1974, p. 5). St. Francis proposed the democratic idea of the equality of all creatures to replace the idea of man's limitless domination over nature or creation.[5] St. Francis' break with the dualism of man and nature is reminiscent of indigenous peoples' awe and respect for nature and indicates a similar spirituality, which may help to bridge, at least to some extent, the gap between the different knowledge systems. It requires, though, a break with dogmatic, hegemonic Christianity's view of nature; stewardship must replace domination and exploitation as the hegemonic Christian axiom, and St. Francis must be recovered in the discourse of ecological survival. White is quite adamant, "we shall have a worsening ecological crisis until we reject the Christian axiom that nature has no reason for existence save to serve man (p.6)," and

I add, unless the unholy relationship between what has traditionally been perceived as *hegemonic* Christianity and capitalism is broken.

The similarity between St. Francis' "ecological" thinking and indigenous peoples' relationship to nature opens up a third space referred to in the introduction for an appreciation of the connections and relationships between knowledge systems that have more or less been camouflaged in the century-long imposition of a specific interpretation of Christianity and reinforced through the hegemonic role of capitalism.

It is, in today's world, necessary for indigenous and Western knowledge systems to co-exist. By co-existence I mean, in particular, a situation where the hegemonic knowledge system talks to the dominated one and acknowledges the urgency of addressing issues that the dominant epistemology seems unable or unwilling to tackle. Its superiority complex must be disbanded in the quest for a sustainable future. Concomitantly, indigenous knowledges should be given space, or rather they must create and demand space, to query hegemonic epistemology.

All societies are hybrid, in one sense or the other, in line with Homi K. Bhabha's cultural hybridity thesis (Bhabha, 1994, 1996) where different cultures and knowledge systems operate in the same space. There is some sort of dialectic here where the one feeds into the other, but there is also a tension and an asymmetry that needs to be addressed. In Bhabha's thinking, the idea of a third space is something that is generated, but not necessarily, caused by what preceded it. The third space is, in my understanding, a space which generates new possibilities by questioning entrenched categorizations of knowledge systems and cultures and opens up new avenues with, and this is important to underline, a counter-hegemonic strategy. In a post-colonial situation where the colonizer "presents a normalising, hegemonic practice, the hybrid strategy opens up a third space of/for rearticulation of negotiation and meaning" (Meredith 1998, p. 3).

Bhabha's third space is a contested terrain and has been critiqued for its presumed lack of historical and political embeddedness. While Bhabha's third space is conceptually and theoretically interesting, one should be wary of being too optimistic given the long history of economic and epistemic subjugation. The epistemological dimension of colonialism should not be underrated and should not be thought of in the past tense. The inherent danger of such a space is the perpetuation of imbalance and asymmetry between the knowledge systems—between the dichotomized space of Self and Other *within* the third space. When exploring the third space one has to acknowledge that all indigenous knowledges are subjugated knowledges, and that the issue of power is central in discussing and analyzing the power relationships between indigenous knowledges and so-called Western science and epistemology. There is a question of negotiation here, but the question is how much can be negotiated when the power relationship between the knowledge systems is so skewed and when there is an issue of domination and subjugation. There is a concern that indigenous knowledges are appropriated by the North to serve North's own purposes or interests, and that they are made to fit the paradigms of Western epistemology. As Agrawal (2005) states: "those who possess indigenous knowledge have not possessed much power to influence what is done with their knowledge" (p. 380).

In many ways, the third space is reminiscent of Freire's (1970) concept of dialogue where conscientization is the ultimate goal. Freire's concept of dialogue potentially provides the foundation for a re-imagining of the teacher-student relationship in this new space. A third space that transcends the teacher-student relationship onto a more trans-personal level indicates some sort of undogmatic, non-entrenched space where both potential nostalgic claims of indigenous authenticity, Western pretensions of superiority, and the inherent contradictions (referred to earlier) in both knowledge systems can be interrogated for new negotiations.

Louis R. Botha (2011), who tries to articulate a way of knowing beyond "the grasp of my Western consciousness," (p. 43) employs:

> Cultural-historical activity theory (CHAT) as a conceptual framework within which mixed methods can be employed to negotiate more appropriate knowledge-making relations and practices between the epistemologically divergent ways of knowing of indigenous and Western knowledge communities (p. 2).

Third generation cultural-historical activity theory (CHAT) (Engeström, 1987, 2001) is relevant when analyzing contradictions within and between the two activity systems of indigenous knowledges and Western knowledge. In CHAT, contradictions are viewed as central sources of change and development. According to Yrjö Engeström (2001), "contradictions generate disturbances and conflicts, but also innovative attempts to change the activity" (p. 137). CHAT is an object-oriented change methodology, so it is therefore essential to analyze contradictions in relation to the object of activity. A crucial object of activity in which Western knowledge systems and indigenous knowledge systems interact is, for example, to combat HIV/AIDS. Relevant questions to ask in order to focus on contradictions within and between these two interacting activity systems working to combat HIV/AIDS are, for example: How has the activity system's relation with the object been developed over time? What are the theoretical ideas and tools that have shaped the activity?

Making use of the cultural-historical activity theory may be seen as a way of operationalizing Bhabha's third space in which indigenous peoples can name and practice their knowledge-making processes and state where and how they would relate to Western knowledge. It is a space to undermine "the position of power that dominant Western knowledge traditions have assumed vis-a-vis indigenous knowledge making" and to expose "how the local and spiritual nature of indigenous knowledges differentiate them from modern, Western knowledges" (Botha 2011, p. 2).

This space then becomes a potentially shared object of activity as shown in Figure 3.3. Potentially shared objectives are objects of activity or problems that motivate collaboration between activity systems. As Anne Edwards, Harry Daniels, Tony Gallagher, Jane Leadbetter, and Paul Warmington (2009) explain:

> CHAT alerts us to the impact of sharing problems or tasks between systems. It was developed to recognize that participants from different systems bring different attributes to work on a common object or problem, which, in turn, is likely to lead to an expansion of the object and systemic learning within the collaborating systems (p. 91).

The model is in line with Semali and Kincheloe's (1999) notion that indigenous knowledges are subjugated knowledges that "can be employed as a constellation of concepts that challenge the invisible cultural assumptions embedded in all aspects of schooling and knowledge production" (p. 32).

CHAT is used as a framework for decolonizing knowledge-making by challenging some of the dominating knowledge traditions that hegemonize Western epistemology by claiming universality. Botha (2011) asks "how we can consciously and deliberately integrate the diverse ontological, epistemological and axiological positions implicit in the project of bringing together indigenous and Western knowledges" (p. 6). CHAT is a tool to mobilize differences between knowledge systems "for the ultimate purpose of bringing the divergent ways of knowing together in a conscious and critical manner" (p. 2). CHAT represents a space, a potentially shared object of activity, where indigenous peoples can name and practice their knowledge-making processes, and relate them to Western knowledge. Concomitantly, CHAT is a way of "demonstrating how Western research can redefine its relationship to people from indigenous/ marginalised contexts" (p. 2). On a micro level it implies creating dialogues across traditional barriers and knowledge systems by breaking down the skewed power relationships and redistributing power. Moreover, such dialogues imply participation (within the redistributive power framework) and open up spaces for sustainable change.

According to Engeström (2001) two interacting activity systems constitute the minimal model for activity theory. CHAT can trace the complex interactions between indigenous knowledges and Western knowledge without losing sight of the many ways in which these knowledges are construed, or of the possibility for new and diverse understandings to emerge.[6]

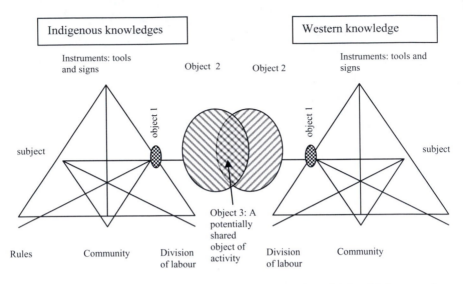

Figure 3.3   Two interacting activity systems as minimal model for third generation activity theory (adapted from Engeström, 2001).

The upper part of the triangle shows how a group of people uses tools to pursue an objective. The use of tools and signs demonstrate the intentionality of human actions, while at the same time tracing a cultural trajectory of the tool users. This means that the nature of a system's activity influences, and is influenced by, the tools it has developed in response to its object orientation. The lower part of the triangle shows the division of labor, and that the activity of this community is regulated by rules.

The starting point in a collaborative activity is the partnership between actors and institutions working towards a shared objective. In our context, a dialogue working towards a shared objective takes place between proponents of the hegemonic Western knowledge system and proponents of indigenous knowledges, for example, to combat HIV/AIDS. The dialogue or negotiations may take the "solution" of the challenge a step further and lead to proposals for a new strategy/new solutions that are based on other contested, contradictory, and alternative proposals. Often such dialogue may create contradictions, and it is therefore urgent to situate the dialogue in a context where both parties, particularly Western hegemonic knowledge, have to yield to create power equity. By identifying contradictions, in our case within and between Western and indigenous knowledge systems in the activity systems, the participants are aided in focusing on the root causes of the problem and thereby aided in creating solutions based on these contradictions. As noted, contradictions are crucial for the development of activity systems (Engeström) and involve what he terms expansive learning (Fig. 3.4 below). It means questioning and reflecting on the current situation, which may lead to new learning and the development of new forms of knowledge.

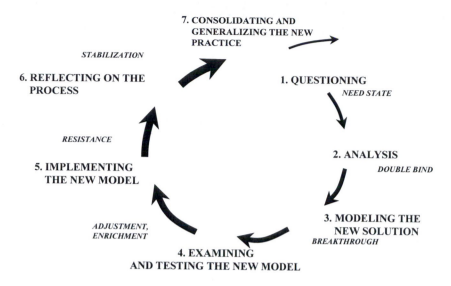

Figure 3.4   Cycle of expansive learning (Engeström, 1987).

As mentioned above the expansive learning cycle starts with individuals questioning the present situation or context and is expanded to collective movements or new solutions. An initially simple idea is transformed into a more complex one and is being implemented, but is again being contested or interrogated, and new practices are being consolidated and revised. It creates a third space, which intends to undermine "the position of power that dominant Western knowledge traditions have assumed vis-a-vis indigenous knowledge making, and how the local and spiritual nature of indigenous knowledges differentiate them from modern, Western knowledges" (Botha 2011, p. 2).

The model is in line with Semali and Kincheloe's (1999) notion of indigenous knowledges as subjugated knowledge that "can be employed as a constellation of concepts that challenge the invisible cultural assumptions embedded in all aspects of schooling and knowledge production" (p. 32). CHAT is used as a framework for decolonizing knowledge-making by challenging some of the dominating knowledge traditions that hegemonize Western epistemology by claiming universality.

Such a space means the unraveling of myths of fixed indigenous knowledges and identities and underlining the dynamism of these knowledges. At the same time there are commonalities between the various indigenous knowledges in terms of the relationship between the Self and the world, which "provides us with fascinating new ways of making sense of realities and compelling topics for intercultural conversations" (Kincheloe and Steinberg, 2008, p. 14).

Ellen Carm (2012, forthcoming) uses CHAT and expansive learning as a tool for analyzing processes that were manifested in transformations and changes at an individual and institutional level as well as within the sphere of micro, meso, and macro interventions in the HIV/AIDS program in Zambia. Two activity systems were involved in the research, one was the public governmental and educational actors; the other was the traditional leadership structure. This opened up dialogue and reflection between the two systems. While the former system, based on "rational" Western epistemology, was not conducive in driving back the pandemic alone, the traditional leaders with their power basis were turned into gate openers and role models "when they took on the responsibility to open up and go out to the communities and openly discuss issues related to sexuality and HIV/AIDS prevention and the need for changing cultural practices" (Carm 2012, forthcoming).

Such a strategy requires many rounds of dialogue and temporary solutions (because of contradictions within and between the knowledge systems) in order to reach new solutions not previously tried out in the battle against the HIV/AIDS pandemic. It shows that carriers of indigenous knowledges have something to contribute in effecting change and creating more sustainable solutions.

From a global perspective, the anti-globalization movement has signaled an alternative route for the sustainability of the planet. Confrontations at various summits have precluded the possibility of dialogue because the global leaders have shown no sign of addressing the real critical issues in a humble way. There is therefore a need to explore the hidden residues of alternative knowledge production *inside* the legacy of Western intellectual history in order for a dialogue to open up, not only at the local or national level, as the example from Zambia shows, but at the transnational and global level.

The Francisization of Western Knowledge Production

In a sense, Freire's (1970) theorizing of the dialogic nature of knowledge production is important here, but it requires that both parties in the dialogue acknowledge that there is wisdom and important knowledges to be gathered from the other dialogue partner. There is a need to acknowledge the significance of contextual, localized, and spiritual knowledges, in educational institutions, in the world of aid, and in societies in the South at large simply because the current epistemic hegemony is not able, as has been repeatedly noted, to address these issues in a sustainable way *alone*. It is with this perspective that White suggests the importance of an alternative Western knowledge system derived from the teachings of St. Francis, which I propose to call the *Francisization* of Western knowledge production.[7] There is a sense that the negotiation of a third space in relation to CHAT, which encompasses different knowledge systems may be facilitated with the inclusion of, or the appropriation of, aspects of this alternative Western knowledge into the hegemonic one. There are, however, difficulties with such an appropriation /inclusion due to the hegemonic power/ knowledge syndrome and also because of a heavy historical legacy.

When emphasizing indigenous knowledge production and epistemologies, it is also important to identify, as many scholars do (see Smith, 2000), indigenous cultures and knowledges not only as oppressed knowledges, but also as knowledges of creativity, holism, ecological awareness, and communality. Indigenous knowledge offers a challenge to Eurocentric epistemology, not only in order to create space for indigenous/Southern self-recognition and emancipation, but also for sustainable alternatives in terms of how we administer our common earth.

3.5   ANOTHER KNOWLEDGE SYSTEM IN THE SOUTH: ISLAMIC KNOWLEDGE PRODUCTION

As was noted in the discussion of Said's *Orientalism,* Orientalism defined and essentialized the East in general, and Islam in particular, as a hostile irrational and culturally inferior Other.

As a matter of fact, Islam was, like other non-European epistemologies, dislocated in the wake of colonialism and imperialist expansion. Orientalism and the West's arrogant Eurocentrism treated Islam as a monolithic entity without acknowledging its plurality and internal differences.

The Qur'an and Hadith contain many statements related to cosmology and epistemology, and to human and divine knowledge. The unity of existence is reflected in the unity of various forms of knowledges and grounded in the unity of God. What distinguishes Western epistemology from Islamic epistemology is that even though the Qur'an is open to concepts that come from different fields of knowledges, they must fit the Quranic perspective. If they cannot be reconciled with Islamic principles, they should be excluded (Abdullah, 1982). The transcendental and spiritual elements of Islamic knowledges were perceived in the West as irrational, feminine, uncivilized, barbaric, underdeveloped, and anti-developmental; from such a perspective Islam and Islamic knowledges had nothing to offer. In Chapter 5, a specific version of Islamic epistemology (what I term Islamist) is explored in more detail in relation to the Islamist education in Sudan and South Sudan and how it collides with a more articulated Western discourse originating in the southern part of the country. Interestingly, while subalternized and dislocated in the Western epistemic universe, Islamist epistemology (embodied by the National Congress Party version in Khartoum) also had and still has hegemonic and Orientalizing tendencies, in our case in relation to the previous southern part of the country.

Since the National Congress Party in Khartoum pursued a very conservative version of Islam (an Islamist rather than a mainstream Islamic policy), co-existence with the non-Islamic South, primarily Christian South,[8] was extremely difficult, as the positions were entrenched on both sides. Modifications of positions in a third space between the hegemonic Islamist knowledge system in the North and the non-hegemonic, primarily Christian, pro-Western knowledge system in the South were difficult to envisage, at least on the political and epistemic macro level.

3.6   EDUCATION IN THE GLOBAL SOUTH: WHAT KIND OF KNOWLEDGES? WHAT KIND OF EDUCATION?

> The development of ecological understanding is not simply another subject to be learnt but a fundamental change in the way we view the world.
>
> —John Tillman Lyle, *Regenerative Design for Sustainable Developments*, 1994, p. 269

It has been argued that it is urgent to start *new* conversations about the world and man in terms of the present economic and ecological crisis, but also in terms of the global architecture of education.

A natural starting point for these new conversations is the school, with its large catchment area. The following section interrogates the state of affairs of educational discourse production globally and queries how nation states in the South, often with a non-hegemonic, indigenous epistemological orientation, prepare the new generation in the South for a sustainable future. Clearly schools and education institutions are important sites where knowledge production takes place.

While education cannot be seen as the miracle cure that can change the situation in these countries for the better, there is little doubt that education and relevant knowledges are important factors in fostering societies that have the potential to reduce poverty and promote sustainable development within the constraints of the global system discussed earlier. By undertaking a survey of educational discourses across the globe, one finds evidence of the global architecture of education (Jones, 2007).

The global architecture of education or the global educational discourse has had, and still has, enormous consequences for how the school systems function in various parts of the world. This homogenous global educational discourse exists in countries with heterogeneous socio-economic and political systems, both in the core and the periphery, and is distributed in substantial part through the World Bank, IMF, UN organizations, INGOs such as USAID, Save the Children, etc., and through state-to-state cooperation on education.[9] With such a perspective, education plays a homogenizing epistemological and a modernizing role. The epistemological transfer, besides its ramifications nationally and internationally, impacts school quality as it contributes, I argue, to alienating students in the South cognitively from

their home environment by introducing them to an alien culture and epistemology in school.

Identity Construction and Alienation in School

Basil Bernstein's (1971) exploration of working-class children's encounter
with the middle-class English classroom is educative in this context since it
exposes the alien culture that the working-class kids encounter at school in
the UK. It is this alienating effect of the classroom culture and epistemology
that is addressed in the following subsection. Since the educational discourses in the South are more or less *a priori* linked to Eurocentric epistemology and knowledge production (confirming the success of the Western
episteme), indigenous students suffer because the knowledges they bring
from home are not being discussed or valued in the classroom. As Adrienne
Rich (1986) states:

> When those who have the power to name and to socially construct
> reality choose not to see you or hear you . . . when someone with the
> authority of a teacher, say, describes the world and you are not in it,
> there is a moment of psychic disequilibrium, as if you looked in the
> mirror and saw nothing. It takes some strength of soul—and not just
> individual strength, but collective understanding—to resist this void,
> this non-being, into which you are thrust, and to stand up, demanding
> to be seen and heard (p. 199).

This alienation causes an epistemological shock, which creates huge
learning problems for the students, a challenge that most governments in
the South do not address in a proper way.

In the chapters on South Africa, South Sudan and Chile, three of our
countries under scrutiny in this book, the alienating effects of schooling
is discussed at some length. In these countries—students bring unofficial,
indigenous knowledges from home to the classroom which are epistemologically of a different nature than those which the policy documents and
on which the curriculum of the schools are based. Since these indigenous
knowledges are not addressed in a serious and comprehensive way in the
school curriculum, the encounter with school is often alienating. Experi-
encing lack of recognition of their cultural and epistemological background
affects secondary socialization and identity construction and signals in a
negative way what are important knowledges and what are not (Darnell
and Hoëm, 1996; Apple, 1993).[10]

Recognition of indigenous knowledges and epistemologies means, as
Horsthemke (2004) puts it:

> Reclamation of cultural or traditional heritage; decolonisation of mind
> and thought; recognition and acknowledgement of self-determining

development; protection against further colonisation, exploitation, appropriation and/or commercialisation; legitimation or validation of indigenous practices and worldviews; and condemnation of, or at least caution against, the subjugation of nature and general oppressiveness of non-indigenous rationality, science and technology (p. 33).

The alienating effect of colonial education is recounted, for example, by Ngũgĩ (1981) in *Decolonising the Mind*:

> Colonial alienation takes two interlinked forms: an active (or passive) distancing of oneself from the reality around, and an active (or passive) identification, with that which is most external to one's environment . . . it is like separating the mind from the body . . . On a larger scale it is like producing society of bodiless heads and headless bodies (p. 28).

Inclusion of indigenous knowledges means that the students' own experience and home environment take on more importance. As Semali and Kincheloe (1999) state:

> The assumption is that when learning is matched with local needs, education, whether indigenous or formal, can have a galvanizing effect on the lives of learners . . . sensitivity to traditional customs and social norms will be ensured by community members, while education will be relevant and lead to culturally appropriate curriculum practice (p. 108).

Ngũgĩ's (1981) experience from his school days tells a story of exclusion rather than inclusion:

> And then I went to school, a colonial school, and this harmony was broken. The language of my education was no longer the language of my culture . . . English became the language of my formal education. In Kenya, English became more than a language: it was *the* language, and all the others had to bow before it in deference. Then one of the most humiliating experiences was to be caught speaking Gĩkũyũ in the vicinity of the school. The culprit was given corporal punishment . . . or was made to carry a metal plate around the neck with inscriptions such as I AM STUPID and I AM A DONKEY (p. 11).

Such experiences, which transcend the language issue, cause self-hatred, inferiority and/or sometimes aggression. There is an Othering here when your own culture and self-understanding is constantly being marginalized and looked down upon. This Othering of the colonized or indigenous and the perception of them as different and inferior is projected onto themselves and resides in the notion of what Fanon (1967) called the Manichean dichotomy referred to earlier in which implacable discursive opposition between colonizer and the colonized is being produced.

Octave Mannoni (1956) explained the situation of the colonized in ethno-psychological terms, and that the colonized suffer from a dependence complex. The issue is well illustrated by Renato Constantino (1971):

> We see our present with as little understanding as we view our past because aspects of our past, which could illuminate the present have been concealed from us. This concealment has been effected by a systematic process of education characterised by a thoroughgoing incalculation of colonial values and attitudes-in-process, which could not have been so effective had we not been denied access to the truth and to be part of our written history (p. ix).

By ignoring the indigenous peoples' own history, cultures, and epistemologies the modernist curriculum privileges a particular view of the world, a view that at certain levels is seldom deemed problematic. Ali A. Abdi (2006) argues that the global architecture of education represents a "current imperialism; some might call this benign colonialism that is still underdeveloping Africa and its people" (p. 17). Abdi also maintains that "globalization is not designed . . . to develop the African people, and its educational prescriptions are making the situation worse for African children" (p. 23).

What is almost completely under-communicated in the South is how the hegemonic educational discourse—across the curriculum of school and university systems and across nations—has helped to promote the capitalist world-system and globalization and defend positions of power. The significance of privileging Western epistemology, beyond its alienating effect, is how the hegemonic epistemology and educational discourse effectively prevents a critique of the present neo-colonial epistemological legacy—the hegemonic world system and its oppressive features.

This is made possible because the hegemonic epistemology and its translation into educational discourse is unrivalled in schools. Such an educational discourse reinforces the epistemic dominance in countries in the semi-periphery or periphery, which already experience the negative aspects of the present world order. To challenge this hegemonic knowledge necessitates a deconstruction of the triad of Western epistemology–(neo)colonization–hegemonic power and implies a decolonizing of the curricula and the educational discourses globally.

The subtle ways in which the Southern mind is colonized is seen in one of our case studies from Sudan. Interestingly, the imposition of an Islamic knowledge system through the educational discourse provoked more aggressive reactions in the non-Islamic Southern Sudan than the modernist, Westernized education curricula from Uganda and Kenya, where the former, besides its negative religious connotations, was rumored to halt modernity, modernization, and development. Such an internalized understanding of knowledge transfer from Europe as natural and the only way to effect change in the South tells the story of an epistemological success story that has swept all over the South.

Ngũgĩ's colonizing of the mind is an appropriate term here. As Tucker (1999) states:

> Some cultures and societies find themselves overdetermined by Western representations to the point that they can no longer recognize themselves in the discourses that claim to portray them. They are saturated with imposed meanings, ambitions and projects (p. 13).

Science/Mathematics Education: The Epitome of Western Education

While Western knowledge is often transferred to the South in a decontextualized way, indigenous knowledges often exist and are generated in specific contexts. It is this contextual embeddedness of indigenous knowledges that can give it a comparative advantage compared to decontextualized Western knowledge.

The question of what kind of education is therefore urgent in relation to teaching science and science education.

Modern science teaching is often regarded as the epitome of modernist education with what is termed Eurocentric mathematics as the core discipline. Eurocentric mathematics is applied and produced from a deductive axiomatic logic and is often regarded as a neutral discipline. However, among mathematicians, there is now controversy about its claims of certainty, universality and absoluteness; some argue that mathematics is socially constructed knowledge and that there are cultural limitations to its claims of universality (Ernest, 1998; Tymoczko, 1986). Moreover, as Ernest (2007a) points out, "the role of mathematics is inseparable from the dominant background ideology of capitalism-consumerism, through which it helps to sustain the economic supremacy of the developed countries of the North" (p. 9).

Ethno-mathematicians have long pointed to the sophistication of alternative, non-Western forms of mathematical knowledges that have been suppressed from the curriculum as childlike and primitive. The choice of one type of math representation over another representation means power to control which representations are "rational" and which are "primitive" (D'Ambrosio, 1997).

Even though the notion that mathematical ideas are culture-free and value-free has proven to be false, and thus has been discredited, the notion has still been maintained by societal interests and pressures. Eurocentric mathematics has until recently rarely been challenged in the classroom, thus, it ignored important mathematical knowledges from the "margins." As George Gheverghese Joseph (1997) states: "The contribution of the colonized were ignored and devalued as part of the rationale for subjugation and dominance" (p. 63), and ideologically supported by the elite in the South who were conditioned by the same education system as in the North. According to Ubiratan D'Ambrosio (1997):

> Ideology . . . takes a more subtle and damaging turn, with even longer and more disrupting effects, when built into the formation of the cadres and intellectual classes of former colonies, which constitute the majority of so-called Third World countries. We should not forget that colonization grew together in a symbiotic relationship with modern science, in particular with mathematics and technology (p. 23).

Moreover, the view that the history of mathematics was primarily the result of developments in Europe and Europeanized countries has been critiqued by ethno-mathematicians arguing "that an Arab renaissance in mathematics between the 8th and the 12th centuries provided for a flow of mathematical knowledge into Western Europe that helped shape the pace of developments for the next five hundred years" (Rivera and Becker, 2007, p. 214; see also Joseph, 1997; Powell and Frankenstein, 1997 for a critique of the Eurocentric foundations of mathematics). However, these knowledges were appropriated by Europe, and mathematics was used as a tool to impose the supposed rationality of the hegemonic power on non-Western, indigenous cultures. The focus on ethno-mathematics is therefore due to both the recognition of the close connection between cognition and culture and the wish to create some sort of historical balance and equity in the classroom. There is research available now that shows how different indigenous groups have developed mathematical competence and practices, in particular "quantitative and qualitative practices, such as counting, weighing and measuring, comparing, sorting and classifying" (D'Ambrosio, 1999, p. 51).

The challenge is to look at mathematics through non-Western/European lenses. This does not mean that mathematics from an anti-colonial perspective should only focus on mathematical practices from their own communities; it should be taken as a point of departure for exploring practices also outside their community. As we have noted in another context identity construction and cultural identities vary within a specific ethnic group meaning that indigenous mathematical practices may not be the same to all members of that indigenous group, and ethno-mathematical practices may even be resisted by members for a number of different reasons. Essentializing specific mathematical practices may prevent members of the group from going beyond these practices to learn other mathematical approaches. Ferdinand Rivera and Joanna Rossi Becker (2007) suggest a hybrid version of ethno-mathematics, which "should bridge the divide between the abstract, universal, and decontextualized nature of Western mathematics and the situated, local and contextualized nature of ethno-mathematics" (p. 219). We are talking of co-existence here, which may help indigenous students from being alienated in school and at the same time provide them with possibilities to gain insight into mathematical practices that transcend their own communities; this may help to orient them in the global world.

There is therefore reason to be cautious about the uncritical transfer of a Eurocentric mathematics curriculum without, as it were, taking into account local needs and contexts as well as resources. There is a need for critical mathematics education, which means, according to Ernest (2007a), to "empower learners as individuals and citizens-in-society, by developing mathematical confidence . . . and to foster critical awareness and democratic citizenship via mathematics" (p. 34). However, such political objectives for teaching mathematics are contested, and except for local cases among disempowered groups, have not been implemented in mainstream education in any country (Ernest 2007a). It goes to show that there so far has been little or no space to interrogate the principles on which the global architecture of education is based.

Medium of Instruction

Quite central in the indigenization of education curricula is the use of mother tongue as the medium of instruction in school. While multiple studies clearly show the advantage of learning and being taught in the mother tongue (Pattanyak, 1986; Akinnaso, 1993; Williams, 1996; Brock-Utne, 2000; Heugh, 2000) there is a sense that neither the heavy international donors nor the African governments want to acknowledge these research findings.

In 1968, UNESCO claimed that it is:

> Through his(her) mother tongue that every human being first learns to formulate and express his(her) ideas about himself(herself) and about the world in which he(she) lives. Every child is born into a cultural environment; the language is both a part of and an expression of, that environment. Thus, acquiring of this language, his(her) mother tongue is part of the process by which a child absorbs the cultural environment; it can, then, be said that this language plays an important part in moulding the child's early concepts. He(she) will, therefore, find it difficult to grasp any new concept which is so alien to his(her) cultural environment and that it cannot readily find expressions in his(her) mother tongue (UNESCO, 1968, p. 690).

The cognitive advantages of being taught in your home language are summed up by stock taking research on mother tongue and bilingual education in Sub-Saharan Africa:

> There are convincing evidence highlighted below to argue for . . . the use of mother tongue or the use of an African language familiar to the children upon school entry as the natural medium of instruction in all African schools and institutions of higher education. This approach reflects better

the socio-economic and cultural realities of multi-lingual Africa. However, it does not advocate the rejection of the official/foreign language. On the contrary, research evidence shows that the use of MT (mother tongue or NL [national language]) as a medium of instruction throughout schooling improves the teaching and learning of the official/foreign language as a subject of learning and will ultimately make it a better medium of specialized learning wherever appropriate (Alidou et al., 2006, p. 10).

The result of being taught in a foreign tongue is that the majority of indigenous children in primary and even secondary school have insufficient linguistic and literacy skills.

As A. Bame Nsamenang and Therese M.S. Tchombe (2011) state:

As national governments in Africa grapple with slim budgets and low resource bases, their education systems are churning out masses of marginally literate school leavers and graduates, increasing numbers barely able to scratch a living from the continent's largely agrarian livelihoods . . . Paradoxically, the African school, the social institution officially mandated to deliver relevant education, has been responsible for Africa's inability to ensure a good life, renew and strengthen its own culture and worse yet to generate and share its culture's knowledge and know- how (p. 8).

Clearly, such a situation impacts negatively on sustainable development. First, it is an economic burden to parents if their child sits year after year in school hardly understanding the subject being taught. This may mean repeating classes with additional school fees and/or extra transport costs, or in the worst-case scenario, that the child may have to drop out of school altogether. Second, spending years in the classroom with illiteracy as the end result is clearly not conducive in terms of nation building and economic sustainability. Linguistic issues thus become "inseparable from issues related to development" (Wolff, 2006, p. 47). In fact, for sustainable development to take place in Sub-Saharan Africa, there is an urgent need to involve the African masses and not only the leaders. Such an involvement necessitates the extensive use of indigenous languages in nation building efforts.

While the situation for indigenous languages as medium of instruction is tenuous at best in South Africa, the situation is similar in South Sudan and in Chile for the indigenous population. As I show in the chapter on Chile, even in the supplementary curriculum for indigenous students, Educación Intercultural Bilingüe (EIB), the medium of instruction is Spanish.

The Issue of Relevancy and Indigenization in Education

Several attempts have been made in Africa as well as in Latin America to contextualize and indigenize teaching and education. Already the missionaries sought to combine mental and manual labor in order to produce Africans whom they considered appropriately educated for their environment (Morrow, Maaba, and Pulumani, 2004). Such an approach was ambiguously received by the students who sometimes felt patronized because they were given what they considered a second rate education.

Julius Nyerere's Education for Self-Reliance

Julius Nyerere's Education for Self-Reliance policy in the late 1960s and 1970s was intended to promote mass education in order to improve production and productivity in the rural sector. Since Tanzania was a poor rural country with an agricultural economy, it was important for Nyerere that teaching should be relevant to the predominantly rural masses. The students were to be prepared to work in the rural communities; the mental and the manual were combined and strong emphasis was put on commitment to the values of rural communities and a communitarian spirit. The focus on African heritage and African cultures was meant to contextualize a curriculum away from a traditional Western academic educational tradition. While the results of this policy's implementation were at best mixed, the policy was short lived due to the structural adjustment policy imposed by the World Bank in the 1980s, which renewed focus on the Westernization of education, particularly in higher education (Buchert, 1994, p. 169). According to the World Bank, "theoretical academic learning and practical work could not fulfill the intended goals, was too expensive, and was not worth while compared with less expensive conventional academic education of a satisfactory quality" (Buchert, 1994, p. 171).

There were multiple reasons for the partial failure of the education for Self-Reliance Policy, some domestic and others international. What is interesting in our context is how quickly the World Bank intervened and imposed a Westernization of the education system without granting the Policy for Self Reliance more time to be implemented. The policy was possibly the most appropriate in a society, which was primarily rural and with a very small modern sector. In the chapter on (South) Sudan, the Tanzanian policy as a model for other Sub-Saharan countries is discussed in more detail.

Bantu Education in South Africa and the Brigades Movement

Bantu education in South Africa also combined classroom education with production. This system was not meant to advance the situation for the blacks or value their African heritage and epistemology; it was to perpetuate their status quo. Bantu education was also rejected by the liberation movements and resulted in mass demonstrations and confrontations in the 1970s (for example, the Soweto Uprising in 1976).

A so-called progressive version of Education with Production was Patrick van Rensburg's Brigades Movement and the Foundation for Education with Production, which was established in 1980 and is now functioning in Botswana, South Africa, and Zimbabwe. Rensburg's approach was a strong focus on practical subjects like agriculture, building, carpentry, metalwork, technical drawing, and typing, whereas the academic curriculum was based on new 'subjects' like "Cultural Studies, Development Studies, Environmental and Social Studies, Fundamentals of Production, Science, Mathematics, Communication (English and an African language), Technical Studies" (van Rensburg, 2005). The purpose of Education with Production was to transfer the students' skills and knowledge to productive work. Goods produced in the schools were meant to provide for the students and the communities. Moreover, the more academic subjects were intended to give the students a tool to critically analyze the societies in which they lived.

The ANC in exile was interested in Education with Production. It picked up ideas from van Rensburg as well as socialist and quasi-socialist approaches to education. Experiences from other liberation movements and examples from Cuba were also drawn upon.

There was, however, some ambivalence about the whole concept of Education with Production. Some ambivalence was related to the tension between political and more academic views of education; another ambivalence was related to the fact that students, socialized in a Western academic education tradition, prioritized the academic subjects and resented manual work. This problem was also experienced in van Rensburg's schools and in the schools visited when we did field-work in Cuba, as many students felt that the focus on production stole time from the more academic subjects that required concentration over time.

While the Education with Production model is still operating in some countries in Sub-Saharan Africa, the model has never been integrated into the nation curriculum of these countries. The model remains at best an alternative to the mainstream curriculum, probably due to economic considerations (pure academic schools are cheaper), and the vocational fallacy thinking that vocational instruction in school will not have decisive influence on the occupational aspirations of students as students want good jobs in the modern sector (see Foster, 1965). There are also considerations relating to producing competitive learners in a globalized world.

Indigenous Knowledge Production Rather than Material Production

It is interesting that the ANC, which was attracted to the education with production policy in exile, has not included education with production in the new curriculum. Instead, the ANC after the new dispensation is, as I show in the chapter on South Africa, gradually adopting a rhetoric that is about to recognize indigenous knowledges as an asset in South African education. It is an African heritage thinking here, which is more based on the importance of non-Western epistemologies and knowledge production in school rather than material production. However, as I discuss at some length in Chapter 4, there is still some way to go before such rhetoric is implemented in the curriculum for primary school after the new dispensation.

Latin America, Indigenous Cultures, and Epistemologies in Education

A similar, but stronger emphasis on indigenous epistemologies and cultures in education is now emerging in Latin America.

At the turn of the 21st century, many countries like Guatemala, Bolivia, Peru, and Ecuador adopted a new discourse of multi-culturalism by recognizing the multi-ethnic character of their nations (Stiegler, 2008).

The adoption of a multi-cultural discourse meant that education was perceived in a new way, and the previous assimilationist policies were, at least in theory, replaced by policies that were intended to preserve indigenous cultures, epistemologies, and languages.

The indigenous languages should be used as the medium of instruction, and the cultural aspects of the indigenous peoples should be treated in the same way as the non-indigenous peoples, where the concept of 'intercultural' implies a dialogue between the dominant and non-dominant cultures in the classroom (Küper and Lopez, 1999). In Chile, a case study in this book, educational reform in the 1990s attempted to address indigenous issues. While the introduction of EIB was a significant educational step in Chilean educational history, it must be noted that what distinguished the Chilean EIB from the EIB of other Latin American countries was that it was a supplementary curriculum developed in indigenous communities only.

Learning Material

This imposition of an alien culture has been reinforced by the distribution of learning material in colonial languages in South Africa, South Sudan, and Chile. In South Africa, with eight million Xhosa-speaking people and nine million Zulus (the two biggest population groups) there are no text books in primary schools in their vernacular languages, with the exception of language-learning books. Even if books were available, there are not enough competent teachers to teach in their vernacular. If textbooks are available, they are in colonial languages. This is a situation unheard of in any country in the North.

In South Sudan there were no textbooks on history in secondary schools that focused on the history and cultures of South Sudan until 2010 (Breidlid et al., 2010). Either the books were written from a Northern Sudanese perspective, or they were imported from Uganda or Kenya. In Chile, the textbooks for the additional curriculum (EIB) for Mapuche Indians are mainly in Spanish and the medium of instruction is Spanish.

Big countries in the North primarily distribute knowledge and control the publishing houses in the South (with some exceptions). There is

Pearson, for example, which is the world's leading education company, providing services to more than 70 countries. There is Macmillan Africa and Macmillan Education Latin America. Heinemann Publishers is best known among educators and learners in Southern Africa, Australia, and New Zealand. There are also some publishing houses that are locally owned, like Heinemann Kenya and Heinemann Southern Africa, that publish for Southern African schools, colleges, technikons, and universities.

The South African government has been concerned about the lack of domestic publishing capacity. In a report to the Department of Arts, Culture, Science and Technology the obstacles to growth in domestic publishing are listed:

> A limited buying market . . . Priorities of government are, by necessity focused on the provision of basic needs. For instance, of the rural schools that exist many are without electricity and water, not to mention libraries.
>
> Lack of trained personnel in certain technical aspects of the publishing industry. High risks of establishing new publishing houses. Uncertainties caused by rapid and continuous advances in information technology . . . Highly competitive foreign publishers impacting on local industry, for instance almost 60 percent of academic books are now imported . . . Limited incentives for local writers. Unfavourable domestic economic climate (DACST, 1998).

There is, therefore, a recognition of the need for a national book publishing sector in South Africa as well as in other Sub-Saharan African countries, particularly to publish educational materials in indigenous languages. However, primarily due to the economic imbalance between foreign and domestic publishing houses, the local or domestic publishing houses are fighting an uphill battle. It means in reality that the big foreign publishing houses dominate the market; they do not provide schools with textbooks in the vernacular, but print books in one of the colonial languages (usually English) so that the books can be widely (globally) distributed across national borders. The publishing houses, therefore, contribute to the spread and imposition of a Western discourse. Governments in the global South (particularly in Sub-Saharan Africa) have neither had the financial capacity, nor paid sufficient attention to protecting their epistemological and cognitive independence.

A Decolonized Curriculum

When the thinking and acting of the majority of the people in a country, that is, their cultural expression, is more or less excluded from the curriculum, particularly in primary education, it does something profoundly damaging to the self-confidence and self-esteem of those people, aside from the obvious learning challenges it creates in school. What the curriculum should do is "to help the people and their elite to capitalise and master the existing knowledge, whether indigenous or not, and develop new knowledge in a continual process of uninterrupted creativity, while applying the findings in a systematic and responsible way to improve their quality of life" (Hountondji, 2002, p. 36).

This exclusion of indigenous knowledges and cultures has major implications for the distribution of power in the country where those with non-indigenous cultural capital are in the driving seat. The democratic problems of such a situation are obvious. The prioritization of non-indigenous knowledges also means an under-utilization of indigenous resources and knowledges in the development of a given society.

The inclusion of alternative worldviews and epistemologies in the education systems has a double objective: to boost the identity formation of the students by including perspectives and worldviews that are not alien to them, and to address knowledge production and development that query the unholy relationship between a capitalist economy or world system and the sustainable development of nation states.

Only when oppressive knowledge production is exposed and interrogated and indigenous knowledges are recovered can indigenous students start reclaiming and reconstructing their identity. These identities will be hybrid and multiple (as I show in my case study of South Africa in Chapter 4), but they will be grounded in recognizable cultural and epistemological sites, and thereby not completely overrun by alien epistemologies when they turn up in school. Such a school and such a curriculum will be concerned with how knowledges are produced, why some knowledge has been subjugated, and what alternative knowledges can be transmitted to the school environment by opening up to multiple knowledges.

Moreover, the opening of a third space will no longer simply convey validated Western knowledge from teacher to student. This process should not happen in isolated spaces for indigenous students or students in the South only. Interrogating knowledge production in the schools in the North is equally important since such interrogation very seldom takes place as the hegemonic, monopolistic Western knowledge is taken for granted. Dealing with Northern/Western interest in indigenous knowledges is problematic, however, if such knowledges are perceived in the same way as indigenous land, that is, to be used for maximum exploitation. Any interrogation of alternative epistemologies should have the intention to open up space for new solutions to issues of sustainability, not only for indigenous peoples' rights and just claims.

It is therefore essential to interrogate the ontological and epistemological assumptions of Western knowledge, and to incorporate knowledges that were destroyed or marginalized during the time of colonization. It is important to ask, as Birgit Brock-Utne (2000) does, in relation to the educational discourse in the South: What kind of education? What kind of knowledges?

Indigenous knowledges are not only important in nations where indigenous peoples are in the minority, like in Chile. What happens all over the South is that the indigenous population (like the majority populations in Sub-Saharan African countries) experiences a form of cognitive genocide, often without realizing it or being conscientized about it. The seriousness of this is not only due to the non-recognition of indigenous peoples' epistemological and cultural background, but as discussed earlier in this chapter, to the undervaluing of indigenous knowledges in terms of sustainable development, for example, in ecological management, agriculture, and indigenous medicines. It is only recently that indigenous knowledges have been recognized in the West/North, albeit as a commodity and not as knowledge systems that need to be included in the school curriculum. Not even the governments in the global South have systematically incorporated indigenous knowledges into the schools.

The idea of the absolute dichotomy between the two knowledge systems, the one living in harmony with nature and the other dominating it, may be up for grabs. While the two systems cannot be completely harmonized, the idea that the two systems might be able to complement each other and co-exist constructively in achieving a more sustainable future must be pursued further. It is in this perspective that CHAT and expansive learning discussed in this chapter are suggested as a basis for a discussion and collaboration in what has been termed the third space. The classroom may be one of the venues for such a third space.

Teaching and Learning in an Alternative Paradigm

Bishop's experiences of teaching Maōri children in mainstream classrooms in New Zealand are, in this context, of particular interest and could be the basis for the negotiation of an alternative learning space in contexts where indigenous groups are involved. His experiences of teaching Māori in mainstream settings provide us "with a picture of the sort of alternative educational relations and interactions that are possible when educators draw upon an alternative culture than that previously dominant" (Bishop, 2007, p. 445).

More concretely, the traditional classroom situation is replaced by a situation where "educators can create learning contexts that will address the learning engagement and improve the achievement of Māori students by developing learning-teaching relationships" (Bishop 2007, p. 445). Bishop refers to five criteria that are necessary to make the classroom situation conducive to optimal learning:

(1) power sharing (where power is shared) between teacher and learners and where the learners have the right to self-determination and sense-making processes;
(2) culture sensitive (where culture counts) in the sense that the students' home culture knowledges are "acceptable" and "legitimate," and the learners can bring "who they are" to the classroom;

(3) dialogue, as reminiscent of Freire (1970), that is, the learning process is dialogic and the learners are allowed to raise questions and evaluate questions and answers. Moreover, the learning is reciprocal and knowledges are co-created. The teacher should create an environment where the learners' knowledges are validated;

(4) connectedness where teachers are connected and committed to the students and their communities and vice versa—school and parents/community work closely together;

(5) a common vision for what is the goal of teaching and learning ("what constitutes excellence for Māori in education" [Bishop 2007, p. 445]). In such a classroom situation, it is not the teacher who is in focus or the only one with the power to define what are acceptable and appropriate knowledges.

The new learning situation suggests that the learners can more easily take meaning from new information and knowledges when there is a link to their previous cultural experiences and knowledge systems. It is a teaching and learning situation where cultural homogeneity between home and school is being reconstructed and where learning is contextualized. According to Yunkaporta (2009), such counter-hegemonic teaching, which is intensely ecological, means that it relates to land and place "within a framework of profound ancestral and personal relationships with place" (p. 49). Moreover, teaching and learning in such a non-hegemonic context implies story sharing, the use of all senses, group orientation, non-linearity, and connection to real-life purposes and contexts (Yunkaporta, 2009, pp. 48–49). Such a teaching and learning situation can be developed "out of the cultural sense-making processes of peoples previously being marginalized by the dominance of colonial and neocolonial educational relations of power" (Bishop, 2007, p. 457).

In mono-lingusitic settings the counter-hegemonic teaching should be conducted in the native tongue of the learners. Moreover, the spiritual aspects of indigenous knowledges are at the centerpiece of teaching. As George Dei and Arlo Kempf (2006) state, "For many, developing the spiritual aspects of this transformation is just as crucial as the development of critical consciousness—indeed these may well come hand in hand . . . Additionally, spirituality may serve as a connection to our histories, and in so doing help us resist amputation from our past, and thus present and future" (pp. 312–313).

Since primary school reaches out to large parts of the population, it is strategically placed to elaborate and practice new ideas for a changed paradigm that encompasses multiple epistemologies and sustainable practices in a decolonizing setting. To undermine "the prescriptive hegemonic paradigms that dominate our ongoing colonial encounter" (Dei and

Kempf, 2006, p. 314) is, however, a formidable task, which requires very committed and conscientized teachers and learners.

What the World Is Doing or not Doing

While many governments in the South have not succeeded in improving the situation of the masses,[11] development assistance from the North to the South has also failed to help the poor escape their dismal conditions. Robert B. Zoellick, the President of the World Bank, expressed his concern after the release of the "Global Monitoring Report" in 2008:

> In this Year of Action on the MDGs (Millennium Development Goals), I am particularly concerned about the risks of failing to meet the goal of reducing hunger and malnutrition, the "forgotten MDG." As the report shows, reducing malnutrition has a "multiplier" effect, contributing to success in other MDGs including maternal health, infant mortality, and education (World Bank, 2008).

According to a report from the MDG Gap Task Force 2010, delivery of official development assistance is slowing down (UN, 2010), and the MDGs are out of reach.

Even though economic growth in Africa has been substantial over the last few years, the African Progress Panel (2011) warns that "a particularly worrying development is the increase in inequality—both within and across African societies . . . the continent's strong economic growth has not translated into widespread job creation and poverty reduction" (p. 28). The Panel also suggests that progress is hampered by insufficient dedication to "sustainable development by both African states and their international partners (p. 28). In Latin America the indigenous population is often marginalized both in terms of politics, culture, education, and wealth. The gap between the original population and the immigrants from Europe is getting bigger (*The Economist*, 2003) at the same time as the indigenous peoples lead a life that is often more sustainable.

The Role of Education

A 2002 UNESCO report on progress, which was prepared for the World Summit on Sustainable Development, states that "much of current education falls far short of what is required' (p. 9), and calls for a new vision and "a deeper, more ambitious way of thinking about Education" (p. 8). Indirectly a critique of the global architecture of education, UNESCO seems to explore new, more ambitious routes of education for sustainability. The report ambitiously states, "Just as we learnt to live unsustainably, we now need to learn our way out—to learn how to live sustainably" (p. 7).

In the discussion below, I explore how, and to what extent, the challenges of sustainable development and education are treated among UN organizations like UNESCO and international lending institutions like the World Bank. While there are differences between the institutions, there is nevertheless a sense that the discussion is almost entirely centered on a Western epistemological and ideological framework.

The UN Organizations

The World Summit on Sustainable Development held at the end of August 2002 in Johannesburg, South Africa, issued the "Johannesburg Declaration on Sustainable Development," which once more reaffirmed the importance of eradicating poverty and achieving a fair and just allocation of resources. Education and training were not, however, mentioned as basic requirements to achieve fairness, but are referred to together with "technology transfer, human resource development, education and training to banish underdevelopment forever" (UN, 2002 a, ¶18).

The Johannesburg Summit underlined, beside the issue of poverty reduction, the importance of the environment in sustainable development. It is in this perspective that indigenous knowledge systems must be seen. Odora Hoppers (2002) is right when she claims, "a major threat to the sustainability of natural resources is the erosion of people's knowledge, and the basic reason for this erosion is the low value attached to it" (p. 7). As has been noted, the neglect and dislocation of such knowledges are a major threat to sustainable development.

While education was not given a prominent place in the Declaration from Johannesburg, the other document from Johannesburg, the Development Plan of Implementation (UN, 2002b) refers to education in a number of paragraphs (¶¶ 116–124). The Plan underlines that:

> Education is critical for promoting sustainable development. It is therefore essential to mobilize necessary resources, including financial resources at all levels . . . to complement the efforts by national governments (¶116).

While what is stated about educational goals may be seen as commendable *per se*, they are marked by a technical educational discourse, which does not ask the important or underlying questions about the relationship between education and sustainable development. Does any kind of educational input promote sustainable development?

The assumption would be that the launching of the United Nations Decade of Education for Sustainable Development 2005–2014 (DESD), (UNESCO 2005a) would explore the relationship between education and sustainable development more comprehensively and critically.

The objectives of the DESD are to:

Integrate the principles, values, and practices of sustainable development into all aspects of education and learning. This educational effort will encourage changes in behaviour that will create a more sustainable future in terms of environmental integrity, economic viability, and a just society for present and future generations (UNESCO, 2005a).

What these objectives in reality mean is outlined in UNESCO's "Media as Partners in Education for Sustainable Development" (2008), a manual written to give the media reliable information about education for sustainable development. The manual asks whether modern societies can be both economically and environmentally friendly, referring to writers who state that sustainable development is a contradiction in terms and that the term is "simply an attempt by business to show that capitalism is environmentally friendly" (UNESCO, 2008, p. 36). The report refers to other commentators who think that sustainability and capitalism are compatible. Referring to Jonathan Porritt, who states "capitalism is basically the only economic game in town," the manual is mainly concerned with keeping the capitalist system alive with an environmental face.

Underlining the importance of education the manual states that "education . . . can shape the world tomorrow, equipping individuals and societies with the skills, perspectives, knowledge and values to live and work in a sustainable manner" (UNESCO 2008, p. 36). Therefore, reorienting the goals of education "to recognize the importance of sustainable development must become a world priority" (UNESCO, 2008, p. 35), meaning that that education should function as a critical complement to social, cultural, and economic policies. However, the manual never addresses the need to go beyond Western-based knowledge systems or educational discourses for a more sustainable earth. Since the present global economic system with its underlying knowledge base is only critiqued up to a point, the exclusion of indigenous knowledges in the training manual (indigenous knowledges are not mentioned once) is logical, albeit alarming.

In 2011, DESD introduced "The Climate Change Starter's Guidebook" (UNESCO/UNEP 2011) that provides an introduction and overview for education planners and practitioners on issues relating to climate change and climate change education. While this guide is also steeped in a modernist rhetoric the message is to delink economic growth from environmental degradation.

The production and provision of goods and services has traditionally caused environmental deterioration. However, advances in policy, technology, resource management, and business thinking have created the possibility for a "green economy," which delinks economic growth from environmental damage (UNESCO/UNEP, 2011, p. 48).

There is an optimism in technology here that neither questions the high consumption levels in so-called developed countries nor the epistemological basis of the global architecture of education:

> Economic growth and consumption levels could be sustained, in principle, whilst also respecting nature and the climate, by using energy more efficiently and by switching to low- and no-carbon energy technologies. UNESCO emphasises the role of education in support of climate change adaptation and mitigation in providing skills and capacities but also through shaping the values, attitudes and behaviours needed to put the world on a more sustainable path (UNESCO/UNEP, 2011, p. 49).

At the same time the guide refers positively, although only twice, to indigenous knowledges and sustainability:

> Education programs that . . . promote indigenous knowledge, sustainable lifestyles and sustainable development will further enhance these capacities (critical thinking and problem-solving skills) (UNESCO/ UNEP, 2011, p. 61).

And:

> Indigenous and local knowledge is a key resource for communities in understanding the environment, and assessing and adapting to climate change impacts. It should be strengthened and integrated into education programs (UNESCO/UNEP, 2011, p. 61).

In connection with the International Day of the World's Indigenous peoples (August 9, 2011) UNESCO reiterates that:

> Indigenous peoples hold some of the keys to tackling global challenges. As we strive to foster sustainable and equitable development, it is vital we listen to the voices of indigenous peoples and that we learn from their knowledge (UNESCO, 2011 c).[12]

Even with these sporadic references to indigenous knowledges, there is no indication that the remaining years of DESD will widen the understanding and scope of education in such a way that it starts exploring critically how other knowledge systems can address the issue of sustainability in a more holistic way and critically interrogate the sustainability of even green growth within the Western epistemological paradigm. Unfortunately, there seems to be no development in UNESCO's thinking on sustainability issues since the launching of the rather promising 2002 Report on Education for Sustainability referred to above. The intriguing assumption in the UNESCO documents is that it is possible to keep the capitalist system alive with an environmental component. This credo is transmitted to education institutions around the globe confirming that the global architecture of education is solidly anchored in a Western epistemological tradition with little vision for a sustainable future.

The World Bank

The World Bank has probably been the most important contributor around the globe in education over the past 50 years; it has been the single largest source of support in the field of international education. The Bank has, since its inception, invested more than $69 billion globally in education through more than 1500 projects. The Bank's support for education in terms of loan commitments was more than $5 billion in 2010 (World Bank, 2011, p. 1).

The World Bank's entire history, its creation, and its rationale are rooted in the post-war reconstruction (and development) of the capitalist economies according to the dominant Western/Eurocentric paradigms that scientific knowledge leads humankind's dominance of nature for endless, linear growth, and development. In the last decades the World Bank has been associated with neo-liberal ideology, and although there have been some changes in the Bank's educational policies over time, its faith in the market, its belief in the philosophy of one-size-fits-all and its belief in the Western educational discourse have remained constant.

Its educational ideology has, however, not been fundamentally different from that of other donors or national governments in the South, even though its embrace of neo-liberal, capitalist economic principles has been more openly articulated.

Despite this focus, the World Bank has in the past devoted some interest to indigenous knowledge systems through the World Bank's Africa office. The Africa office has been in partnership with communities, NGOs, development institutions, and multi-lateral organizations. However, the Bank's references to indigenous knowledges seem to be marginal at best. Its latest webpage update is from 2006.

Indigenous knowledges' marginality in the World Bank universe can be seen from its newest strategy, "World Bank Education Strategy 2020" (World Bank, 2011), which focuses on three areas: knowledge generation and exchange, technical and financial support, and strategic partnerships. While UNESCO at least refers to education and sustainable development as well as other knowledge systems in its policy documents, the World Bank strategy paper not once mentions the UN Decade of Education for Sustainable Development or indigenous knowledges. Conversely, the conventional economic criterion, economic growth, is referred to on almost every page with statements like "Education is fundamental to development and growth" (World Bank, 2011, p. 1), and "The new strategy focuses on learning for a simple reason: growth, development, and poverty reduction depend on the knowledge and skills that people acquire, not the number of years that they sit in a classroom." (World Bank, 2011, p. 3). Not even green growth is referred in this strategy paper, underlining the complete lack of communication between the UN bodies and the World Bank on this important issue, as well as the World Bank's lack of will with regard to creative and new thinking towards 2020.[13] The World Bank perpetuates the hegemonic Orientalist epistemological discourse, probably more one-dimensionally than other players in the field of international education. It is a discourse that is never questioned by the Bank and is designed in Washington with a macro-approach toward all countries in the South. This one-size-fits-all approach, besides its modernist and unsustainable profile, neglects the fundamental differences in educational topography in the various countries where the World Bank enters to assist. This is not a new development for the Bank, but it is worrying due to the Bank's enormous influence on education policy across the globe.

The World Bank education policy has long been the subject of harsh criticism (see Samoff and Carrol, 2003; Brock-Utne, 2000; Arnove and Torres, 2007). Steven Klees (2008) captures his critique of World Bank policy in education over the last 25 years in the title of his recent article: "A Quarter Century of Neo-liberal Thinking in Education: Misleading Analyses and Failed Policies" (See also Klees, Samoff and Stromquist, 2012).

The Norwegian Educational Trust Fund (NETF)

In an analysis of the Norwegian Educational Trust Fund (NETF,2002) administered by the World Bank, Avenstrup et al. (2003) found that the World Bank's educational interventions in Africa neither strengthened local educational systems nor institutional capacity, lacked national ownership and did not contribute to knowledge transfer to local partners.[14] The lack of national leadership is exemplified in the statement from the NETF Report below:

> There were cases where ministries felt that their own planning of sector programs had not been accepted and that donors and the World Bank, thus including NETF, were imposing a different approach upon them by developing their own programs of support (Avenstrup et al, 2003, p. 22).

The NETF story underlines a more general tendency in World Bank interventions in education in Africa. In line with Klees' analysis above, the World Bank's educational achievements are not, according to the NETF-report, a success story. The Bank's focus on a one-size-fits-all strategy and its epistemic paradigm means, in reality, a neglect of the context where the educations systems are situated; thus, it supports school systems that do not emphasize cultural relevance and sustainability. The World Bank's top-down imposition as referred to in the NETF Report means an Orientalization of education aid, and it signals a superiority/inferiority knowledge relationship that reiterates the asymmetry in the relations between the North and the South. It is worth noting that Cuba has managed better in educational terms than most countries in the South without any assistance from the World Bank or the IMF.

The dislocation of indigenous knowledges in development assistance perpetuates a skewed power relationship from the colonial days where indigenous knowledges were dismissed. As there is this embedded power asymmetry in the development activities in the South (underlined in dichotomies like donor-recipient, developed-developing, rich-poor) with a systematic transfer and imposition of Eurocentric knowledge implying progress and development, there is a need to inject alternative paradigms into a donor community that is predominantly steeped in a Eurocentric epistemic logic. The feeble attempts to include indigenous knowledges in education are primarily window dressing exercises with no fundamental influence on the donors' ideological or epistemological basis.

Alternative approaches from the North and "solutions" based on indigenous knowledges in the South are hardly listened to, and even more seldom applied as a basis for alternative visions in development work. Scholarly reports on change and development that question the assumptions on which the donor discourse is based are basically not read, and indigenous knowledges are not perceived as central in the processes of change in the South (Agrawal, 1995; Batiste and Youngblood, 2000). There is a sense that there is a re-invention of the wheel in terms of education interventions in the South, even though this reinvention shows poor results in terms of positive change. The reasons for the contemporary situation among donors are probably multiple and justified by them on both epistemological and empirical grounds. A scenario where indigenous knowledges are accepted as a supplement to imported hegemonic Western knowledge might jeopardize the power and authority of the external experts and the aid community, that is, the whole relationship between us and them.

In an endnote to Chapter 5, I discuss briefly how UNESCO and Save the Children in their education policies in South Sudan stick to the hegemonic educational discourse and that do not refer to indigenous, local, or traditional knowledges in their policy papers. In the analysis of the South African primary school curriculum after 1994 (Chapter 4), I show how the ideological and epistemological content is heavily influenced by the educational discourses in the West. The implication is that the African National Congress (ANC) has been reluctant to undertake a more radical reorientation in educational policies that includes innovative educational strategies to meet the needs of the majority of South Africans even though there has recently been a change in rhetoric if not in implementation.

Many countries in the South (like South Sudan) rely heavily on aid or loans from the World Bank or other international actors and do not have the capacity to question the educational discourse imposed from the North.

Nor are many governments interested in multiple knowledge systems in the curriculum, since the government officials are trained in the Western educational system and believe that there is no other way to shape the education system and prepare the young people for the future (as in South Africa and Chile). In Chile there seems to be little interest by the authorities to include indigenous knowledges in the main curriculum beyond exotic elements. Since the Indians, the original population in the country, represents a minority, there is no demand from the majority community to indigenize the curriculum.

It is only Cuba and (North) Sudan, among the case studies in the book, that pursue an educational policy not based on the global architecture of education that is supported by the big donor institutions and the countries in the North.

4 Indigenous Knowledges and Education
The Case of South Africa

4.1 INTRODUCTION

The South African Context

South Africa emerged from apartheid in 1994 with the legacy of a segregated education system. The apartheid system had offered different educational opportunities for blacks and whites (as well as other ethnic groups). The Bantu Education Act (No 47) of 1953 (enacted by the apartheid government) created the Department of Bantu Education which was established to produce a curriculum that suited the "nature and requirements of the black people" (Boddy-Evans, 2011). Dr. Hendrik Verwoerd (then Minister of Native Affairs, later Prime Minister), stated:

> [I]ts aim was to prevent Africans receiving an education that would lead them to aspire to positions they wouldn't be allowed to hold in society. Instead Africans were to receive an education designed to provide them with skills to serve their own people in the homelands or to work in labouring jobs under whites (Boddy-Evans, 2011).

What is important for our purposes in this book is to underline that the content of the Bantu Education Act was specifically designed in such a way that the inferior position of blacks in the South African society was confirmed and strengthened. In other words, the content of the Bantu Act intended to further racial discrimination and preserve social and economic inequality. There was no attempt to exploit the resources of indigenous knowledges to elevate the blacks to the same playing fields as the whites; on the contrary, Bantu education was introduced to secure the *status quo*. As Vuyisile Msila (2007) states:

> The problem with colonial education and thus apartheid education in South Africa was that they spelt the end of traditional values learning in education. Currently, education faces these challenges in accommodating indigenous knowledge systems (p. 156).

It was this racist education policy that the ANC government, which came to power in 1994, wanted to radically reshape in the new South Africa in order to give the same educational opportunities to all population groups in the Rainbow Nation. The result of the work was Curriculum 2005 (1997), sometimes referred to as Outcomes Based Education (OBE), with a later revision, the Revised National Curriculum Statement, in 2002. Education Minister Khader Asmal stated of the education system after the new dispensation that "Challenging the past and moving beyond the legacy of apartheid is how the South African Department of Education plans to work towards social justice and equity with the introduction of the new curriculum titled 'Curriculum 2005'" (Ocampo, 2004).

Since the inception of Curriculum 2005, there has been a debate in South Africa about the Africanization of knowledges in the curriculum, and many voices have argued for the use of African indigenous knowledges in schools (see Msila, 2007). The indigenization of South African schools has been advocated by the African Renaissance movement and promoted by the former presidents Mandela and Mbeki, as is discussed later in this chapter.

4.2   AFRICAN RENAISSANCE

The interest in, and focus on, indigenous identities and knowledge systems has been fuelled by the emergence of the African Renaissance rhetoric proposed by Nelson Mandela and more consistently and frequently by former president Thabo Mbeki.

Their focus is related to building a nation where African values, knowledges, and heritage are central. While the rhetoric around African Renaissance and a new birth for Africa goes back a long way (Zeleza, 2009), my focus in this chapter is the use of the concept in South Africa after the liberation of South Africa in 1994.

In 1994, Mandela had already referred to African Renaissance at a summit of the Organization of African Unity, saying, "Africa cries out for a new birth. We must, in action, say that there is no obstacle big enough to stop us from bringing about a new African renaissance" (Mandela, 1994).

Thabo Mbeki (1996) followed this up with a strong focus on African identity construction by stating that his people, "whatever the circumstances they have lived through and because of that experience, they are determined to define for themselves who they are and who they should be." A few years later, he reiterated his argument:

> We must proceed with ongoing African studies and research, into our rich creative and cultural past and rekindle into African knowledge systems, so as to make younger generations aware of the achievements emanating from our continent and impress upon them their inherent creativity, that is setting the stage for new developments and discoveries

... for building mental universes of their own, for Africa's progress and prosperity (Mbeki, 1999).

While African Renaissance took a step back to focus on the past (as well as exploring the present) in order to construct an African identity/identities based on African heritage, African values, and indigenous epistemologies and knowledges, the concept is also future-oriented ("who we should be"), that is, a new beginning for Africa yearning for a better future. African Renaissance's focus on African heritage, identity construction, and a usable future may seem to be couched in some ambiguity or lack of direction, but it may also imply a dual orientation—a political, future-oriented development that, at the same time, retains a focus on African heritage, identity, and indigenous knowledge systems.

The return to the past is a way of signaling that what was negated during the apartheid regime, the "Africaness" of South Africa and its indigenous knowledge systems and values also meant a negation of African identity, which now needs to be restored to effect a viable future. African Renaissance, in Mbeki's rhetoric, means that (South) Africa and African identities are to be "shaped by African philosophies and not be limited by Western constructions" (Kubow, 2009, p. 47). African philosophy and indigenous knowledges seek to establish an indigenous identity/indigenous identities and affirm core African values in the face of and as a response to globalization.

An African Renaissance that does not degenerate into essentialism has, according to Mbeki, the potential to change the lives of many Africans who have been ravaged by the continuing legacy of colonialism. African Renaissance thus embraces the view that Africa is destined to make considerable progress in economic, political, and spiritual values by suggesting some sort of a rebirth where South Africa has a leading role to play.

It is this dialectics between African past/present, including indigenous knowledges, identities, and spiritual values in addition to the political, future-oriented world that addresses globalization on its own terms, that may seem to constitute this rebirth. While space does not allow me to probe into this duality/dialectics in detail, suffice it to say that there may be an underlying contradiction here between the repeated references to the continent's scientific accomplishments in metallurgy, astronomy, mathematics, engineering, medicine, and writing systems (see Diop, 1974) versus the emphasis on African spirituality, *ubuntu*, and communal aspects of indigenous knowledges. It is as if Africa intends to compete on the Western playing fields in terms of material and scientific accomplishments and simultaneously emphasize non-material, communal values.

The chapter seeks to explore the "cultural and epistemological world" of African Renaissance, that is, African heritage/identity and African indigenous knowledge systems as a potentially constitutive element of Africa's rebirth and a new future. Such an exploration is done through a brief ethnographic journey among the Xhosa, one of the largest black groups in South Africa. This is the only case study in the book where indigenous knowledges are examined in some detail based on field-work. As I underlined in the first chapters and again in this chapter, an epistemological analysis does not imply that indigenous knowledges are perceived to be the same among all the Xhosa or among other indigenous groups in South Africa. However, avoiding essentialized images of what indigenous knowledges means does not imply that there are no common threads that bind indigenous knowledges together, a point I briefly take up in the Xhosa section.

What are the characteristics of so-called indigenous knowledges as found in the black communities in South Africa? To what extent do they differ from the values and the knowledge production in the West? How is black, in this case Xhosa, self-being constructed? Have the indigenous values and worldviews been overrun or worked over by colonial and epistemic imposition or can we find traces of epistemic and spiritual resistance among the blacks? In other words, has the Xhosa mind and soul been colonized by Western epistemology?

Against the backdrop of this discussion the relationship between indigenous identities, knowledge systems, indigenous values, and worldviews are analyzed in comparison to worldviews found in South Africa's new curriculum (Curriculum 2005 and the later revision). How do the home values of the indigenous students concur with those of the new curriculum after 1994? The rationale for this focus is related to the question of whether the South African primary school is "their school," that is, the school for the majority of South African children in terms of cultures and knowledges. Moreover, what was the epistemological basis of the curriculum after the ANC came to power? Do we find traces of African Renaissance in Curriculum 2005? Finally, does the epistemological basis of South African schools promote a sustainable future for the new nation? These are questions that inform the discussion in this chapter. In the next subsection I discuss the ethnographic journey to two Xhosa communities in search of African indigenous knowledge production.

4.3   XHOSA WORLDVIEWS AND KNOWLEDGE PRODUCTION

As already noted, the ethnographic research[1] in South Africa was conducted among the Xhosa in Western Cape and Eastern Cape. The term Xhosa here is used to denote "Xhosa-speaking Africans as a particular sector of the Bantu population of South Africa" (Pauw, 1975, p. 1). The Xhosa are of Nguni stock like the Zulu.

The name Xhosa is a generalized term for a diversity of proud clans, the Pondo, Bomvana, Thembu, and the Xhosa tribe itself. Red and the orange of ochre were the traditional colors of the Xhosa, Pondo, Tembu, and Bomvana ('the red ones'). 'Red people' are illiterate people, according to the Xhosa.

The selection of the Xhosa was based on the fact that it is the second largest ethnic group in South Africa and because the Xhosa played a very important role in the political development of the country after the new dispensation in 1994.[2] Since the data used in this chapter are from the locations of our field-work, other Xhosa communities and people may have deviating cultural practices/world outlook. It must be said, though, that the findings of the research fit well with the literature in the field. While not a static or monolithic group, there are certain basic features of Xhosa cultural values, indigenous knowledges, and identity construction that seem to recur and cut across location, age group, and gender. There are, however, pockets of resistance against and deviations from a homogenous Xhosa identity description. This is briefly accounted for in the following sections.

The Locations

Mamphela Ramphele describes her role as an outsider as she approaches Langa, the site for our field-work in Cape Town in her book, *A Bed Called Home* (1993).

> Driving off the N 2 near Cape Town's D. F. Malan airport towards these hostels, one cannot help feeling uncomfortable. The smell from the Athlone sewerage system alerts one to the turn-off into Langa, as do the billowing fumes of the Athlone power station. The temptation to hold one's breath is overwhelming, but reality precludes such action. The streets are pot-holed and teeming with people and vehicles. The "flowers of the Cape Flats," flying bits of plastic litter, are in evidence everywhere (p. 19).

Although our research was done a decade after Ramphele's research, the atmosphere driving into Langa had not changed much apart from the smell that was not as nauseating as it might have been earlier. Driving into Langa, however, one observed that the township's existence was not only a matter of hostels and shacks, but also of big houses with nice gardens behind big fences. Some change had taken place since Ramphele's observation and some of the constraints observed in her book had changed, even though the full impact of post-1994 was not easy to measure.[3]

Visiting villages in the Eastern Cape was not markedly different from visiting villages in other African countries apart from the fact that the roads were, on the whole, much better, at least before you turned into the side roads leading to the villages. The major changes that had occurred in Peddie in the Eastern Cape since liberation were, we were told, electrification and tap water, a tremendous leap forward for a rural village.

Politically, the role of the chiefs seemed to have been minimized to the advantage of ANC officials. Educationally a new curriculum, Curriculum 2005 (C2005) was being introduced both in the townships and in rural schools.

The Xhosa Knowledge System

To recover, in the parlance of African Renaissance, African heritage and indigenous knowledges means, in reality, to recover an African or Bantu identity/identities on the basis of African epistemologies and African cultural practices and outlook. An exploration of this identity construction necessitates an exploration of the lens through which Africans perceive themselves.

The apparent ambiguity of the African Renaissance rhetoric referred to above signals the complexity of recovering meaning and identities related to African heritage. While there is a temptation to relapse, as Massey states, "into past traditions, of sinking back into (what was interpreted as) the comfort of Being instead of forging ahead with (assumed project of) Becoming" (Massey, 1994, p. 84), there is an equal temptation to relate Xhosa culture and identities to a postmodern, fluid perception where nothing is stable and where any coherent description is undermined.

This ethnographic journey into rural and urban Xhosa territories tries to make sense of what Monica Hunter (1979) called, referring to the Xhosa culture, a widely different culture compared to its European counterpart, and at the same time, being cognizant of Adam Kuper's (2000) warning that "appeals to culture can offer only a partial explanation of why people think or believe as they do, and of what causes them to alter their ways" (p. x). Particularly in a South African context, explanations in terms of culture have often racist overtones: "It is because of his culture." Moreover, while all our informants were part of the Xhosa ethnic group, the situatedness of that culture meant, as Daphna Oyserman and Spike Wing Sing-Lee (2007) argue in another context, that a culture is neither perfectly transmitted to all members nor is perfectly uniform across all members (p. 255). Clearly one's place within a society influences one's understanding of that particular culture or community and which aspects of the culture and epistemological orientation are accessible. One should also be wary of the tendency to underestimate differences within an ethnic community or exaggerate the differences between communities.

From the above one can deduce that the journey we undertook does not claim authenticity *per se* since any essentialization of Xhosa identities and knowledge systems would be to deny their complex historicity. All notions of fixed or essentialist identities are problematic, also in the case of the Xhosa, partly because even the most traditional indigenous societies are not static; they are all exposed to external influences. Hunter underlines in her investigation that the Xhosa did not constitute one group where all members were uniform in terms of beliefs, traditions, impact of foreign influence, etc. Nevertheless, there is a sense that the recovering of an

African heritage is linked to tradition, not necessarily in terms of nostalgia for a utopian past, but in terms of the lived lives in Xhosa communities.

The focus in this section is on religious and spiritual influences, primarily because they impact heavily on Xhosa identity construction and world outlook. Clearly, the influence of foreign forces on the indigenous communities allows, as David Rubinstein (2001) states:

> Interpretive interplay between them, a process suggested by the concept of intertextuality. That is, a rule or a norm can be read in light of another rule or norm. Readers do not encounter cultural messages as blank slates but as encultured agents whose "horizons of expectations . . . shape their receptions of cultural objects" (p. 75).

This intertextuality notwithstanding, the journey underscored Hunter's claim of difference where identity construction is seen as a process where the Xhosa, to a very large extent, are born into traditional ties where choice and agency are limited and where tradition and place are guarded. The postmodernist insistence of identity as something always fluid, with hardly any boundaries, does not quite fit the terrain of our ethnographic research in Xhosa territories. While there is border crossing among the Xhosa in terms of identity construction, there is also an anxiety "about the breakdown of barriers supposedly containing an identity" (Massey, 1994, p. 122).

Tradition and Modernity

While the concept of African Renaissance is an alien concept, the Xhosa cultural practices are part of everyday life. As has already been noted, Giddens (1991), employing the terms 'tradition' and 'modernity', argues that modernity makes a radical break with tradition, whereas Paul Heelas, Scott Lash, and Paul Morris (1996) ask whether it:

> Is really reasonable to suppose that 'traditional' societies can swallow up the person to the extent of muting or denying the exercise of autonomous voice, or to suppose that dwellers in 'modern' or 'post-modern' societies are content, let alone able, to live with little or no guidance from determinate others (pp. 7–9).

While Heelas et al. are right that tradition and modernity co-exist both in 'modern' and 'traditional' societies, it is nevertheless my contention that the degree of co-existence differs depending on the potentials of human agency and choice in the societies in question. It is well known, for example, that the potentials of human agency under apartheid were fairly circumscribed in oppressed communities (Breidlid, 2002) where various types of constraints made change and options difficult. Moreover, scholars like Hunter and others indicate, in line with the results from our research, that traditional societies like the Xhosa society are very conservative and not as prone to change as are more modern societies. Tucker's (1999) rejection of the polarities of tradition and modernity referred to in Chapter 2 is based on the notion of modernity as used to indicate "a normative development trajectory" and that so-called traditional societies that deviate from the European techno-economic standards are defined as traditional or primitive despite the fact that they are "contemporaneous with those who label them as such" (p. 8). While this is true in a Eurocentric value-loaded context where tradition is Othered and labeled as inferior, the discussion here attempts to explore important aspects of indigenous knowledges and worldviews, not in terms of a Western development trajectory, but in terms of their intrinsic meaning.

Identity Construction in Xhosa Communities: Place and Space

Even though there are obvious differences between rural and urban Xhosa communities, certain fundamental issues seem to transcend the urban-rural divide, most notably linked to identity construction. I will first argue that the identity construction among the Xhosa is very much linked to the notion of place. Then I move on to analyze the link between place, indigenous religious practices, and identity construction. Finally, I argue that despite what I call the Xhosa multiple identities that interplay between various cultural and religious practices, these identities are to a large extent defined in terms of indigenous place specificity and are not worked over by modern values.

According to Giddens (1991), the notion of place is more or less a traditional, pre-modern notion that is about to be replaced by a notion of space due to the advent of modernity:

> Place is best conceptualized by means of the idea of locale, which refers to the physical setting of social activity as situated geographically. In pre-modern times, space and place largely coincide, since the spatial dimensions of social life are, for most of the population, and in most respects, dominated by presence—by localized activities. The advent of modernity increasingly tears space away from place by fostering relations between "absent" others, locationally distant from any given situation of face-to-face interaction. In conditions of modernity, place becomes increasingly phantamagoric: that is to say, locales are thoroughly penetrated by and shaped in terms of social influences quite distant from them (pp. 18–19).

As referred to by Heelas et al., the deterritorialization of place is not as clear-cut as Giddens seems to suggest, as there is also, in both pre-modern and modern societies, a recapturing of place as a constitutive element of identity construction. As Escobar (2001) states:

> People continue to construct some sort of boundaries around their places, however permeable, no matter how changing and hybridized those grounds and practices might turn out to be (p. 147).

Nevertheless, place, defined as "the experience of, and from, a particular location with some sense of boundaries, grounds, and links to everyday practices" (Escobar 2001, p. 152) constitutes an important reference point in the construction of Xhosa identities, both in the rural and urban areas, most notably, but not exclusively in terms of indigenous, religious practices.

The focus on the concreteness and territoralization of place, as opposed to the more abstract notion of space can, from a Western perspective, be interpreted both as a defense of *status quo* and a way of sustaining or reconstructing alternative worlds. In a way, this tradition and place-related identity may seem to represent resistance to the attempted dislocation of place and rootedness in postmodern thinking as well as resistance to the imperialistic aspects of modernity and globalization. In other words there is a sense that this identity contributes to creating some sort of boundaries against colonial and post-colonial imposition or the fluidity of postmodern identity construction. The importance of place may also be seen as a way of establishing some sort of security among subaltern groups in the middle of insecurity, powerlessness, and fragmentation.

Whatever the rationale, conscious or unconscious, the importance of place and boundaries as a sanctuary and a location of identity construction in the Xhosa world are unmistakable. It does not mean that the construction of identity is fixed or unchangeable, but it means, particularly among rural Xhosa, that identity construction is bound to a geographical place or location.

Place is both a physical location and a carrier of meaning which is, I argue, more prevalent in Xhosa communities than in most Western societies. While it is true that postmodern identities are negotiated by the convergence of multiple places and cultures, there is a sense that the postmodern migrant identity derived from frequent border crossings is counterbalanced in Xhosa communities visited by the defense and maintenance of place as a concrete vantage point. While the focus on place and territory in a sense indicates withdrawal from domination, it also transcends the Western preoccupation with land as something exploitable since place and territory are something sacred and imbued with spirituality.

This does not mean that place in a Xhosa epistemological sense is only a bounded area that carries meaning solely in that area. As will be discussed later in this chapter, place also functions as a porous area where impulses and relations stretch outside the contained place referred to above. However, transgression of place is counterbalanced and to a certain extent resisted by place specificity.

Identity, Indigenous Knowledges, and Worldviews: Place and Religious Practices

While identity construction among the Xhosa is very much linked to place as a constitutive factor, place is again linked to indigenous knowledges/ worldviews in spiritual and religious ceremonies, rituals, and other practices. Even though there are aspects linked to indigenous cultural practices other than religion or spirituality, religion and spiritual practices are the *sine qua non* of Xhosa identity. Ver Beek (2000) defines spirituality as:

> A relationship with the supernatural or spiritual realm that provides meaning and a basis for personal and communal reflection, decisions, and action . . . So while one could be spiritual without being religious or vice versa, in practice the two are commonly intertwined as people experience and describe their spirituality through a religious perspective (p. 32).

Among the Xhosa, and commonly among other indigenous peoples as well, spirituality and religion are very much linked to nature/place, and it is the holistic nature of the interrelationship between place/nature, man, and the supernatural/spiritual which is foundational in Xhosa communities and differs from the Western hegemonic perception of knowledge, which separates people from their environment physically and through the systems of knowledge, belief, politics, and economics that it imposes.

This close interconnection between supernatural forces, nature, and man is also well argued by Lesiba J. Tefflo and A. P. J. Roux (2000):

> African metaphysics is holistic in nature. Reality is seen as a closed system so that everything hangs together and is affected by any change in the system . . . (p. 138).

In Europe, on the other hand, this holism was undermined by the Protestant reformation (Delanty, 2000, p. 39), which played an important role in the rise of modern science (and the separation between the secular and the spiritual) and, therefore, the advent of modernity. The characteristic feature of indigenous cultural practices is not only that there is no separation between the temporal and the sacred/spiritual, but there is also little separation between the present and the past, the living and the dead. While it comes as no surprise to observers of Africa that spirituality plays an extremely important part in the lives of the Xhosa, religion and spirituality were strikingly democratically distributed among the vast majority of the informants, whether they were educated or non-educated, or whether they lived in rural and urban areas.

The Ancestors

In the Xhosa religious system the ancestors stand out as one of the most important pillars. Prior to the advent of Christianity, Xhosa religion was, according to Chidester (1996) "an integrated system like any non-Christian religion" (p. 110) where there was no clearly defined supreme deity, but where "the Xhosa devoted their ultimate attention to the ghosts of the departed [and] they attributed to these all the powers ordinarily ascribed to Deity " (p. 109). While the belief system today is supplemented by

Christianity, important elements of the indigenous religion are still being practiced.[4] The informants underlined the importance of rituals in their veneration of the ancestors. As a rural male teacher told us:

> In our tradition we worship the ancestors. That is our connection with God. We believe something is superior—ancestors. I must do things for the ancestors. Spiritually I have to go to church, but the traditions must also be there. If you don't do what you are supposed to do, bad things happen (2002).

Several informants, including an 11-year-old rural school child, repeated the almost legalistic perception of the rituals:

> I strongly believe in ancestors. It is normal to do traditional beliefs with ancestors. Before my father starts the ceremony he pours out a little bit of brandy and *umqombothi* to the ground for the ancestors to drink and after that he will first serve his family, kinship, and other family of the farm. So everyone drinks in peace and they sing traditional songs and (dance) traditional dance (2002).

Another informant among the same group of students reiterated the same experience:

> My mother makes *umqombothi* and prepares for the ceremony. My father [is] in the kraal and [the animal] cries when they slaughter it . . . that means that the ceremony was accepted by the ancestors (2002).

The various types of rituals that take place in the homestead function as communication channels to the ancestors where people also ask for advice on matters like marriage, jobs, etc. Homesteads, therefore, function as a site for negotiations between the living and the dead and are places not only of identity construction, but also of cohesion. As the internalization of ancestral cultural values is reinforced, such communicative practices clearly underline the sense of belonging in the Xhosa community. This is also underlined by Berthold Adolf Pauw (1975), who states:

> The enduring presence of the ancestors is closely associated with the homestead, particularly with the cattle kraal where homestead heads were buried, and the rear position of the hut . . . there was a strong sense of the presence of particular effective dead, the ancestors, with their living descendants, especially in the homesteads of their successors (p. 130).

Pauw also mentions that the ancestors are sometimes referred to as *imilondekhaya*, guardians of the home (p. 131). This means that the ancestors are seen as protecting the living and the place from dangers and sending blessings, or they, as Pauw states, "send misfortune to express their annoyance about bad behaviour, or to draw attention to the need for ritual to be performed" (p. 140).

The pressure to conform to these practices was unmistakable and only a few of our informants rejected ancestral veneration, like a mother from the rural village:

> I don't believe in those things. The church is what I believe in. They don't do it. No dreams any more. I believe I am protected by the spirit of the church. I still take my son to the bush because that is done in the Bible (2002).

By refusing to identify with the traditional religious system of the village she seemed to construct an understanding of the world and a perception of herself, which was not place-specific, but was acquired through interaction with other places and in opposition to the hegemonic discourse. In the example above, the mother still took "her son to the bush" as it could mix with her Christian belief. The importance of sacrificing to the ancestors was reiterated time and again:

> If you keep on saying to your ancestors that you don't have the money, they will think you are not trying hard enough. Bad things will happen. . . . You must do everything right. However, things are always connected to these things. Bewitching really takes place. Happens if people are jealous (mother and grandmother, rural village, 2002).

There is a kind of sacrificial deficit here which must be balanced, and there is a spatial cleavage that must be bridged. This is clearly manifested in a narrative we were told about a goat that was chasing people who hadn't sacrificed to the ancestors. The chase stopped, according to our informant, when the people said that they would slaughter a beast as soon as they got money (female teacher, rural village). A similar goat story, with its mythical overtones, is reiterated in Bessie Head's novel *Maru* (1971) and is obviously a trans-ethnic narrative that sums up the significance of the ancestors or the supernatural in the daily lives of black people in Southern Africa.

The ancestor cult is, according to Hunter (1979), a sanction for the respect for seniors upon which the social and political system is based (p. 266). In societies where social security and safety nets are all but absent, the ancestors may seem to play a role, not only of cohesion, but also of social security. There is a sense that the ancestors are guarantors that the social and moral world will not collapse and that the solidarity of the group will be maintained. The ancestors are, as Idowu (1982) states in another context, "factors of cohesion in African society" (p. 184).

The ancestors not only play an important role in the lives of ordinary people, they also play a role in national politics. In the last elections in

South Africa (2011), President Jacob Zuma warned voters of the wrath of the ancestors if they didn't vote for the ANC, but not all indigenous peoples heeded that warning (*Mail and Guardian,* 2011a).

Xhosa Religion and Christianity

It has been noted how the close relationship between Western epistemology, with its universalistic truth claims and colonialism, meant hegemonic control over epistemologies that did not have universalist pretensions and often were called superstitious. Interestingly, the overwhelming majority of our informants who seemed comfortable with their Xhosa religious identity also confessed to be Christians.

As one informant from the black township stated:

> We are mixing it [Christianity and traditional beliefs] . . . However, if the ancestral thing is religion, then we are believing in two religions. Qamata is respected. And God is respected. Qamata is only the same as God. Just different names. The values are the same. And respect. Our ancestors are dead, but they are still alive . . . We talk to them so that they talk to the Lord. It is a link (a devout Christian from the township, 2001).

As Mbiti (1969) states, "Christianity, Islam, and traditional religions overlap in a number of points, and this makes it fairly easy for a person to be a convinced Christian or Muslim and yet incorporate in his life elements from traditional religion" (p. 275).

This is in line with our informants:

> Even the Christians are performing the traditions. That is in the weekends. Each family has its own way of doing things. In our culture we have to slaughter if the father is dead. The cow has to be slaughtered to accompany him to the other place. Even in the urban areas they are still doing that (ANC informant, rural village, 2002).

Oppositional voices against this type of syncretism were rarely heard. Here is an exception: "Most people practice ancestral beliefs, but I can't serve two masters at the same time" (a lay preacher in the rural area, 2002).

When illness strikes, Christians frequently serve two masters at the same time. According to our information it was quite common to go to both the medical doctor and the traditional doctor for any sickness.

The Dialogic Nature of Identity Construction

This is not the place to discuss the theological implications of this duality, but it goes to show that the Xhosa identity construction is nurtured from various sources where the boundaries of the traditional communities are being challenged. Only in rare cases is it, however, being threatened.

A specific place may be experienced in multiple and complex ways (Dillabough and Kennelly, 2010) depending among other things on the primary socialization process. Moreover, time spent in certain places with influences from the external world impacts identity construction (Berger and Luckman, 1966), implying a strengthening or a shifting of relationships to place(s). The construction of identity is thus socially embedded where the traditional intersects with other places and/or space.

The strong influence of Christianity does not, paradoxically enough, seriously shake the place-boundedness of the Xhosa belief system. While it is clear that Christianity, as such, is a foreign import often associated with a form of modernity, Christianity has also become, as Terence Ranger (1987) states, "Africanised" (p. 43). Christianity has to some extent been incorporated into the indigenous belief system where the territories that these belief systems occupy are not, according to the majority of our informants, mutually incompatible; on the contrary, there is an interplay or a dialogue that nourishes both systems.

The dialogic nature of identity construction is underlined by Appiah (1992):

> It is in dialogue with other people's understanding of who I am that I develop a conception of my own identity . . . but also because my identity is crucially constituted through concepts and practices made available to me by religion, society, school and state, and mediated to varying degrees by the family. Dialogue shapes the identity I develop as I grow up (p. 154).

Premised on this dialogue between indigenous religion and Christianity, most of our informants can be said to incorporate and transcend what can be termed indigenous identity. Geir Skeie (1998) defines indigenous (traditional) identity as an identity where the basic stories in a culture are seen as important elements in an identity-building project, or even more strongly, an identity that relates to one tradition or culture. While we have seen that relating to only one story does not seem to be a typical trait of Xhosa identity, our informants nevertheless stressed that even though their identity consists of several stories (for example, indigenous and Christian) there is, at the same time, one coherent story. In a sense, our informants have multiple identities that still seem to deviate from the fluidity of post-modern multiple identities as well as from what Skeie (1998) terms "transversal identity." Transversal identity refers to a kind of identity continually being reconstructed when confronted with the plurality of society. My understanding of Xhosa multiple identities seems both similar and dissimilar to Skeie's transversal identity in the sense that it relates to indigenous and modern stories, yet is dissimilar in the sense that the rootedness and place specificity of the indigenous value system is not fundamentally shaken by other cultural messages, even though this will vary from person to person.[5]

Our research findings go to show that the multiple identities among the Xhosa are a complex construct where border crossings are taking place, where identities are multiple due to the multiplicity of influential relations, where these relations are located differently in terms of significance, and where place and home are in most cases the most important constitutive factor. It is from this perspective the "cultural world" of African renaissance must be seen. This accounts for Hunter's statement that the Xhosa (Bantu culture) is widely different from European cultures.

Moreover, any internalization of non-indigenous discursive practices, a phrase coined in Fanon's book *Black Skin, White Masks* (1967), or in Christianity in particular, should therefore not be interpreted as a surrender to foreign, modern influences or as a dislocation of traditional place. Interestingly, Western epistemic hegemony, also ambivalently embodied in a "modernist" religion (Christianity), has influenced, but apparently not conquered, the soul and mind of the Xhosa. Since Xhosa identities are constructed on the basis of both traditional and modern stories, Gyan Prakash's (1992) statement that the post-colonial subject has been thoroughly "worked over" by colonialism and its legacies (p. 9) is somewhat misleading in our context. There is a sense that, despite the intertextuality and dialogic exchange between various value systems, the indigenous cultural values are retained, not only as a means of social cohesion, but as a fundamental element of Xhosa indigenous identity construction. Spirituality in an indigenous sense is retained as a very important epistemological marker among the Xhosa (and not only among our informants) (Hunter, 1979; Pauw, 1975). Research from other indigenous communities in Sub-Saharan Africa indicates a similar worldview and epistemological orientation (Mbiti, 1969; Idowu, 1982, Chabal and Daloz, 1999). Since indigenous can be defined, according to Semali and Kincheloe (1999), primarily in terms of the shared experience of domination, Xhosa identity construction can also be seen, at least from a sociological perspective, as a kind of low-key cultural and epistemological resistance.

4.4   LAND, SUSTAINABILITY, AND SUSTAINABLE DEVELOPMENT

While sociological explanations of Xhosa belief systems may be interesting up to a point, one should be wary of reinterpreting Xhosa spirituality in terms of symbolic representations, and hence interpreted as 'rational' from a Western perspective (see Appiah's discussion in chapter 3). There is a sense that a "rational" explanation of the belief in ancestors and spirituality, even among African scholars (for example, Idowu), does not take the worldviews and epistemological basis of the Xhosa seriously.

One consequence of the importance of place and territory among the Xhosa is their view of land as sacred. This is strikingly similar to the belief system of the Mapuche discussed in Chapter 7. Jacques L. Hamel (2005) states that many Africans, and the Xhosa among them:

> Organize their lives by following the guiding beliefs and principles of animist or similar knowledges. This keeps them close to the environment, with the environment, inside the environment, fitting in the environment and respectful of its providence (and its spirits). They tend to adapt to the environment and to adopt the environment. For them the natural environment is god. It is not something to be viewed as an economic resource to be exploited for prosperity. In this context material development is not a myth that is pursued aggressively and *homo economicus* is overwhelmed by *homo mythologicus* (pp. 11–12).

Or put differently—instrumental rationality in modernity "has no coherent meaning or conceptual validity for indigenous peoples" (Tucker, 1999, p. 20).

Conversely, *homo mythlogicus* is an alien notion in hegemonic Eurocentric knowledge production; its imposition in Africa has impacted and transformed the environment and its sustainability, often negatively. While the replacement of *homo mythlogicus* with *homo economicus* may contribute to short-term economic success, it may not only challenge identity construction and self-esteem among indigenous peoples, but cause unsustainable development as well. The trajectory of "development" in the North is in this way telling: *homo economicus* contributed to "the economic successes and the environmental failures of the industrialized North" (Hamel, 2005, p. 34).

Our journey into Xhosa territory has exposed a situation where Eurocentric epistemic imposition has not, however, succeeded in being hegemonic in the lives of the majority of our Xhosa informants despite the long history of colonial and post-colonial imposition. The Xhosa have retained a holistic worldview where spirituality/religion and the awe of nature are a fundamental aspect of Xhosa identity construction and epistemology.

That is why it is so urgent to incorporate indigenous knowledges in future conversations about sustainable development. It necessitates giving space to notions of the sacred and spiritual that transcend utilitarian, economic considerations and have non-instrumental, but ecological significance (Bhabha, 1990, p. 24). As the only economic superpower in Africa, South Africa has a long way to go in terms of sustainable development in the country. As a matter of fact, South Africa contributes about two percent to the world's greenhouse gas emissions and is among the world's top 20 emitters (*Mail and Guardian*, 2011b). This means that the South African government, which has not had a very aggressive policy toward alternative forms of energy, has a major responsibility to prioritize this on the political agenda and to take action. What has been high on the political agenda in South Africa, however, is the resistance to biopiracy and the theft of indigenous knowledges of nature discussed in Chapter 3. While it has been noted that there has been some success in combating the powers of the pharmaceutical corporations in South Africa (for example, the withdrawal of the case by pharmaceutical corporations against South Africa in relation to affordable HIV/AIDS medicine in 2001), there is no reason to lower the guard in terms of protecting indigenous knowledges.

The multi-national food corporation, Nestlé, has recently been accused of biopiracy in South Africa in relation to patent applications related to the use of the Rooibos and Honeybush plants. Rooibos and Honeybush are found in the South African Western and Eastern Cape provinces and have been used as medicine for a long time in the area. The Swiss non-governmental organization, the Berne Declaration, and the non-profit environmental organization, Natural Justice, stated in this context that:

> The second bio-piracy case in South Africa in less than a year again demonstrates how big corporations neglect their obligations to seek prior informed consent and to share benefits when using genetic resources from the developing countries as obliged by the CBD [Convention on Biological Diversity] (*Times Live*, 2010).

According to the Berne Declaration, Nestlé uses illegally accessed material to build up its business and prevents South Africa from sharing profits. The consequences of biopiracy are alarming; resistance to the theft of indigenous knowledges is ultimately a resistance to the recolonization of South Africa.

It is therefore of vital importance to include the protection of indigenous knowledges in the national political discourse in South Africa. Moreover, their inclusion is equally important in the conversations about South Africa's future development, which necessarily will also take place in the classrooms around the country.

4.5   EDUCATION POLICY IN SOUTH AFRICA AFTER 1994

While our study of indigenous knowledges is restricted to select groups of the Xhosa, studies of other ethnic groups, not only in South Africa but across Sub-Saharan Africa, confirm a picture of indigenous knowledges and worldviews that have strong elements of spirituality and ancestral beliefs (Leclerc-Madlala, 1999; Mbiti, 1969). It means that the majority of school children in South Africa (as well as in other parts in Sub-Saharan Africa) come from backgrounds where the key concepts and epistemological orientation that are linked to a modernist education system are alien. This is where encounters with such an educational discourse education might cause problems.

In the next part of this chapter the cultural, epistemological, and ideological underpinnings of the South African national curriculum after the new dispensation in 1994 are under scrutiny. To what extent is the "cultural world" of the indigenous population taken into account in the outcomes-based Curriculum 2005 and its later revision?

The introduction of Curriculum 2005 (C2005) in South African schools in 1997[6] was looked upon by the South African government as an important tool in the transformation of the South African society. This is clearly manifested in the introduction to C2005 (DoE, 1997a), which quite naturally is set against the former ideological impositions in schools through the apartheid state:

> In the past the curriculum has perpetuated race, class, gender and ethnic divisions and has emphasised separateness, rather than common citizenship and nationhood. It is therefore imperative that the curriculum be restructured to reflect the values and principles of our new democratic society (p. 1).

Only adherents of the old apartheid regime would question this new point of departure in South African schooling. In fact, a new narrative needed to be written to construct some sort of unity in the fragmented nation. The Rainbow Nation is such a narrative. As Howard D. Mehlinger (1981) states:

> Every country employs a wide range of social institutions to induct new members into its society, transmit the cultural heritage to the young and to develop in its people a feeling of national pride. The major means for accomplishing these goals is through educational institutions . . . [and] within the schools, the major responsibility falls on the social studies program (p. 25).

According to the Task Team for the Review of the Implementation of the National Curriculum Statement, Curriculum 2005 was well received, "falling on fertile ground ripe for alternatives to the divisive apartheid curriculum . . . Quite simply, the nation, particularly teachers and the media, embraced the story it told and the *ideological* turn it promised" (DoE, 2009, p. 12, my italics).

However, soon critical voices were heard, not so much on the ideological content, but more on the pedagogical implications and on the fact that the curriculum focused more on general than specific aims. As the Task Team wrote, "To this day the legacy of lack of specificity in the curriculum remains . . ." (p. 14). Moreover, the committee selected to undertake a comprehensive revision of Curriculum 2005 was mandated to simplify and clarify the curriculum.

The message that supported the implementation of the Revised National Curriculum Statement in 2002 was not, however, that it was a *new* curriculum. For the grassroots, teachers, and administrators, the Revised National Curriculum Statement was therefore blended into the original C2005, or looked upon as a further development of C2005. In the analysis of the curriculum that follows, I refer to the original Curriculum 2005 as C2005 and the revision in 2002 as the Revised National Curriculum Statement.

The Task Team sums up the changes in the Revised National Curriculum Statement in the following way:

> It explicitly attempted to change the curriculum agenda from a local, primarily skilled-based and context dependent body. . . towards a more coherent, explicit and systematic body of knowledge more suitable for a national curriculum in the twenty first century and more able to take its place amongst other regional and international curricula (DoE, 2009, p. 13).

While it is debatable that C2005 from the inception was very "context dependent," it is interesting that the Task Team perceived the Revised National Curriculum Statement as more adequate in dealing with internationalization and globalization, and thus, by implication, not so context dependent and localized. The important question for the purposes of this chapter is: What happened to the African Renaissance rhetoric and Mbeki's focus on African heritage and local, indigenous knowledges? Has the African Renaissance in any way functioned as an ideological compass for the curriculum writers? Is there an ideological or even epistemological difference between C2005 and the Revised Curriculum Statement in this respect?

Ideology, Knowledge, and Power

Since the main objective of this part of the chapter is to analyze curriculum ideology and epistemic foundation, this subsection explores, albeit briefly, the concept of ideology. In my discussion of ideology I underline that ideology is associated with knowledge as power. This is in line with Henry Giroux (1983) who states, "ideology refers not only to specific forms of discourses and the social relations they structure but also to the interests they further" (p. 144).

Ideology is in many ways an elusive concept, and the relationship between ideology and curriculum is problematic. My understanding of ideology is mainly derived from Louis Althusser (1969) who, by dissociating himself from traditional Marxist thinking about ideology as "false consciousness" or illusion, defines ideology as "bodies of representations existing in institutions and practices" (p. 155).

What is important for our purposes here is that ideology, as John B. Thompson (1984) states, is seen as responding:

> To the individual's quest, conscious or unconscious, for knowledge about the complexity of the world. Ideology functions as the relation through which human beings live in relation to the world (p. 90).

In that sense, ideology has a real relationship with the world, but the relationship is also "imaginary" in the sense that it does not tell the whole "truth" about man's relationship to society; it conceals real contradictions in society by trying to establish a sense of security and recognition among its subjects. Thus, dominant ideology has the function of obscuring from the subaltern classes the "real" state of their own lives and exploitation.

Althusser's important observation is that society in a certain sense addresses ("interpellates") the subject and recognizes the individual as a subject with value and identity. This means that subjectivity or personhood is itself formed in and through ideology, as the interpellation idealizes the individual and its real situation in order to conceal the real contradictions of society. When the subjection of selves cannot easily be achieved due to indomitable contradictions, repression replaces the mechanism of interpellation.

In a school context, ideology is an important and complex concept, which may help us to understand the links between the dominant, hegemonic society and the school with its students and teachers. The constitution of subjectivities in schools can be partly understood on the basis of various ideological interpellations of which C2005 is considered important.

Michel Foucault's idea of power is not very different from Althusser's notion of ideology in the sense that while power *per definitionem* is coercive, its campaign/use is often secretive or veiled, similar to Althusser's ideology. In this sense power is at the same time seductive and coercive, establishing some sort of dependence among those who are coerced by it. Like ideology, power is viewed as an all-pervasive phenomenon, which, if not interpellating the person (as with ideology) is, as Foucault (1980) insists, employed and exercised through a net-like organization (p. 98). While (hegemonic) knowledge gives rise to power, knowledge is also a product of power.[7]

In the South African context after 1994, and particularly in relation to C2005, the government interpellated the population into believing that the transformation of the educational system was under way by bombarding the people with important ideas like democracy, social justice, equity, and equality (DoE, 2001, p. 2). Needless to say, these were ideas or concepts that had to become part of the education system if the transformation of South Africa were to take place. However, as will be documented later in this chapter, these ideas were situated in an educational, ideological, and macro-political context, which made the implementation of some of these principles in schools really problematic. Moreover, the ideological thrust of the government's school policy was so massive that interrogations into the ideological foundation of the curriculum and any other counter-hegemonic interventions into the education policy were very difficult, if not impossible.

Curriculum 2005 and a New Vision for South Africa

As I will try to show in this subsection, C2005 was in many ways a very ambitious curriculum plan, which clearly was meant to contribute to a new beginning in South Africa.

The objectives of the C 2005 were:

> A prosperous, truly united, democratic and internationally competitive country with literate, creative and critical citizens leading productive, self-fulfilling lives in a country free of violence, discrimination and prejudice. (DoE, 1997a, p.1)

This is an interesting statement, which admittedly might have been a quotation from any curriculum in the Western world. In a slight conversion of the motto of the University of Cape Town, South Africa wanted to become a "world class African country." The pressing question in our context is, however, on whose premises was such a new South Africa going to emerge. The proposition of C2005 that "the curriculum be restructured to reflect the values and principles of our new democratic society" (DoE 1997a, p. 1) is probably intentionally so vague and ambiguous that that one wonders what was to be included and excluded from the variety of values, worldviews, and knowledge systems in South Africa—with the exception of apartheid values.

Constructing a New National Identity

When C2005 proposed to establish "a shared understanding of a common South African culture" (DoE 1997a, p. 16), the question arises: Is this possible? What is a common South African culture? Since it is difficult to find a nation with a clear-cut culture, and since individuals, also in the South African context, construct multiple identities, such a national identity has to be constructed. A national curriculum is, in a way, a sense of constructing a national identity where certain cultural values are promoted and others are not. Such a selection is indeed very contentious because it most certainly means that the cultural heritage of many schoolchildren is not being valued in the new curriculum. As Bernstein (1971) states: "How a society selects, classifies, distributes, transmits and evaluates the educational knowledge that it considers to be public reflects both the distribution of power and the principles of social control" (p. 47).

Emile Durkheim's (1956) view that education is the image and reflection of society and imitates and reproduces the latter is true in so far as it refers to the hegemonic power structures in a given society. South Africa was in a special situation here because the curriculum was designed not to replicate the *status quo* but, on the contrary, to contribute to change. There was, however, some reason to be pessimistic here about the possibility of implementing a *new* educational discourse due to the pervasiveness of the global architecture of education (see Ross, 2000, p. 42).

Both versions of the curriculum (C2005 and the Revised National Curriculum Statement) are clearly *in principal and rhetorically* ideologically counter-hegemonic to the dominant hegemony of the apartheid days. As we have seen this was stated quite explicitly in the preamble of C2005. The apartheid hegemonic ideology is replaced by an anti-racist and anti-sexist curriculum. Beyond its ideological break with apartheid ideology, C2005 is modeled on a Western discourse, depending heavily on different international contexts, especially from New Zealand and Australia (DoE, 1995). The aims and objectives of C2005, that is, the Outcomes Based Education (OBE), are to "ensure that learners gain the skills, knowledge and values that will allow them to contribute to their own success as well as to the success of their family, community and the nation as a whole" (DoE, 1997a, p. 10). Concepts like "critical and creative thinking," "organise and manage themselves . . . responsibly and effectively," "critically evaluate information," "use science and technology effectively," "problem solving contexts do not exist in isolation" (DoE, 1997a, p. 10) are familiar to anyone with some knowledge of curricula from the North. At the same time, the special outcomes of the curriculum in the human and social sciences specify that it is important "to demonstrate a critical understanding of how South African society has changed and developed and to participate actively in promoting a just, democratic and equitable society" (DoE, 1997a, p. 56). Other concepts of modernity like progress and development also figure prominently in the policy documents, concepts I will return to later in the chapter in the subsection on sustainable development (DoE, 1997a, p. 66). Moreover, the linkage between education, modernity and a "competitive international economy" is underlined as the prime engine in education policy (DoE, 1997b).

While nobody will dispute the importance of these skills or outcomes in a globalized world, the contribution of indigenous knowledges in the transformation of South Africa in C2005 is only vaguely referred to as "salvag[ing] elements of indigenous culture which are constitutionally aligned and therefore worthy of preservation for prosperity" (DoE, 1997a, p.193).

There is, however, a difference between the original C2005 and the Revised National Curriculum Statement (2002) in this respect.

The Revised National Curriculum Statement (2002) initiates a discussion of how the school children move between different worldviews and knowledge systems in a day:

> The existence of different worldviews is important for the Natural Science Curriculum . . . Several times a week they cross from the culture of home, over the border into the culture of science, and then back again (DoE 2002, p. 12).

This epistemological movement and border crossing was confirmed in our research on the Xhosa and by Cynthia G. Fakudze (2003b) who states that "the African child finds him/herself having to cross the cultural border between his/her African worldview and that of school science as he/she learns scientific concepts presented to him/her in the science classroom" (p. 132).

As was exposed by our field-work, many teachers, like the students, cross cultural and epistemological borders on the same day, teaching Western science at school and taking part in traditional practices at home. How do students and even teachers cope with a knowledge system in school, which is alien to their home universe? As one science teacher in Eastern Cape told us, "I am a science teacher at school and a traditional practitioner at home" (2002) The implication here is that the teacher operated with two fairly different knowledge systems, which do not seem to mutually nurture each other. The sustainability of such a situation is certainly debatable in a more national, South African context. Fortunately, the Revised National Curriculum senses a critical challenge here, asking:

> Is it a hindrance to teaching or is it an opportunity for more meaning-ful learning and a curriculum, which tries to understand both the cul-ture of science and the cultures at home? (DoE, 2002, p. 12).

As noted in Chapter 3, the cultural border crossings have been identified by Bernstein (1971) as a big problem for working-class youths in middle-class schools in England. These border crossings, important and difficult as they may be, seem of a much more limited, linguistic-cultural character than what can be observed in South African schools. Among Xhosa children it is not only a matter of linguistic code-switching, but of a collision of knowl-edge systems, which is of a far more serious and substantial character than class barriers in school in England. The Revised National Curriculum signals that these challenges will be dealt with in the development of a curriculum:

> Science curriculum development, which takes account of world-views and indigenous knowledge systems is in its early stages and will be addressed with enthusiasm by many educators. This Revised National Curriculum . . . is an enabling document rather than a prescriptive one (DoE, 2002, p. 12).

The importance and seriousness of these epistemological challenges referred to above is underlined by Meshach B. Ogunnyi (2003), who states, "The concept of worldview is central to science education because it is the knowledge that a learner brings into the science class. Research has shown that such knowledge has a great potential for hindering or enhancing the learning of science" (p. 27). Research on worldviews and knowledge sys-tems held by three groups of students in Form IV classes in some high schools in Swaziland confirms the complex picture described above and shows an intriguing mixture of worldviews embodying magic and mysti-cism with a more rational outlook. Fakudze (2003a) concludes her research by stating that the students, "regardless of their gender, age and interest in science, hold varying degrees of traditional as well as scientific notions about selected phenomena, that is, they hold a multiplicity of worldview presuppositions" (p. 61). As mentioned earlier, our field-work among the Xhosa confirms such multiplicity of worldviews and knowledge systems, but it simultaneously underlines that the indigenous core values are retained as the basis for identity construction.

The crossing of epistemological borders to accommodate the modern, "rational" world of science means that the student, according to Ogunnyi (2003), is "involved in negotiating and navigating a complex array of conflicting mental states. He must synergize these conflicts into a more comprehensive world-view capable of accommodation of the new experience within the framework of intra/intersubjective life worlds, which provide him/her a sense of social identity" (pp. 27–28). The complexities of these negotiations and navigations should not be underestimated. Moreover, as Olugbemiro J. Jegede and Glen S. Aikenhead (1999) suggest, indigenous students' encounter with modernist schools and Western science alienates them from their indigenous worldview and epistemological orientation.

> [W]hen the culture of science is generally at odds with a student's life-world, science instruction will tend to disrupt the student's worldview by trying to force that student to abandon or marginalize his or her life-world concepts and reconstruct in their place new (scientific) ways of conceptualizing (p. 47).

Even though the Revised Curriculum Statement started a discussion about including students' indigenous knowledges in the schools, the revision was not primarily aimed at such an inclusion. On the contrary, the revision attempted, as the Task Team writes explicitly, to revise the curriculum from its local, context-based body to a curriculum "more suitable for a national curriculum in the twenty first century and more able to take its place amongst other regional and international curricula" (DoE, 2009, p. 13).

4.6   INDIGENOUS KNOWLEDGES, EDUCATION, AND SUSTAINABLE DEVELOPMENT

The policy document on indigenous knowledges (Indigenous Knowledge Systems Policy) from the Department of Science and Technology (DST) (2004) signals, however, a commitment to African heritage and knowledge production:

> The White paper on Arts, Culture and Heritage (1996) views education as part of culture, and acknowledges that culture itself is transmitted through education . . . It is therefore critical to ensure that the national education strategy is synergistic with and nurturing of IK. In the development of the New Curriculum Statements, there has been a strong drive towards recognizing and affirming the

critical role of IK, especially with respect to science and technology education (p. 17).

The department's IK policy states that it will provide "a basis upon which indigenous knowledges can be used to make more appropriate interventions" (DST 2004, p. 3) as well as to affirm African cultural values in the face of globalization. Moreover, the policy document underlines the importance of creating incentive mechanisms to make African indigenous knowledges more geared towards economic growth. At the same time the document underlines the sustainability of indigenous knowledges in many communities in South Africa without, as it were, capitalizing on the possibility of indigenous knowledges to strike an alternative course of sustainable development beyond market liberalism and capitalism. On education, the policy document states that the new education system after the new dispensation is the key to "sustainable technological capacity" and that it is "critical to ensure that the national education strategy is synergistic with and nurturing of Indigenous Knowledge Systems" (DST, 2004, p. 17). The very existence of a policy document on indigenous knowledge suggests a pledge on the part of the South African authorities to put indigenous knowledges on the political agenda.

Even though sustainability and sustainable development are not recurring concepts in the Revised National Curriculum Statement, education is clearly seen as an important tool in achieving change and sustainable development. Moreover, the Revised National Curriculum Statement emphasizes the significance of a critical approach to economic sustainability:

> It takes the view that a "balanced" economy is desirable. Here, a "balanced" economy means one, which aims to achieve sustainable growth, reduce poverty and distribute wealth fairly, while still pursuing the principles of an open market and profitability. It promotes respect for the environment, human rights and responsibilities (DoE, 2002, p. 5).

While the Revised Curriculum Statement tries to mitigate the worst excesses of an economistic approach—market liberalism and capitalism—it is worth noting how indigenous culture and indigenous knowledge systems are absent from the discourse on sustainability. Given the strong emphasis on indigenous knowledges in the IK policy document, there is a sense that coordination between the departments is somewhat deficient since sustainability in the Revised Curriculum Statement is more or less exclusively linked to a modernist, Western approach with a dash of poverty reduction strategies.[8] Not even the concept of "balanced" economy in the Revised Curriculum Statement transcends the borders of the imported, Western knowledge system. This is problematic for the simple reason that one is doomed to fail to communicate with those who are going to be the pillars of transformation in the country. As Ntuli (2002) states:

For any development to succeed with rural people, and even with many township dwellers in South Africa, the role of divine beings, ancestors, sacred places (like *isivivane*), sacred people and sacred objects needs to be addressed. To touch on these issues is to compel our Westernised intellectuals to experience severe conceptual violence, and yet many of them secretly subscribe to these beliefs (p. 63).

Moreover, when indigenous knowledges are emphasized more comprehensively, like in the IK Policy paper, the discussion of including indigenous knowledges takes place, as Botha (2011) states, on the modernist playing fields:

Evidently, in the context of South Africa's bid to make formal learning inclusive of indigenous knowledges, both students and teachers are struggling with crossing cultural borders. This article takes the position that most of these efforts aimed at including indigenous knowledges proceed from epistemic and practical models that are located outside of indigenous ways of knowing so that indigenous peoples are most often the ones having to make the cultural journey, and are seldom the culture brokers (p. 151).

It is in such a situation that there is a need to explore another space for negotiations between the two knowledge systems. Since indigenous knowledges are epistemologically different from the modernist Western knowledge that hegemonizes the education system in South Africa, the coming together of these knowledges requires, as Botha (2011) states, "a theoretically clear, reflexive framework for implementation." (p. 170). CHAT's expansive learning as introduced in Chapter 3 offers such a framework. In the case of the Revised National Curriculum it would mean that the contradictions and differences between the two knowledge systems "inherent in a collaborative indigenous-Western knowledge framework negotiate for new forms of cultural expression within the national educational discourse, expanding and distorting the theory and practice of education in perhaps radical ways" (Botha, 2011, p. 170). It means that while taking account of the differences and contradictions between the knowledge systems (they do not necessarily constitute completely irreconcilable differences in the learning space), such a "collaboration" requires acknowledgement and accommodation of both knowledge systems.

As David Turnbull (2007) states:

Given the lack of universal criteria of rationality the problem of working disparate knowledge systems together is one of creating a shared knowledge space in which on the one hand equivalences and connections between differing rationalities can be discursively constructed; and on the other hand where no common ground can be created (p. 13).

This collaboration to create a third space (Bhabha) or third spaces/ interstitial spaces (Turnbull, 1997, p. 560) is based upon the assumption or understanding that knowledges are not only perceived as representation but as performance as well. This enables seemingly different knowledge systems to work and "talk" together so as to produce knowledges in a new space. Based on CHAT and cultural-historical activity theory as outlined in Chapter 3, this collaboration aims at generating knowledges beyond the borders of both knowledge systems. The unit of analysis here is the education system in South Africa with the objective of including indigenous learning and knowledges as an integral part of the education system. In a South African education context, one can envisage two interacting activity systems, the modernist Western educational discourse represented by the Department of Education (DoE), with their formal structures, institutions, and curriculum, and indigenous knowledge systems, represented by indigenous communities with their institutions and practices. Representing various voices and opinions that negotiate and conflict with each other and the presence of the divergent knowledge systems in the third space will potentially create innovation and new knowledges, thus indicating the potential for expansive transformation in activity systems. This is realized when "the object or motive of the activity are reconceptualised to embrace a radically wider horizon of possibilities than in the previous mode of the activity" (Engeström 2001, p. 137). In the two interacting activity systems discussed here, indigenous learning and knowledges are transported from the state of oblivion and Othering into the center of learning and provide the possibility of generating cultural centered knowledge in the third space.

In the classroom such collaboration can take place based on the cultural-historical activity system discussed above, or what could be called a "generative" model, where knowledges are generated by incorporating both knowledge systems into the pedagogical process to inspire new insights and knowledges in interactions inside a shared third space. Such an approach is reminiscent of Bishop's classroom teaching from New Zealand referred to in Chapter 3, and there is no reason why his experiences cannot provide the basis for pedagogical and epistemological discussions in a South African context, particularly if it is imitated at the local level and is then slowly developed to encompass bigger parts of the education system as well as teacher education. Such negotiations and interaction in the third space will contain both process learning and content learning; thus, knowledges will complement and enhance each other.

Nsamenang and Tchombe (2011) state that such a model "enables you to focus on the co-construction of concepts and practices relevant to school learning in the local community through the consideration of both indigenous and Western knowledge systems" (p. 17). Similar to Freire's (1972) concept of dialogue such a "generative" model focuses on interaction between the facilitators and the learners in order to liberate or generate education that "consists in acts of cognition, not transferals of information" (p. 53).

Such teaching-learning transactions provide the possibility for creating a third space where knowledges are negotiated and fought over, reproduced, and modified, but where innovation and creativity are also generated.

A "generative" model would imply that the question of relevance is anchored in the security of the students' own background, from where they gradually move on to acquire knowledges that also make them competent to negotiate in the global village. Such negotiations in the third space necessitates ideally not only a revision of the Revised Curriculum Statement, but a different teacher training and in-service training that prepare teachers to walk in the worlds of both knowledge systems. This is easier said than done, since most teachers "fail to emancipate themselves from dominant oppressive pedagogy of *received knowledge* which they deposit on their students" (Nsamenang, 2011, p. 63). This is due to their socialization and training in the Eurocentric tradition and to the guidelines in the curriculum. Moreover, since instruction from grade four is in English (a language that is not their mother tongue), the teachers are often squeezed for time just to deliver the basics required (code-switching is often necessary and very time-consuming), and the education bureaucracy is complex, slow moving, and not susceptible to alternative routes. Emancipation from the given script in the schools is more or less utopian. It is therefore crucial, as Botha (2011) maintains, "to start at the micro level of local interactions, so that it is immediately available as a practice-based tool for guiding the implementation and bottom-up development of interventions related to indigenous knowledges" (p. 168). Such a bottom-up approach is probably also the best way of making the third space a breeding ground for sustainability and sustainable development.

Medium of Instruction and Sustainability

The seriousness of the breakdown of communication in education in South Africa is not only related to the alien knowledge systems of the various learning areas; the task of bridging the gap between knowledge systems is also related to the issue of language in the classroom. If one agrees that quality education is an important tool for creating sustainable development, the focus must be on the negotiations between knowledge systems and the question of the language in which these negotiations take place.

In South African primary schools, the mother tongue is supposed to be the medium of instruction during the first three years of schooling. In the later grades, the provisions in C2005, the National Revised Curriculum Statement, and the Language in Education in Policy document (DoE, 2002) are unclear and confusing. The National Revised Curriculum Statement states that the idea is to keep the home language ("is to be sustained") until "the learner is able to learn effectively in the language of learning and teaching. [Then] the home language should continue alongside the additional language as long as possible" (DoE, 2002, p. 5). Moreover, the

Revised Curriculum Statement underlines that "the curriculum provides strong support for those learners who will use their first additional language as a language of learning and teaching (DoE, 2002, p. 4). Such a statement suggests that the policy acknowledges that some home languages will not be used as languages of learning and teaching after third grade.

The confusion is discussed in the Task Team's report:

> Both reports of teachers and research show that many schools are delaying the introduction of English until Grade 3—the year before learners are expected to learn through the medium of English . . . Students' proficiency in English by the end of Grade 3 is not sufficient for them to make the transition to English as the Language of Learning and Teaching (LOLT) in Grade 4 . . . Recent proposals encourage the teaching of mother tongue until Grade 6, whilst at the same time developing English in preparation for adopting it as the LOLT. However, clear curriculum guidance as to how this may be achieved is not provided . . . (DoE, 2009, pp. 41–42).

Our field-work in rural and township schools in Eastern and Western Cape confirmed a situation where the medium of instruction from Grade 4—even in homogenous Xhosa-speaking classes—is English, not Xhosa. Moreover, all textbooks and all exams are in English. This does not mean that teachers use English consistently in their teaching. On the contrary, the teachers make use of code switching or code-mixing, where Xhosa is most often used to explain the content matter in the learning area (in violation of the regulations from the education authorities). Clearly, this is a sensible solution in terms of the students' cognitive development, but causes problems when the same students sit at the exam table and are forced to answer in English. The efficiency of learning under such conditions is highly questionable. During our research in South Africa we found that Xhosa-speaking parents in Eastern Cape wanted their children to be taught in English in the primary school, not their native tongue, even though the parents did not have the command of the language themselves. While it is not difficult to understand that the parents, from a pragmatic and strategic point of view, see the social, cultural, and economic value of competence in the globally dominant English language, it nevertheless illustrates the hegemonic role of English. In other words, the strategic reasoning of the parents in Eastern Cape is right in the sense that it is necessary to acquire a good command of English, but they are wrong in their insistence on English as the medium of instruction from day one.

In our field-work we noted that the language barrier (despite code-switching or code-mixing) created huge problems even for students with a talent for math or science (Appel and Muysken, 1987). As one teacher told us: "I have several Xhosa students who excel in math, but who might fail because the exams are in English" (2001).

Our field-work confirmed that students who have successfully navigated between various knowledge systems when taught in their mother tongue are still classified as failures when the exam results are out due to the language barrier. While not enough space and time is set aside to negotiate the various cultures, worldviews, and knowledge systems in class, the curriculum makes these negotiations and navigations even more difficult because the dominant school language is alien to the majority of primary school children in South Africa (Alexandre, 1972; Alexander, 2000).

The result is that the majority of indigenous children who graduate from primary and even secondary school in South Africa have insufficient language skills in English and insufficient skills in the basic subjects. It has already been noted how this situation has negative consequences on sustainable development.

4.7   CONCLUSION

Education is still very problematic for the majority of black South African students. According to Cape Argus,

> out of the 1.2 million black students entering the public school system in 2007, only 3.5% emerge functionally literate. Also, the chief executive of the Institute of Race Relations reported that up to 80% of South Africa's public schools are dysfunctional despite a decade of increases in public spending on the education system." (Cape Argus, 2009).

Compounded by the apartheid legacy and economic realities, the present crisis in South African education is undoubtedly aggravated by what has been the central focus of this chapter, viz. the pervasiveness of the alien, Western knowledge system and the colonial language as medium of instruction. I have argued that this situation undermines attempts to make the schools functional for all population groups. Frank Darnell and Anton Hoëm (1996) discuss the negative consequences of the discrepancy between home and school:

> The degree of integration between an entire system and its subsystems will determine how and to what degree the system will function . . . Where there is cultural homogeneity or a complementary relationship between the home and the school, each will reinforce the other . . . Conversely, if the cultural background of the students and the culture of the schools lack symmetry there will be conflict. The cultural influence of the school will tend to weaken the self-concept and identity of the students, render their . . . background irrelevant and desocialization and resocialization will occur (p. 271).

The seriousness of this privileging of the dominant discourse in school is well summed up by Bernstein (1990):

> The talk, the values, the rituals, the codes of conduct are biased in favour of the dominant group . . . However, there is also another distortion at the same time; the culture, the practice and the consciousness of the dominated group are misrepresented, distorted. They are re-contextualised as having less value (p. 171).

The South African school system functions as a good illustration of Bourdieu's *habitus* theory (Bordieu and Passeron, 1990), where the school system reproduces the socio-economic profile and value system of the nation by using the habitus of the hegemonic ideology as a basis. Ntuli (2002) agrees:

> Our education system seems to move farther and farther away from indigenous knowledge . . . There is no attempt at any level to examine the indigenous knowledge systems awareness of the essential interrelatedness of all phenomena—physical, biological, psychological, social and cultural (pp. 64–65).

When indigenous cultures are introduced in school it is often in terms of what Gyekye (1997) calls "a truncated and hence impoverished conception" (p. 107), such as local cultural expressions like dancing and singing. Important as these events may be, they do not really address the underlying epistemological foundations of indigenous cultures and therefore become isolated from the general thrust of the curriculum.

The government's economic policy underlines the distribution of power in South African society where the majority of the population, that is, the blacks, plays second fiddle, even though the government is black and ANC-dominated. The power of the hegemonic ideology rests on economic realities—the distribution of economic power has not substantially changed since the days of apartheid. In the case of South Africa, those with non-indigenous cultural capital are in the driving seat (whites and the black elite). The democratic problems of such a situation are obvious since the "privileging of some knowledge over others will extend a degree of power to those who hold that knowledge . . ." (Sillitoe, 1998, p. 233). A more comprehensive inclusion of indigenous knowledges and epistemologies may threaten the power hegemony based on Western knowledges and the reproduction of hierarchical structures benefitting those in power.

Besides the power issues referred to above, there seems to be a fear that innovative and transformative educational strategies designed to meet the needs of the majority of South Africans will leave South Africa out of the process of globalization (see Crossman and Devisch, 2002, p. 107). Moreover, the authorities may worry that a more contextualized curriculum (note the DoE Task Team report, 2009) might leave the successful school leavers at a disadvantage internationally, even though research has clearly shown that the present educational system under the ANC regime puts the majority of school children at a disadvantage. The issue is rather that a decontextualized curriculum may backfire on the ambitions to make South Africa a competitive nation in a global setting if the majority of the students do not acquire the basic skills and the competencies necessary in the alien education system. This is one reason why the sustainability of the present system is questioned in this chapter.

However, the situation is not completely bleak. Odora Hoppers' work from 2002, in response to the South African Parliamentary Portfolio Committee on Arts, Culture, Language, Science, and Technology, signals a curiosity or even willingness by the South African authorities to look into the potential of indigenous knowledge systems. Whether her work and the work of others will influence the next revision of the curriculum remains to be seen. The IK policy document on indigenous knowledge systems from the Department of Science and Technology (DST, 2004) referred to earlier in this chapter, which attempts to pave the way for the incorporation of indigenous knowledge systems into mainstream institutions, confirms the authorities' interest in indigenous knowledge systems, as does the discussion of indigenous knowledges in the Revised Curriculum Statement (2002). There is, however, a sense that the interest is primarily rhetorical and that implementation is on hold or delayed due to macro-political and power considerations discussed above (see Jansen and Sayed, 2001).

The discussion earlier in the chapter of cultural-historical activity theory and the generation of knowledges in a third space may open up to the possibility of negotiation between indigenous and Western knowledges, deconstruct the absolute dichotomy between the two knowledge systems, and indicate a course for a more sustainable future. It is, however, dependent on a commitment from the ANC government that transcends rhetorical promises and goes beyond paying only lip service to African heritage and African Renaissance. As we have seen, indigenous knowledges do not only need to be valued in school; indigenous knowledges are an important asset to the South African natural heritage and need to be protected against the invasion of Western governments and pharmaceutical multinational corporations.

5 Education in Sudan and South Sudan

Tension and Struggles between Epistemologies

5.1 INTRODUCTION

The Sudan Context

The armed conflict between the Khartoum government in the North and the Southern regions of Sudan, which ended with the Comprehensive Peace Agreement (CPA) in 2005, lasted for 50 years with certain intermissions (for example, the ceasefire between 1972 and 1983). In 1955, one year before Sudan achieved independence, the first resistance against the Khartoum government started when soldiers in the South mutinied, refusing transfer to the North. The mutiny was eventually suppressed, but it saw the beginning of the protracted resistance by different Southern Sudanese liberation movements against the various Khartoum regimes in the years to come, whose policies resulted in wide-spread discontent and rebellion in the Southern regions. The issues of contention and conflict were many, for example, economic and social underdevelopment in the South, religious, political, and social oppression, as well as lack of educational opportunities. The Addis Ababa Agreement in 1972 kindled a hope for peace when Southern Sudan was established as an autonomous region. The ceasefire reached in 1972, however, came to an end when Sudan President Gaafar al-Nimeiry issued a decree in 1983 to incorporate Sharia law into the penal code in the Southern region as well. In this situation, Army Colonel Dr. John Garang de Mabior from Southern Sudan went underground and established the SPLM/SPLA (the Sudan People's Liberation Movement/the Sudan People's Liberation Army) to fight Islamic imposition, both ideologically and militarily. After the Northerner Sadiq al-Mahdi won elections with his Umma party in 1986, the new Sudanese government rescinded Nimeiry's decree and initiated peace negotiations with the SPLM/A. However, the hopes of a negotiated peace were smashed when the Islamist military regime led by General Omar al-Bashir came to power following a coup in 1989.

The CPA of January 9, 2005, between the National Congress Party (NCP) and the SPLM/A, defined a 6-year period (to end in 2011), after which a referendum was held to determine whether Sudan would remain a single country or be divided into two. In the interim, the two parties were tasked with finding solutions to a range of hotly disputed political issues, from the distribution of the oil revenue to the profile of the education systems (see Thomas 2010 for an assessment of the CPA). The referendum in January 2011 resulted in a decisive vote for independence for South Sudan, and on July 9, 2011 South Sudan became the newest nation in the world and Africa's 54th nation. Still, after the independence many hotly disputed issues are yet to be resolved.

The reasons why the South voted for separation from the North in January 2011 were multiple, and were often attributed to some of the grievances that had been voiced by the Southerners throughout the 50-year conflict, that is, the fundamental religious and ethnic differences between the Southern, non-Arab populations and the Northern, Muslim, Arab-dominated government of the NCP. Another reason was the struggle over the abundant oil and natural resources (Jok, 2001, 2007; Johnson, 2007; Lesch, 1998). The experience of being denied educational opportunities was, according A. H. Abdel Salam and Alexander De Waal (2001), an important reason why youth in the South readily took up arms against the NCP government during the civil war. Since the NCP came to power through a *coup d'etat* in 1989, the education system in Sudan has been based on an Islamist ideology,[1] which provoked the Southerners, who are primarily Christians or belong to an indigenous religion. During the last phases of the civil war the Education Secretariat of the SPLM produced a curriculum for the South which was based on more modernist, secular principles.

Some Theoretical Considerations: Attribution Theory

One basic problem with research in conflict areas is to label groups and define their ideological positions. As Tim Allen (1994) says:

> It is an issue confronted by the actors themselves in the conflict, because they need to state who they are and who their enemies are . . . In a different way, it is an issue confronted by social analysts, because they want to avoid a straightforward acceptance of the actors' perceptions of what they are doing, and also want an objective interpretation of ideologies and events (p. 113).

While an objective interpretation of ideologies and events is indeed very problematic and perhaps impossible (who determines what is objective?), it is clear from my research in Sudan that discourses in both the North and the South were often, if not always, produced to harmonize one's own position and demonize and homogenize the enemy's position.

On this basis, and since the focus of this chapter is on epistemological differences and impositions, I make use of attribution theory to explore the ways in which knowledges are produced in relation to the political and educational discourses and in relation to how parties on both sides of the conflict "attribute" epistemological positions to the Other, attributions which were seen as more or less innate and thus difficult to change. This led to a problematic polarization between the South and the North, and more than anything else, decided the outcome of the referendum in the South.

The theory of attribution can be traced back to Fritz Heider (1958) in his book on interpersonal relations. Since Heider, attribution theory has been extended and employed in studies of international relations, by Robert Jervis (1976) on perceptions in international politics, by Daniel Heradstveit (1979) on the Israeli-Arab conflict, by Deborah Welch Larson (1985) on containment policy, and by Heradstveit and G. Matthew Bonham (1996) on Arab perceptions of the first Gulf War. Moreover, Robert C. Prus (1975) has explored attribution in a negotiated context without as it were explicitly referring to an international context.

Attribution theory assumes, as Prus (1975) states:

> That objects have stable properties and that, over a period of time, persons would be expected to accurately characterize humans in terms of their dispositional properties . . . Attitudes, beliefs, intentions and sentiments are seen as relatively enduring qualities, in much the same way as the height, width, depth, and weight of a cube of metal (p. 3).

While dispositional attributions, according to Heider, refer to causality ascribed to internal or more or less innate factors, situational dispositions refer to external factors outside the control of the agent. Not surprisingly, blaming the Other is usually linked to dispositional attribution, that is, some inherent attribution of the Other. Similarly dispositional attributions are used to explain our own success, whereas situational attributions assign causes to situations and external factors outside our control.

According to Ross (1977), there is a tendency in social attribution "to underestimate the impact of situational factors and to overestimate the role of dispositional factors in controlling behaviour" (p. 183). Consequently, behavior attributed to the innate nature of Self and Other makes behavior more predictable and gives a sense of control. On the other hand, dispositional explanations may blur the complexity and ambiguity of "reality" (Renshon, 1993; Heradstveit and Bonham, 1996, p. 274), creating versions of "reality" that are fixed and not easily subject to change. As Heradstveit discovered about Arab and Israeli respondents, they were "overwhelmingly dispositional when observing their own good behavior (and their opponent's bad behavior) and situational when attributing their own bad behavior (and their opponent's good behavior)" (Heradstveit, 1979, p. 57).

5.2 THE ISLAMIST HEGEMONIC POLITICAL DISCOURSE

In order to understand the struggle over the educational discourses in the North and the South it is important to discuss how ideological and epistemological domination during the civil war created an atmosphere of tension and mutual suspiciousness between the two regions. What is particularly important for this book is the discussion of how political, ideological, and epistemological assumptions of the warring parties spilled over into a conflict over the epistemological basis of the educational discourses. The focus of this chapter therefore, as in the preceding chapter on South Africa, is about cognitive justice and epistemological domination.

Moreover, such a discussion inevitably brings up the question of the potential Africanizing and indigenizing of the curriculum, particularly with reference to South Sudan and issues related to a sustainable nation-building process for the new country.

As in South Africa, the recognition of epistemological diversity is a highly contested terrain because it involves not only the recognition of contradictory or supplementary epistemologies, but also divergent political and economic interests. The battle over which knowledges count is also a battle of political and economic hegemony and domination, which is true for both South Africa, Sudan and South Sudan, and as we shall see later, also in countries in Latin America.

"Domination occurs," Peter L. McLaren (2000) states, "when relations of power established at the institutional level are systematically asymmetrical, that is, when they are unequal, therefore privileging some groups over others" (p. 80). Analyzing domination and hegemony in Sudan helps us to understand how relationships between the various groups were distorted and manipulated by relations of power and privilege at the macro, political level and at the micro level, in our case education. Such distortions can easily lead to fragmentation because the relations of domination "are sustained by the production of meanings in a way which fragments groups so that they are placed in opposition to one another" (McLaren, 2000, p. 80). Since knowledges are deeply rooted in power relations there is a need to expose these power relations in education.

What differentiates this chapter from the chapter on South Africa is that the suppression of indigenous knowledges by the imposition of Western knowledges in South Africa was replaced by an Islamist epistemic imposition on Muslims and non-Muslims alike in the old Sudan. In a sense, the Islamist educational discourse suppressed other knowledge systems in such a way that it may be termed a form of epistemicide, as we will see in this chapter. Islamic epistemic hegemony is a good example of an imposition of a system that denies diversity; that is, an epistemic mono-culture, which is as rigid and one-dimensional as the Western epistemic mono-culture.

In the South African context, we have seen how epistemological or epistemic one-dimensionality has more or less been accepted even by the ANC government (although with some rhetorical concessions to indigenous knowledges) as a necessary tool for development and modernity. However, the lack of diversity in the Islamist educational discourse is framed within a different rhetoric, which is religiously motivated more than economically driven. Such a hegemonic discourse requires both an insistence on unity in diversity, and at the same time the hegemonic discourse requires the creation of the Other as inferior and therefore in need of a hegemonizing, all-encompassing discourse.

The complexity of the situation in Sudan, and now in the two Sudans, is that while South Sudan does not acknowledge the imposition of an Islamist knowledge system there is little discussion in South Sudan over the imposition of Western knowledge. Such knowledge is, as we shall see, very much linked to the rhetoric around development and progress, as the Islamist discourse is seen as hampering progress. It does not seem that the South Sudanese, however, in the wake of Islamist educational fundamentalism, the civil war, and the CPA, are ready for an exploration of how indigenous knowledges can be integrated in the classroom, although there are voices in the South Sudan society that are critical to certain aspects of modern epistemology.

In order to understand the conflict and the rigidity of positions that led to South Sudan's independence, it is important to understand how individuals and groups of people as well as governments in the North and South of Sudan perceived their own and others' views and actions. It is particularly important for the purposes of this book to discuss how ideological and epistemological domination during the civil war created an atmosphere of tension and mutual suspiciousness. It is to this conflict I now turn.[2]

A necessary point of departure for exploring epistemic power relations in Sudan is to analyze the educational discourse, which was administered by the Government of Sudan (up to 2005) and the Government of the National Unity prior to the independence of South Sudan on July 9, 2011, with the exception of those areas in the South controlled by the SPLM/A.

The current education system in the North was introduced by President al-Bashir in 1990, one year after the *coup d'etat,* which brought him to power. It is an education system that has not changed substantially since 1990. Since al-Bashir is still in power after the separation of South Sudan (May 2012), there is no reason to believe that the education system in North Sudan will change fundamentally in the immediate future. On the contrary, al-Bashir has announced that he will reinforce Sharia Law after separation:

> If South Sudan secedes, we will change the constitution, and at that time there will be no time to speak of diversity of culture and ethnicity . . . sharia and Islam will be the main source for the constitution, Islam the official religion and Arabic the official language (*The Guardian,* 2011).

In order to understand the educational discourse in the "old" Sudan as well as in the current (North) Sudan, it is important to explore the ideological, epistemological, and religious foundation of the Sudanese state, and the role of Islamism in particular. When Nimeyri introduced Sharia law in the South as well as North in 1983 the South took to weapons. The Southern revolt was set in motion due to the political and epistemic imposition by the Islamist government in the North.

This part of the chapter analyses the ideological and epistemological foundation and the set of values upon which the government party in the North, the National Congress Party (NCP), builds. The second part analyses the primary education system in relation to the value universe discussed earlier, and discusses, in particular, the school system's relationship with the various ethnic groups, cultures, and religious backgrounds in Sudan.

It is the Muslim Arabs (a minority in the country) who, since independence in 1956, have had full control of the state apparatus with the exception of the liberated areas in the South controlled by the Sudanese People's Liberation Army (SPLA).

One of the most important reasons for the repeated failures of the peace talks between the Government of Sudan(GoS) and SPLM/A prior to the Comprehensive Peace Agreement in 2005 was the unwillingness of the governing elite in the North to recognize the ethnic diversity of the country, even though the rhetoric at times was multi-ethnic and in line with the Constitution of 1998.

While it is well known that Islam is practiced in varying ways across Sudan, from the Sufi orders to the Muslim Brotherhood (MB) and the National Islamic Front (NIF), it is the dogmatic version of Islam (Islamism) through the governing party, the NCP, that has strong links to groups like MB and NIF, which for years has imposed its version of Islam on other Muslims and also on non-Muslim groups. The NCP political leadership that is part of the riverain elite in and around Khartoum has, besides its political hegemony, a financial foundation unrivalled in the country based on Arab investment, Sudanese expatriates in the Gulf—and the oil revenues from 1999. Moreover, the Sudanese Arabs possessed and still possess, in Bourdieu's terms, a cultural and ideological capital of immense dimensions in terms of the dominating role of the Arabic language and the privileged status of Arabic in Islam.

Even though Islamism today is a common denominator for a range of different movements, their common objective is to establish an Islamist state founded in Sharia. In Sudan Sharia has been practiced to some extent in the North, but not in the Southern region despite Nimeyri's attempt in 1983. It is this normative Islam that controls the hegemonic discourse in the North and permeates most political decisions, even after the establishment of the Government of National Unity (GNU) in 2005. Opposition movements that did not want a government based on Islamist principles were, and are still, seen as opposing the will of God. This hegemonic discourse interprets the Qur'an literally, in contrast to the Islamist modernists who interpret the Qur'an in a contemporary context. Al-Bashir is clearly inspired by the political philosophy of Hassan al-Banna (1906–1949), the founder of the Muslim Brotherhood, whose philosophy sees political power as an integrated part of Islam. The laws of the Qur'an are to be implemented by the political authorities. Since these laws are seen as God's own laws, the Islamist state is superior, both socially and economically, to other states based on other principles (Eidhamar and Rian, 1995).

In the official policies of the NCP, knowledge of Islam was, and still is, prioritized above all other knowledges. Nothing exists outside of Islam and thus, "everyone is potentially a Muslim. And since nothing exists outside of Islam, the mode of convergence . . . is Islam" (Simone, 1994, p. 143). The development of NCP's Sudan places ultimate importance on religious, epistemological, and ideological factors, therefore, scientific, economic, and social principles are reformulated on this basis. It means that consensus "on specific political and economic issues is usually difficult to attain" (Simone, 1994, p. 86). There is and has been an effort to enforce closure on the multiplicity of meanings and interpretations that is Islam in Sudan. The political and ideological constraints imposed on modes of thought that seek to transcend the fundamentalism of NCP Islamism are multiple and all-pervasive, ignoring, as it were, the heterogeneity within Islamic cultures. Moreover, secularism in the eyes of NCP is seen as absolutely Western and is only maintained through the dominance of Western modernity and colonialism.

Self and Other: The Unity of All Things

A fundamental idea of Islam reflected among the governing elite in the North is the concept of *tawhid,* which means unity, unity of Muslims, or faith in monotheism. The notion that everybody is potentially a Muslim is based on the understanding that there is some sort of fundamental unity in all existence.

While insisting on the unity of all existence and the totality of Islam, the Islamists at the same time, however, confirm the Qur'anic differentiation between believers and infidels, which effectively marginalizes people of other convictions, paradoxically confirming the Self/Other dichotomy in Orientalism. The official religious and political signals from Khartoum reflect Said's (1993) concept of the East and the West (and West here not only a geographical entity, but as much a worldview) as opposites and impossible to unite, and at the same time Khartoum preaches cohesion and unity across the divide. Moreover, by also underlining the ontological superiority of the Muslim and Arab mind and by focusing on the decadence of the West in terms of secularism (also used to characterize the Christian south), the NCP seems to have reversed the Orientalist interpretation of the West-East dichotomy by romanticizing the East (Arabs) and demonizing the West.

The notion of *tawhid* and the unity of all in Islam has always been anathema to the Southern Sudanese, who are predominantly Christians or believers in indigenous religions and who view the Islamists' talk of unity as that of another order that does not give space to others. When the Isla-mists refer to the Qur'an as "A common space . . . In fact, the space exists in order to join together and assemble individual differences into a funda-mental unity of purpose" (Simone, 1994, p. 134). For many non-Islamist Muslims as well as non-Muslims and Southern Sudanese in particular, the rhetoric of unity and togetherness is viewed as a theological abstraction with no substance in contemporary, political practices; the NCP has used power and force since 1989 to propagate and impose its views and has suppressed the identity formation of the Other. As a Southern Christian politician working in Khartoum reported, "It is unity premised on Islamic principles and totally unacceptable to us" (2004).

The resistance by the South against the NCP was therefore based on resistance against the representation of Islam as an ideal episteme in oppo-sition to all other ideological and epistemic representations. The result of the referendum in 2011 seems to confirm such a view.

Contradictory Discourses

What makes the attempt to understand the situation in the North some-what problematic is the operation of contradictory discourses produced by the NCP. A good example of these contradictory discourses is the Constitu-tion of 1998 and the educational discourse of 1990.

Although the Constitution of 1998 is couched within a Muslim frame-work, it is in many ways a pluralist document, safeguarding the rights of minorities by accepting citizenship rather than faith as a basis for equal rights and duties. Article 27 states that:

> Every sect or group of citizens has the right to keep their particular culture, language or religion, and to voluntarily bring up their children within the framework of these traditions. It is prohibited to impose one's traditions on children by coercion (helplinelaw, 2000)

The contentiousness of such a Constitution can be seen in the response from the Muslim hard-liners, who in 1998—before the Constitution was passed—criticised, to no avail, the draft version of the Constitution for putting a Muslim and an infidel on an equal footing and enabling a non-Muslim to assume office in an Islamist state (Agence France-Presse, 1998). The educational discourse of 1990 will be discussed in more detail later, but suffice it to say here that it is based on a more fundamentalist Islamist ideology that has little space for alternative views or multi-ethnicity.

One reason for the discrepancy between the Constitution and the edu-cational discourse was possibly the time lapse in the production of the two discourses. The 1990 educational reform happened at a time when the fun-damentalists were on the offensive (one year after the *coup d'etat*) and Pres-ident al-Bashir was more concerned with establishing his Islamist regime than paying attention to world opinion. Sudan's relations with the outside world were at an historically low level, and the IMF suspended all co-operation with Sudan in 1990. Seven years later, the IMF re-instated its link with Sudan, and President al-Bashir was eager to "normalize" the country's relations with Western nations. The wording of the new Constitution of 1998 can be understood as a "charm offensive" to appease Western criticism, but possibly also as a sign of more moderate forces within the government coming in from the cold. The constitutional critique from hard-liners and the exclusion of Hassan al-Turabi, Secretary General of the Muslim Brotherhood since 1964, may seem to support such a view. The Constitution of 1998 notwithstanding, the educational discourse of 1990 underwent no dramatic changes after 1998, signifying that constitutional reform has had little impact on practical policies in education or elsewhere. Since 1989, it has been the Islamists' universalizing discourse that hegemonizes political and cultural life in Khartoum. The Constitution never functioned as a hegemonic discourse. Al-Bashir's comments about the situation in the North after the separation of the South, saying that the Constitution will be altered in line with the NCP's Islamist policy may therefore have few practical consequences, but seems to signal the real sentiments of the NCP policy makers.

The fundamental religious and epistemological dimension of the conflict was confirmed by politicians in the NCP as well as Muslim informants in the North who did not have positions within NCP. Southerners were ascribed negative attributions linked to their ethnicity and religion. As one Muslim politician said, "The war is about Islam against the infidels in the South" (2003) Another Muslim informant, an educationist, stated, "Southern Sudan is an obstacle to the spreading of Islam further south in Africa. That is why it is important to Islamize the South" (2003). This is in line with the statement from the leader of the National Islamic Front, Hassan el-Turabi, "Yes, we are fighting a jihad, and we have always been fighting a jihad in Sudan . . .We want to plant a new civilization in the South. It is our challenge" (in Peterson, 2000, p. 186).

The contempt for Southerners and their cultures was also evident in the streets of Khartoum, where Southerners were/are sometimes labeled not only 'infidels' but as 'slaves' and other negative characteristics. Several of our Southern informants in Khartoum confirmed such attitudes among the Northerners they encountered; several Northern Muslims we interviewed also acknowledged such attitudes (2002–2003). This sense of civilizational and epistemic superiority may be traced back to past and contemporary slavery of residents in the South (see Jok, 2001), an issue to which our informants in the South referred repeatedly and critically.

During the middle of the civil war, the Sudanese academic Francis Mading Deng (1995) summed up the underlying reasons for the conflict in this way:

> The crisis . . . emanates from the fact that the politically dominant and economically privileged northern Sudanese Arabs, although the

products of Arab-African genetic mixing and a minority in the country as a whole, see themselves as primarily Arabs, deny the African elements in them, and seek to impose their self-perceived identity throughout the country (p. 484).

NCP's imposition of dogmatic Islamism resulted in fierce reactions from Muslims and non-Muslims alike. It explains the volatile and tense situation during the war and also during the transition period after the Comprehensive Peace Agreement. While the NCP throughout claimed to pursue a policy that reflected the will of the people, the NCP was obliged to use military force, refusing democratic freedom for Muslims and non-Muslims alike.

As Timothy Abdou Maliqalim Simone (1994) states, "In the rush to establish 'the rule of God,' basic human rights among residents in the periurban areas, both Muslim and non-Muslim, have been largely trampled. Forced and enticed conversions are the order of the day" (p. 144).

5.3   THE ISLAMIST EDUCATIONAL DISCOURSE

The prophet prayed, "O my Lord, do not let the sun set on any day during which I did not increase my knowledge" (in Haneef, 1985, p. 162).

The educational discourse of the Khartoum government is interesting in our context because it deviates from the global architecture of education discussed earlier. In the following section, there is an attempt to show how the educational discourse is based on the Islamist discourse discussed above, and that such a discourse is epistemologically at loggerheads with the Western hegemonic knowledge production discussed in the previous chapters. These epistemological differences notwithstanding, the educational discourse under the al-Bashir government is similar to its Western counterparts in the sense that it is a social system, which sustains a specific symbolic order by classifying people and naming the world (Bourdieu and Passeron, 1990). In a sense, any pedagogical act is a symbolic act of violence, since it more or less takes for granted that a certain knowledge system and certain pictures of how the world is perceived (hegemonic discourses) are more legitimate than others. Only those with the right ownership of cultural capital can thus gain access to the power spheres of society.

As discussed in the chapter on South Africa, the achievement of cultural capital, that is, the smooth process of socialization of students into school, is predicated on a complex interaction between various entities in society, for example, between home, social class, and school. Any value clash between school and society with the student's home context and society may impair socialization and learning (Darnell and Hoëm, 1976). Symmetry between home and school seems to facilitate the socialization and learning process, as our case from South Africa indicated. By interpellating those students whose socialization/learning process is "hampered" by an ideologically "undesirable" background, the schools are seen as an important tool for homogenizing the population in line with certain value systems, but also, clearly, in areas of political strife. The national curriculum is here an important 'interpellator" where a certain knowledge system is promoted and other systems are not, and where the cultural heritage and epistemological background of many school children are not being valued (see also Breidlid, 2003, pp. 86–87).

There are two issues at stake here. First, the nature of the education system must be seen in terms of the contested issue of the nation- state. Second, the privileging of certain cultural values and knowledge production at the expense of others opens up for a system of exclusion and inclusion, or what I have called epistemic or cognitive injustice (compare the situation in South Africa as discussed in the previous chapter).

Educational Reform

In consultation with leaders of the Muslim Brotherhood and Islamist teachers and administrators, who were the strongest supporters of his regime, al-Bashir proclaimed in 1990 a fundamental educational reform, that is, new philosophy of education. This educational policy paralleled the reforms in the civil service and the military forces. The new regime of 1989 targeted the Ministry of Education to conduct their "Islamist crusade," replaced administrators and teachers with NCP sympathizers, and prohibited alternative political student movements. The rationale for this change in the education system was underlined by President al- Bashir- (2004):

> To strengthen faith and religious orientation and conviction in youngsters so that they may become free, Allah-devoted and responsible persons. Guided by spiritual dedication and righteousness, education shall promote and develop the cultural and social values of society (p. 55).

As evidenced by President al-Bashir's statement above, the main objective of the National Curriculum was to transfer the Islamist principles based on Islam and spirituality, both individually and institutionally, from one generation to the next in the heterogeneous Sudan.

It enforced an Islamist curriculum upon all schools, colleges, and universities and consisted of two parts: an obligatory and an optional course of study. The obligatory course to be studied by every student was to be based on revealed knowledges within and across all disciplines. All the essential elements of the obligatory course were to be drawn from the Qur'an and the recognized books of the Hadith (Metz, 1991).The optional course of study permitted the student to select subjects according to individual preference. In short, the educational reform set the stage for an all-encompassing normative Islamist value universe where the post-modern idea of cultural cross-fertilization or hybridity was taboo (see Breidlid, 2005a and b).

Abdul-Rahman Salih Abdullah (1982) notes that Islamist education differs from Western secular education. In the Islamic educational theory:

> The door is left open for concepts which come from different fields of knowledge provided that they fit the Qur'anic perspective. All elements which cannot be reconciled with Islamist principles should be excluded. It has been pointed out that traditional philosophy which gives excessive weight to reason cannot offer any help to our theory. Hence, traditional philosophy of education which tries to resolve educational issues by reliance upon philosophical assumptions is not applicable (p. 43).

This is in line with Aziz Talbani (1996), who states that subjects such as science, technology, and history can only be permitted if they pass the "test of validity and effectiveness in fostering a deeper awareness of the Divine Presence in the universe" (p. 77). By viewing divine authority as the basis of education, Islamist education as interpreted here is based on the acceptance of revealed knowledge as *a priori* knowledge and becomes the key guide in selecting and validating knowledge in the education system (see Fataar, 2005). Considering Islamist schools as totalizing institutions organized around the production of an Islamist discourse of power, Talbani (1996) sees these schools as producing an ideologically biased and a closed form of education whose role is to reproduce Islamist culture and promote the Islamization of society (p. 67). In other words, there is an epistemic one-dimensionality here that, in principle, is not very different from Western hegemonic knowledge.

The removal in 1991 of the National Committee for Refugee Education, which was responsible for the Southern Sudanese refugees in Khartoum, was a natural consequence of this new policy. The responsibility for refugees was delegated to each state and the Ministries of Education in each state were to take control over all refugee schools, including those established by the NGOs. The objective was to phase out all schools not under the control of the authorities and integrate the students into state schools (Kenyi, 1996).

Since this revolution in the education system sparked controversy in many parts of Sudan, I asked one member of the National Curriculum Committee in Khartoum closely associated with the NCP about the wisdom of imposing an Islamist curriculum on a culturally and religiously diverse country such as Sudan. Dismissing the question as unwarranted, the respondent insisted on the inherent unity between the South and the North and that multi-culturalism was taken care of and subsumed under the umbrella of *tawhid*: "Sudan is one country based on cultural and religious unity" (2003).

Curriculum and Textbooks

The curriculum and textbooks for the primary schools in the North were prepared by the National Curriculum Centre (NCCER) in Khartoum. The members of the committee are political appointees of the government and are experienced educators.

As part of the normal process of the Islamization of education, the curriculum and textbooks were prepared in line with the ideology of the NCP. Education was looked upon as an efficient ideological tool and the members of the committee interviewed supported the universalist perception that the multi-cultural dimension of the curriculum was by definition taken care of, given the cohesion and unity of the Islamist universe. The privileging of Islam was often supplemented by an Arab bias in the textbooks for the primary school produced by the curriculum center.

For instance, Christine Oyenak (2006), based on her analysis of 41 textbooks of English and Arabic languages for primary schools produced by the National Curriculum Centre in Khartoum, concludes that the Arab-Muslim bias is overwhelming and Southern Sudanese history, religion, and cultures have been almost completely left out of the textbooks (see also Kenyi, 1996).

Visits to schools confirmed pervasive Islamization and Arabization in the classroom. As one teacher in a government school in an IDP area in Khartoum told us, "You know, culture here is related to religion. We are Muslims. The most important subject is religious studies" (2003). The importance of schools in nation building was repeatedly stressed in statements like, "The new curriculum emphasizes the identity of the Sudan." Another teacher elaborated the issue rather apologetically:

> Actually, there is something important I want to say. African writers write about the colonizers in a critical way. However, now we have interaction between cultures also outside Africa. In our curriculum, for example, there is knowledge of cultures outside. The curriculum says that we must respect all human beings (2003).

While it is clearly the task of the Sudanese curriculum to construct identities in line with the dominant discourse, it has been noted that the identities of other Sudanese were projected as non-existent or inferior. The similarity with the situation in South Africa is striking, despite the differences in epistemological foundation between the two educational discourses. In other words, this epistemic one-dimensionality is, in principle, not very different from the hegemonic Western knowledge production, which is pervasive in most countries in the global South (as well as in the North).

Even though the Islamist curriculum was basically taken for granted by most Northern educationists to whom we talked, there were dissenting voices among the Muslims. As one Muslim teacher said, "The problem [with the curriculum and textbooks] is not only that they focus on Islam, but the Arab orientation. Most Muslims in the North are not Arabs" (2003). Clearly, quite a few Muslims in Sudan felt the imposition of an Islamist educational discourse was suffocating and wanted reorientation. Some Muslim intellectuals have even tried to reform the traditional structures of Islamic societies by linking the Arab world closer to Europe. As Taha Hussein states, "we must follow the path of the Europeans so as to be their equals and partners in civilization, in its good and evil, its sweetness and bitterness, what can be loved and hated, what can be praised and blamed" (in Hourani, 1983, p. 330). However, al-Bashir's Islamist regime has shown no traits of such a reorientation.

The children of the 1 to 2 million migrants from the South who lived in and around Khartoum during the civil war, many of whom were not Muslims, were affected by the change in the curriculum. When asked about the new national curriculum and textbooks, which were developed at school and university levels, one teacher in the IDP camp in the Khartoum area said, "The National Curriculum is planned by few people. It is not designed according to the whole area. It is designed . . . just for Muslims, not Christians" (2003). Similarly, a concerned parent from the South said, "All songs are in Arabic. There are no tribal traditions, no vernaculars, no songs in my school" (2003). A teacher from the South residing in Khartoum expressed a similar concern, stating, "This is wrong! We cannot teach our culture until we go back . . . They [Northern authorities] see the South as a block, a stumbling block, hindering Islamization to the rest of Africa" (2003).

The NCP perceived the education system as a hegemonic tool, a means of constructing and solidifying the nation state and reproducing cultural capital and the existing power and epistemic relations. The problem was and still is that what many Muslims as well as non-Muslims outside the state apparatus found most problematic was *the forceful way* the NCP government throughout employed an ethnic model of the nation- state and an epistemic mono-culture which sought to homogenize a heterogeneous ethnic, religious, linguistic, epistemic, and cultural landscape, and by implication ignored and often suppressed these differences. The identity of the country was defined in terms of an *Arab* Islamist understanding, which also excluded many *non-Arab* Muslims. To provide a pluralistic sentiment where differences were recognized as legitimate and accounted for was, and still is, perceived as a secular logic that made little sense to the governing elite.

The Islamists' homogenizing efforts on the basis of the dominant discourse had, however, a negative effect by creating a fierce reaction and effectively destroyed any hope of a nation-state and a national narrative where non-hegemonic groups could feel at ease. By attributing everything non-Islamist as negative (despite the *tahwid* rhetoric), the NCP policy rather solidified a Self/Other dichotomy based on the Islamists' feeling of superiority and cemented identities along ethnic and cultural lines with a focus on a common origin and a common set of rituals, heroes, symbols, and values. This lack of recognition of the Other, both in the North (Muslims outside the riverain elite) and in the South, contributed greatly to the fragmentation of Sudan as a nation.

5.4   THE POLITICAL DISCOURSE IN THE SOUTH

While the SPLM/A during the war fiercely resisted the imposition of an Islamist ideology in the education system, the Secretariat of Education (SPLM's Ministry of Education) introduced a more secular, modernist education policy in the liberated areas in the South modeled on the global architecture of education. This policy paralleled the counter-hegemonic political discourse, which was marked by inversion of the hegemonic Islamist discourse of the NCP government.

An exploration of the political terrain in the South during the civil war can, therefore, primarily be understood and defined in relation to the Muslim and Arab North. The political and ideological climate in the South was marked by a pervasive animosity against the Muslim Arabs, an attitude which seemed more or less inherited from one generation to the next and which cut across tribal affiliation. This political discourse derived its meaning from, and was grounded in, that which was perceived as historical oppression over decades (and even centuries) and was firmly confirmed by the Antionovs (bomber planes) and other brutalities of the NCP regime during the civil war. Moreover, as Deng (1995) states:

> Southerners generally believe that the differences between them and the Arabs are genetic, cultural, and deeply embedded. They also acknowledge that their prejudices are mutual . . . Southern scorn for the Arabs lies in the realm of moral values, which they believe to be inherent in the genetic and cultural composition of identity (pp. 409–410).

Regrettably this essentialist notion gave little or no space for ambivalence and ambiguity. The war was therefore not merely a war of resistance against Islam, but racial or ethnic resistance against the dominant discourse in the North, which, as has been noted, implicitly and often explicitly laid claim to being racially and culturally superior to that of the black Africans. Deng (1995) sums up the underlying reasons for the conflict in this way:

> The crisis . . . emanates from the fact that the politically dominant and economically privileged northern Sudanese Arabs, although the products of Arab-African genetic mixing and a minority in the country as a whole, see themselves as primarily Arab, deny the African elements in them, and seek to impose their self-perceived identity throughout the country (p. 484).

Despite different opinions about the SPLM/A, there was a common discourse among the Southerners we interviewed when describing the Arab North. Not having access to the multiple representations of Islam that existed in the North, the informants in the South attributed a specific, uncompromising, and dogmatic Islamist policy to the Arab North, and not only the NCP. This created a polarized Self/Other dichotomy (see also Johnson, 2007; Jok, 2007). This animosity was voiced in the following way by one of the teachers from the South:

> You just have to submit to the Arabs. We feel that there is a very big gap between the Arabs and the Southerners. Their way of forcing us into their system is another form of imperialism. We need a change, for

good or for bad . . . As in South Africa . . . our rights are based on our ethnic group (2002).

Southerners' perception of Muslim Arabs during the war thus hinged on the former group's African ethnic and cultural identity and their identification with Christianity and indigenous religions.

Negative opinions were pervasive among all our Southern informants, young and old, women and men, educated and non-educated. The following response from an elder was typical:

> The Arabs despise African culture and see the Africans as inferior to them. Most of our people see the Arabs of the Sudan as killers, slave traders, and greedy people. We do not like to be ruled by Arabs, because the Arabs want us to be Muslims and Arabs. However, we are Africans and Christians. Arabs want to take over our land for themselves and want to take all the resources for themselves. . . . Arabs want us to practice the Islamist way of life and we don't like it (2003).

Similar attributions, like "we cannot trust the Arabs," "they are robbing our country and our religion," "they are not like us," reflected deeply ingrained perceptions of a Self/Other dichotomy similar to that among Northerners, albeit in reverse. It was not the situation of the civil war that had caused the bad behavior of the Arabs; rather it was the innate, dispositional character of the aggressors that made the civil war inevitable. A chief in the South explained that "The Arabs don't want to develop the South. Arab culture does not help to make our country more developed. That is not in their interest" (2004).

In contrast, Southerners explained their own intentions and good behavior in terms of dispositions (for example, the SPLA's good treatment of POWs from the North), whereas blatant violations of basic human rights in the villages in the South by the SPLA during the war were sometimes explained by the situation rather than the dispositions of the Southern actors. According to an elder from the South, "The soldiers looted many the villages, but they were forced to [do so] due to lack of food" (2003).

The devastating consequences of the war for the population in the liberated areas voiced by one informant came across as quite typical:

> The war has ruined my life in all aspects and not only my education. It cut me off from the outside world for over 12 years staying in the bush and made me not progress with my education after secondary school . . . The war has brought poverty to our community and me in general. The war has destroyed schooling and renders many children to grow without education. The war destroyed basic need facilities such as health. My brother was killed at the battlefront during the war. Many of my other relatives were also killed (2004).

A schoolboy said, "We are very poor. We are hungry at school every day. Many of us have lost our mothers. It is because of the war. It is because of the Arabs" (2003).

In a country where war has been the life-long companion of everybody under 50 (with certain intermissions), the singling out of war as the overarching reason for their despondency was not unexpected and was certainly also influenced by the singular discourse of the SPLM/A propaganda machine.

A Common Southern Discourse

The surfacing of a Southern discourse was repeatedly underlined by our informants. One said, "Many of us learned good things from other ethnic groups. We are more a nation than before." Another informant added, "Another prominent factor that minimizes traditional education to its death are multiculturalism or mixed ethnicity" (2003). In fact, this informant was unambiguous that cultures that disunite people should be discarded "because they promote ethnic segregation." The positive impact of more ethnic integration was underlined by another informant:

> The war made South Sudanese/Africans to have stronger bond and developed unity to confront the common enemy. The war made us to understand the enemy better and made us more determined to fight for our human rights, dignity and total freedom. The war has already created a unity of the oppressed people of the Sudan (2003).

While it was almost impossible to detect multiple, alternative voices against the dominant discourse, a multiplicity of discourses flourished in relation to the activities of the resistance movement, the SPLM/A, often linked to ethnic affiliation. The divergent opinions on SPLM/A did not, in accordance with the discussion above, relate to the liberation army's ultimate goal of freeing the South from the Arabs, but were related to the overall public objectives by Garang (the then leader of SPLM/A) of a united, secular Sudan (many informants wanted an independent Southern Sudan), the ethnic composition of the SPLM/A leadership (informants voiced their skepticism toward what many perceived to be Dinka domination), and the tactics and behavior of the SPLM/A on Southern territory.

While many of our informants pointed to a common Southern identity by living together in constituted communities as a reaction to foreign imposition such a situation did not, however, necessarily invoke commonality and closer affinity. It could also exacerbate tensions and conflicts, as we discovered in Yei, a medium-sized town in the southwest of South Sudan, where the consensus on who constituted the Other (that is, the Arabs) was counteracted by competition and conflict between various ethnic groups. In Yei, the conflict between half-nomadic cattle people and the resident farmers created a very tense situation where the cattle seemingly had been given free rein and encroached upon the territory traditionally occupied by the farmers. Several Southern Sudanese communities found themselves in this ambiguous ethnic terrain and the glue of the communities we have explored sometimes was the exclusion of the Other rather than the inclusion of the various Southern groups.

The discourse of resistance was, despite the compact front against the Arabs, both solid and volatile at the same time, and it is still, in the first months of 2012, too early to say if inter-tribal identity and a Southern discourse will survive the tensions of ethnic conflict or if ethnic conflict will re-emerge on a grand scale and tear South Sudan apart. Ethnic clashes in Upper Nile and other areas signal that much work by the authorities remains if a Southern discourse is to be more stable. What can be said is that our exploration of the sentiments among the Southerners towards the Arab Muslims during the war was clearly voiced in the results of the referendum in 2011, and that the final vote was therefore not surprising.

5.5   EDUCATION IN THE SOUTH AS "SECONDARY" RESISTANCE

Said's (1993) distinction between "primary" and "secondary" resistance is useful in the exploration of Southern resistance to Arab imposition during the war; "primary" resistance refers to the literal liberation struggle, whereas "secondary" resistance is associated with ideological resistance (p. 252). As was noted in another context, "primary" resistance comprises "physical resistance as expressed in liberation movements, mass demonstrations and similar high profile actions, more low key resistance activities which include . . . false compliance, foot-dragging, dissimulation, desertion," etc. (Breidlid, 2002, p. 14). "Secondary" resistance focuses on ideological, intellectual resistance like resistance literature, pamphlets, and propaganda as well as counter-hegemonic education. However, also the rebuilding of "a shattered community, to save and restore the sense and fact of community against all the pressures . . ." can, according to Basil Davidson (1978), be termed 'secondary" resistance (p. 155). The rebuilding of Yei County based on a common political discourse was thus one indication of "secondary" resistance.

Besides being a tool in developing Southern Sudan, education functioned as an important means of "secondary" resistance by impressing an ideological message of political liberation, which tried to foster a Southern identity construction across the ethnic spectrum. Schools were not seen merely as instructional institutions, but as cultural and political sites as well. As Giroux (1983) states, "resistance must have a revealing function, one that contains a critique of domination and provides theoretical opportunities for self-reflection and for struggle in the interest of self-emancipation and social emancipation" (p. 109).

In this way, the education plans and policies of the Secretariat were consciously used by the guerrilla movement and helped to build the communities under SPLM/A control, thus solidifying the epistemological dissociation from the educational system supported by the NCP. In this complex terrain, modern schooling in Southern Sudan functioned as an important bedfellow for the resistance movement (SPLA) by buttressing the dominant political discourse of the South.

It has been noted that one of the reasons why youth in the South readily took up arms against the NCP government during the civil war was the experience of being denied educational opportunities (see Salam and Waal, 2001). This was also confirmed by both SPLM spokespeople and community leaders who participated in the interviews in 2002 and 2003. When asked about why the war started in the first place, one community leader from the South said, "Denial of education is one of the main causes of the war" (2003). Moreover, the ideological basis of the education system and the epistemic exclusion of non-Muslim knowledges were severely criticized. The Southern Sudanese experienced Islam as a totalizing epistemology, which not only claimed epistemic universality, but also imposed its view on everyone. This was confirmed by one of the politicians from the South, who stated about Southern students in the government schools:

> When they reach Grade 8, there is the national examination. It is very difficult for them to pass. They do not speak Arabic well, they do not speak English well, and many do not speak their own language well. Many forget their culture. This is how the government treats us. Our children do not learn where they come from. They do not learn anything about our history, culture and language. A tiny number of schools [use] English as the medium of instruction, but with the retention of the Islamist curriculum (2003).

As is the case in other fragile states (Rose and Greeley, 2006), Southern Sudanese communities supported primary schools during the war. However, the longevity of the conflict made the running of these schools very difficult, exposing a very serious situation around the turn of the century (Nicol, 2002; Brophy, 2003; JAM 2005b; Sommers, 2005). According to Michael Brophy (2003), in Southern Sudan only about 30% of an estimated 1.06 million school age children were enrolled in primary school. These figures deviated dramatically from the North, where 78% of the students took the eighth grade exam (JAM, 2005b, p. 176).

A Western Modernist Curriculum

In the so-called liberated areas controlled by the SPLM/A during the conflict the few primary schools in operation pursued a Western, modernist educational curriculum and used a local language as medium of instruction for the first three years of primary school (or English from the first grade in the multilingual towns under SPLM/A control). In Grade 4, English was introduced as the medium of instruction in all schools. The modernist curriculum used was either a Southern Sudanese curriculum that did not, however, cover all age groups, or a curriculum imported from Uganda, Kenya or Ethiopia. The education plans and policies of the Secretariat of Education consciously contrasted with the educational system supported by the Khartoum-based NCP, reducing the all-pervasive focus on religion and focusing instead on education's role in socio-economic development, environmental awareness, scientific, technical and cultural knowledge, democratic institutions and practices, and international consciousness (*Syllabus for Primary Schools*, 2002, p. 4).

Most of our Southern interviewees mentioned this curricular distinction between the two systems. As one teacher stated:

> Recently [the Khartoum government] said that they wanted to impose Islamist education on us with no concessions to Christians. I told them, if they do, this is why the war broke out in the South. You know that this community doesn't belong to the Muslim community! We are supposed to have rights. We are talking bitterly to them . . . We have the right to practice our Christian faith! I just told them: "If you want to kill me, it's OK, but I want to die as a Christian" (2004).

A member of the Secretariat of Education of Southern Sudan made a similar point, while also identifying the need to reduce dependence on foreign curricula:

> First of all we need to have our curriculum as distinct from the curricula now used from Kenya and Uganda. However, we also need to have a curriculum which includes our history and our roots, and not a curriculum that imposes Islam on us Southerners (2003).

The replacement of an Islamist discourse with a modernist discourse where Western epistemology and science were promoted as the only knowledge system was thought to be relevant for progress and liberation in the South, often at the expense of indigenous epistemologies and values. When asked about the curriculum in the South one Southern teacher stated, "With modern education you acquire scientific knowledge and positive change . . . It also advocates gender balance and sensitivity" (2003). Another Southern teacher explained, "Science teaches ways to get modern medicine and other ways of living. It gives people knowledge about agriculture, health, caring for environment and many others for good way of living" (2003).

The modernist bias was clearly at loggerheads with the curriculum issued by the NCP and used in the big towns under NCP control in the South during the civil war. According to our informants, particularly members of the SPLM, the modernist curriculum in the liberated areas was seen as an important tool against Northern religious and political imposition. When asked about the significance of education, one SPLM representative reported:

> In the movement we regard education as number one among our priorities. It is the backbone of development. Some people think we can liberate this country by only using the gun. We need different ways and strategies to liberate the people of the Sudan—modern education is one of them . . . (2002).

Modernity

It can be claimed that British colonialism introduced Southern Sudan (now South Sudan) to modernity. Modernity introduced Southerners to what was considered part of modernity: both Christianity and literacy. Even though colonialism in many ways rejected some of the promises of modernity, such as rapid economic change and political emancipation (which was not the focus of British colonialism in the South), it also opened the door to the same promises through, for example, modern schooling (although accessed by a minority). Clearly, Christianity was interpreted on the basis of the Southerners' own cultural and historical context and was appropriated as their own, African religion. However, Christianity was also used in the resistance struggle against the Islamist north and as a pathway to development and freedom. It is worth remembering that among the first leaders of the resistance movement, Anya Anya, was a Catholic priest, Father Saturnino Lohure (Breidlid et al., 2010). The Southern Sudanese attitude towards and experience of modernity was ambivalent, premised on both denial and appropriation. This promise of modernity was broken when the North tried to impose Islamism on the Southerners from 1955 onwards. The Islamist crusade to the South was gradually felt to run counter to modernity and progress, and nostalgia for the promises of modernity via the British was re-echoed among many of our informants. Clearly, for many informants there was a close, positive link between modernity and Europe and the West, not unlike the perceptions in the Arab world, where the concept of modernity was associated (albeit not necessarily positively) with Europe itself.

While I suggested in the chapter on South Africa that its education system has a problematic situatedness in the crossfire between the emancipatory logic of the ANC government and the residues of a Western, alienating educational discourse (see also Breidlid, 2003), the situation in South Sudan is somewhat different. While it is often claimed that an education system is "the repository, carrier and transmitter of a society's myth, the institutionalization center for that myth's contradictions, and the locus of the ritual which reproduces and veils the disparities between myth and reality," the education system in South(ern) Sudan does not quite fit this understanding (Illich, in Higgs, 2000, p. 6). Conceptualized within a Western or European frame of reference, the education system during the war in the liberated areas and also after the CPA was, and is, rarely nurtured by the myths of the traditional Sudanese society, or it hardly conveyed these myths at all. Since a civil society hardly existed during the war and schools were islands or pockets in a society marked by a patriarchal hierarchy with little experience of how modern schooling functions, schools often seemed to operate outside of, rather than embedded within the rationalities of the traditional regional or local communities. What schooling in Southern Sudan during the war probably did, at least indirectly, was to explore the incongruities of the cultural practices and myths of the society in which the school was located and to elevate an alien knowledge system to the only system that was thought to be relevant for progress and liberation of the South. It is therefore possible to say that the modernist education system in the South during and since the war, as is the tendency of modernist systems, transported and solidified myths about the unique relevance of Cartesian epistemology, and if it did not discard, it at least neglected indigenous epistemologies.

The perception of modernity and modern education in Southern Sudanese societies was not uniform across the board. While all our informants were part of a specific Southern Sudanese culture, the situatedness of that culture meant that it is neither perfectly transmitted to all members nor is perfectly uniform across all members. Clearly, one's place within a society influences one's understanding of that particular culture and determines which aspects of that culture are accessible. In our sample, the majority of informants were from the educated part of the communities where we did our research, which clearly impacted upon how modernity and modern education was viewed. The introduction of modern schooling was, however, welcomed, not only by those with a vested interest in education—that is, the teachers, school administrators, students, or others with education—but also, generally speaking, by the majority of the community leaders and the elders. "In fact what is called school is the key to the brain . . . If there is no education there is no life. Even if you are a farmer you need to write and read" (2003). A chief underlined the need for both home and school learning:

> At 7 years the child now belongs to the teacher at school. The teacher becomes the father or mother to take care of the child. When he is at home I give him home education but much learning he gets from school, like reading and writing. The teacher opens his eyes to the world (2004).

There was a perception of modern schooling, however vague and unarticulated, as a vehicle for a more sustainable Southern Sudan in which the majority of our informants saw modern education as an indispensable tool in development. The population (probably due to the imposition of Western ideology and discourse since the beginning of the 20th century) hardly questioned the supremacy of Western education that had, so the understanding was, generated so much wealth in Europe and the West. Moreover, its pro-modern, somewhat anti-Islamist bias was welcomed in a situation where any ideological or epistemic transfer from the North was resisted wholeheartedly. The strong sense of the importance of modernist values coupled with Western epistemology in schools as a counter-force to Muslim ideology was repeatedly underlined.

Indigenous Practices as Anti-Modern

While lack of development and change was primarily ascribed to the civil war and the Arabs, some informants attributed traditional practices as another obstacle to change. Modern education was thought to modify not eradicate such practices. As one informant stated, "The purpose of education is not to abandon traditions, just to upgrade and modify them. Modern education upgrades skills to improve life effectively" (2003).

Many informants mentioned sensitization and training of rural people as an important aspect of schooling, partly in relation to girls' education. Girls' education was a matter of serious concern and highlighted the gap in thinking among certain segments of the population in the South. In a way, modern schooling in the South engaged in an ideological war on two fronts—against Islamist imposition and also against certain, if not all, indigenous cultural practices.

As another informant stated, "I want to have a bright future. I don't want to be in darkness like my ancestors. I don't want to suffer like people who are uneducated" (2003).

The issue of awareness and education was raised by several:

> The good things are: creating awareness. It is really good in the way that it teaches you to do things in a better way. As people begin to discover the world, things change (2004).

And another:

> Education builds awareness about many things, for example about HIV and AIDS and how to prevent it. Condoms are not brought to make people prostitutes, but to protect [them] from the dangers of disease (2004).

Other informants underlined the importance of education in eliminating problematic cultural practices, such as, one informant told us, "female circumcision, and the lack of women's empowerment" (2003).

A teacher focused on the importance of education in relation to traditional culture and change:

> One of the problems in our society is the resistance to change. If someone brings in an innovation, the people first have to study it critically. Some also want to look at the others and see how they succeed. They are afraid of changing their traditional practices and habits . . . This is a very big problem (2004).

Yet another teacher confirmed the first teacher's view:

> Most of us are living in accordance with our culture. Educated people have changed their way of culture. Those who are not educated have a narrow type of life. They themselves think that they are the only people in the world. They don't notice that changes are taking place (teacher, 2004).

Education as Inclusive?

It has been noted how the Islamist educational discourse functioned in an exclusive way, since its epistemic foundation did not address the values and worldviews of the Southerners. The Southern educational discourse during the war was, and still is, a more *inclusive* discourse for the Southern population than the Islamist discourse in the sense that it was (is) perceived to be more in line with the sentiments among people in the region, despite its non-indigenous and modernist bias. Whether the new discourse manages to change the gender imbalance among school graduates remains to be seen.

Gender Disparities

According to Arnot and Fennell (2008), gender education reform in the South is often "expressed through an ideologically diverse group of INGOs, grass roots activists, projects and initiatives or through government policy statements developed in response to international pressure" (p. 4). As noted in Chapter 2, global educational policies such as those of the World Bank, the UN organizations and the INGOs homogenize national educational policies and are therefore playing what can be termed a neo-colonial role in identifying pivotal themes and topics in education across the world such as gender equality, literacy, and quality education in local contexts. Although many of these themes have universal appeal and relevance, they are often steeped in a Western logic, which is not always culturally relevant or conducive.

While literacy skills are extremely important in South Sudan where fewer than 2% of girls complete primary education (UNICEF, 2005), the imposition of a certain set of values on the female population in South Sudan through internationally driven campaigns to send more girls to school is therefore not unproblematic within a culture where most girls are seen as important breadwinners to ensure the basic survival of their families. There is an ethical issue here beyond women's liberation and gender equality that is not easily addressed with impoverished households struggling for survival. While the situation in South Sudan necessitates a continuous preoccupation with access, enrollment, and retention among girls, it is also necessary to go beyond the number game and the issue of basic literacy and ask: What kind of education? What kind of quality? What kind of knowledges? These are questions hardly raised in the debate about female participation in schools. Does a modernist education imported from the West offer girls in South Sudan the tools needed to transcend their impoverished environments? Why are indigenous knowledges marginalized in the new curriculum in South Sudan? If school only prepares students for jobs in the modern sector, does schooling lure girls (and probably to a less extent boys) to school with promises that in most cases cannot be kept? These are questions and dilemmas that need to be addressed in the campaigns to reach Millennium Development Goal (MDG) number two by 2015, that is, "ensure that, by 2015, children everywhere, boys and girls alike, will be able to complete a full course of primary schooling" (UN 2010). Gender equality and girls' participation in school, although seen as positive by many of our informants, are also disputed notions in the communities we visited. Since girls' schooling often encourages a certain type of female empowerment which may open avenues earlier closed to the girls, it may threaten, according to some informants, the social fabric of these communities (see Breidlid and Breidlid, forthcoming, 2012).

The Modernist Curriculum as Exclusive

The inclusivity of the educational discourse referred to above may be termed somewhat illusionary since our research in South(ern) Sudan has shown that the indigenous cultural beliefs are very pervasive and cut across differences of gender, age, and educational background (thus not very dissimilar from those in South Africa referred to earlier). The belief system among the indigenous groups in Yei is often characterized by syncretism, that is, an overlap between Christianity and indigenous religion; the indigenous belief system lacks modernity's separation between the temporal and the sacred; and the relationship between nature, man, and the supernatural seems to conflate in a more holistic understanding of the world. This conflation is underscored in the belief in ancestors. As one informant stated:

> They say when a person die[s] he becomes in a prison state, so this people [*sic*] go together with "Malaika" [God]. When a person dies he is still alive. They used to see you what you are doing in the house,

whether you respect them or not. If you don't respect them they come and make something in which they kill you (2003).

Not surprisingly, a modernist educational discourse therefore also has its detractors.

Some informants referred to the alienating influence of modern schooling. As one informant stated, "some of the things the children learn, pull them away from their culture."

When asked what he meant, he replied:

> For example pictures and photos in textbooks. They are related to a different life and culture. Modern education imposes things instead of building on their own existence. Things are brought from above (2003).

For many of the nomadic people, education was perceived as completely meaningless and counter-productive:

> Most of the cattle holders in our area are nomadic. The Baggara use children to take the animals to other areas. Taking the children to school without a permanent settlement is a big problem. Certain things have to be provided. And you need to know why they are running away, and to provide what they need. Some of the nomads reject the issue of education itself. It conflicts with their traditional values. They don't like their children to go to school. And if they come to town, they don't go back. Those who go to study, they don't empower them economically (2003).

While the civil war may have weakened what some Sudanese call the authenticity of certain indigenous traditions and practices ("The war has now scattered everybody, so people are no longer following their traditions properly" (2003)), the actual co-existence between indigenous practices, belief systems, and modernity (even among educated people) would seem to necessitate a re-evaluation of the epistemic mono-culture which was, and still is, hegemonic in the schools in South(ern) Sudan.

5.6   THE NEW NATION SOUTH SUDAN AND SUSTAINABLE DEVELOPMENT

As South Sudan now is emerging as a new nation, the government in the South acknowledges that there is a need for a new national narrative and a South Sudan identity that encompasses the various ethnic groups and the competing knowledge systems in South Sudan.

The establishment and development of a national identity (among multiple identities) based on territorial solidarity and a common cultural heritage is the glue necessary for the new nation-state to survive. In a South Sudan context, what are the implications of an exclusion of indigenous epistemic traditions in the official discourse in relation to South Sudanese identity construction and a national narrative? During the war, a Southern Sudan identity or a Southern discourse was, as has been noted, more easily defined and nurtured in opposition to the Other (the North). People from diverse ethnic groups discovered commonalities across ethnicities during the war, and wanted, as has been noted from our Khartoum field trips, indigenous cultures to be included in the school curriculum so that their past was not lost. The challenge in the new nation South Sudan is to re-establish such an identity in the absence of the Other, or to minimize suspicion/animosities in relation to another Other (that is other ethnic groups) on South Sudanese territory. The hugeness and complexity of such a challenge is seen in the many inter-ethnic clashes in the wake of the independence of South Sudan in July 2011.

As scholars have stated earlier, education can both contribute to conflict and facilitate peace processes (UNICEF, 2000; Smith and Vaux, 2003; Davies, 2004), and one goal of the new South Sudanese education system is to foster inter-tribal reconciliation (see also McEvoy-Levy, 2006). In communities so steeped in indigenous values, the exploration of their own value universe and epistemological orientation in school is important if alienation is to be avoided. Simultaneously, it is urgent to promote the basic similarities in worldviews and knowledge production that exist between the various ethnic groups to stretch loyalties and recognize commonalities beyond ethnic borders.

Since identities are constructed on the basis of multiple historical, contextual, and cultural influences, a modernist educational discourse that *per definitionem* narrowly defines which knowledges should be celebrated and counted undermines attempts to establish identities that are grounded in, but not restricted to, indigenous knowledges, experiences, and cultures. A modernist discourse thus marginalizes and Others, through the domination of Western science and epistemology, the people who constitute the new nation and who, somewhat paradoxically, are attracted to that very same discourse. Ngũgĩ's "colonizing of the mind" is an appropriate term here. It is in this paradoxical terrain that the education authorities of the new nation have to navigate.

It is in the same terrain that the Islamist educational discourse is gradually being withdrawn from the schools in the big towns in post-war South Sudan that were occupied by the NCP during the war. While the withdrawal of Islamist schools from the South can be understood on the basis of the civil war—which entrenched positions on both sides of the conflict—there is a sense that a new educational discourse in South Sudan could benefit in some way or another from the bringing together of the three worlds of discourses related to education, viz. the Islamist educational traditions, Sudanese indigenous knowledges, and Western knowledge. Unfortunately, the educational discourse in the North has been "polluted" by a dogmatism and a Self/Other rhetoric that has camouflaged aspects of Islamic education philosophy (rather than Islamism) that in some respects are akin to indigenous epistemologies and worldviews, for instance, its emphasis on spirituality and religious values.

The Success of the Western Epistemic Mono-Culture

The very fact that the South has fought off the imposition of one epistemic mono-culture (Islam) does not, as we have seen, imply a goodbye to another epistemic mono-culture like Western education. This epistemic mono-cultural focus re-echoes the sentiments in our previous case study, South Africa, and shows the tremendous success of Western epistemic expansion. While there are multiple reasons why the South Sudanese ascribe negative attributions to Islam and an Islamist educational discourse, the problem with the Western epistemic success story is the delegitimizing of the non-hegemonic indigenous knowledges, as voiced by some of our informants. One reason for this is the fact that South Sudanese policy makers and academics, like their South African counterparts, are Westernized Africans who have internalized the hegemonic Western epistemology. Change and sustainable development means adopting the ways of the West and competing on the globalized playing fields, that is, an education system based on a Western epistemic model. Moreover, the heavy influx of Western NGOs in the education sector in the South has augmented its Western bias and has increased the gap, not only between Western and indigenous knowledges, but between the educational discourses in South Sudan and Sudan (see Breidlid, 2010).

A Modernization Bonanza

The political leaders in South Sudan envisage change and development in the new nation as inextricably linked to a Western development paradigm. There is, for example, a modernization bonanza in the capital of South Sudan, Juba, reputed to be the fastest growing city in the world, where the presence of an ever-increasing number of INGOs has resulted in a building boom that has made the city notoriously expensive. The living costs in the city has made life in Juba unaffordable for ordinary Sudanese, and the pervasiveness of corruption (Deng, 2011) and mismanagement means the city is unsustainable in social and economic development. In the countryside, however, little development has taken place and frustration is growing.

The news that the government of South Sudan has decided to relocate the capital to the Lakes state only confirms the impression of a governing elite whose focus is modernization and not service delivery to the population *in toto*.

Foreign Investments in Land

Quite recently, information has emerged that big tracts of fertile land have been acquired by foreign investors through leases with local communities or government institutions. A report released by the Norwegian People's Aid (2011) found that during the last four years "foreign interests sought or acquired 2.64 million hectares (26,400 sq km) in the agriculture, forestry and biofuel sectors alone—an area that is larger than the whole of Rwanda" (*East African*, 2011). Even if this can stimulate rural development, and generate employment opportunities, the report warns that:

> If investments are structured to benefit a small transnational elite at the expense of the rural poor; if the country's arable land is used to grow food and biofuels for foreign populations, pushing communities onto increasingly marginal lands; if commercial land deals concentrate land and natural resources in the hands of a select few, they risk becoming sources of food insecurity, instability, social unrest and conflict (Deng, 2011, p. 36).

The heavy foreign investments are, according to the NPA, mostly based on "centralized business models that take advantage of economies of scale to maximize returns to the investor. . ." (Deng, 2011, p. 4). Moreover, foreign companies can often use the political capital of their domestic allies "to facilitate the land acquisition and may not need to rely as heavily on social capital within the communities. This may avoid some of the *ex ante* costs of negotiations involving affected communities, but it makes for weaker agreements and less sustainable developments in the long term" (Deng, 2011, p. 4)

The maximization of returns and the exclusion of indigenous peoples are just a continuation of post-colonial oppression in the name of national economic development assisted by the indigenous elite.

The Gradual Erosion of Non-Hegemonic Knowledges

In the context of South Sudan there is, as the NPA report referred to above suggests in terms of land resources, an urgent need for the Sudanese authorities to take control of the efforts of national development. Sustainability is under pressure as South Sudan faces critical environmental challenges in terms of severe soil degradation, deforestation, deterioration of water resources, desertification, and deterioration in biodiversity (UNDP, 2011). The gradual erosion of non-hegemonic knowledges may have a serious negative impact on conservation since it is acknowledged that such knowledges can contribute to, according to Berkes et al. (2000), "The conservation of biodiversity . . . rare species . . . protected areas . . . ecological processes . . . and to sustainable resource use in general" (p. 1251). Given the poverty of the new nation, the positive role of the international community is in this connection extremely important, not only in relation to land issues, but more generally in terms of a sustainable national development. Not unexpectedly, South Sudan is rapidly becoming one of the darlings of the international aid community, and the fear is that the influx of funding[3] may jeopardize a sustainable development in the country. In view of the developments referred to above, with the massive allocation of resources to urban development in a predominantly rural society, foreign investment, and purchases of large chunks of land where the indigenous communities often are marginalized, the question is whether it is possible for a South Sudanese government that lacks competence in most sectors to exert control in their own land.

Tanzania: A Model to Copy?

Whether the birth of the new nation might open up space and time for a discussion of how to come to terms with South Sudan's cultural and epistemological roots is an open question. However, there is an urgency here, which the NPA report to some extent foreshadows.

Tanzania pursued a policy after independence that may have some relevance to the post-independence situation in South Sudan (see also Chapter 3). Tanzania was also a very poor country after independence, but had a strong leader in Julius Nyerere who was intent on following an independent course.

Perceiving education as the engine for achieving real independence, self-reliance, and development, Nyerere wanted an education system based on African heritage cultural values. Critical of the colonial education as having colonized the mind of the African, he wanted an education system that conscientized the African and liberated him/her "from the mentality of slavery and colonialism by making him aware of himself as an equal member of the human race, with the rights and duties of his humanity" (Nyerere, 1974, p. 48). The policy of Education for Reliance was launched in 1967. The policy of Education for Reliance was launched in 1967. The curriculum was "'Africanized,' 'politicized,' and directed to developing needed manpower skills in accordance with the manpower development strategy" (Buchert, 1994, p.114). The Education for Self Reliance Policy, however, was hard hit by severe resource restraints and structural adjustment policies and implementation was fragmentary. On a positive note, primary education became almost universal, textbooks for use in primary school were Tanzanianized, and Kiswahili was used as the medium of instruction. Despite its problematic implementation, Lene Buchert (1994) suggests that there might be positive lessons to be learnt from the Tanzanian experiment:

> With due incorporation of the local communities, with due attention to their wishes and needs, and with due understanding of the interaction between educational and non-educational variables at different national and sub-national levels, then, perhaps . . . Education for Self-Reliance . . . is the most appropriate for societies which suffer from lack of growth of the modern sector of the economy . . . and from a continuously dominant rural sector operating at low technological levels (pp. 171–172).

Examples from Tanzania (and Cuba, which will be discussed in Chapter 6) indicate the importance of a strong, committed leadership in order to pursue a national, independent policy agenda. What the experiences from these countries show, however, is the complexity and difficulty of pursuing an independent national development program in terms of economic and education policies.

The Need for Modern and Indigenous Stories: The Schools

In South Sudan there is yet to emerge a strong leadership group with clear visions for the new South Sudan. The South Sudanese government is therefore easy prey for foreign influence and domination, economically as well as epistemologically. What a non-divided South Sudan needs is a new national narrative promoted by the political leaders based on a variety of stories, modern and indigenous, that can complement and feed into each other to avoid alienation, fragmentation, conflict, and unsustainable development.

The initial location of such stories should be the schools in order to reach as many citizens as possible. In the case of South Africa, such stories (as we have seen) are slowly starting to emerge in the policies of the Departments of Education and of Science and Technology, and they have tentatively crept into the Revised Curriculum Statement even with little consideration for their implementability (see Jansen and Sayed, 2001). However, South Africa, in comparison to South Sudan, is an economic superpower with a capacity to design comprehensive and multi-faceted policy documents for the development of the various sectors in the country. South Sudan, on the other hand, is one of the poorest countries in Africa with a workforce that lacks competence in most areas and is entirely dependent on assistance from the donor community to deliver. The proposition to integrate indigenous knowledges in schools is not, as Bhola (2003) states, "to save the indigenous from the modern (which is an impossibility), but to organize a dialectic that is neither cannibalistic nor exploitative, but mutually enriching" (p. 10). This dialectic between the knowledge systems is now missing in the discussion about a new educational discourse in South Sudan. This may, to some extent, be due to the consequences and complications of war and the lack of space, time, and competence during times of hardship to be able to indulge in a more comprehensive reflection over the ideological content of the education system, apart from insisting on its non-Islamist and secular orientation. The task of integrating and, in some way, institutionalizing indigenous knowledges in the education system is complicated; it involves a conscious process of epistemological comparison, translation, and questioning that cannot be left to the individual teachers. The optimism voiced by many of our informants about the merits of modernist education should not be rubbished, but put in perspective: how can education in South Sudan be designed in such a way that it is also takes cognizance of the indigenous knowledge universe of the majority population, thereby serving the population at large and at the same time contributing to a sustainable future? There is some reason to be pessimistic, at least in the short run. The embrace of Western, modernist knowledge in education and the gradual disregard of indigenous knowledges in this context is serious not only in terms of alienation and lack of self-recognition, but also in terms of sustainability. Despite the fact that recognition of the merits of the sustainability of indigenous knowledges is beginning to be acknowledged also in some academic and activist circles in the North in terms of pedagogy, ecology, and conservation (Berkes et al., 2000), there are few signs that the international aid business working in South Sudan will deviate from the development agenda of the past and question the pursuit of a Western education hegemonic discourse.[4] If the opinion of Abel Alier, an earlier president in the South, is anything to go by, the situation is problematic: "If we have to drive our people to paradise with sticks, we will do so for their own good and the good of those who come after us" (in Alvares, 1992, p. 226).

There is a sense that little has changed since the days of Alier 20 years ago and that the goal of national economic development continues to be guided by a neo-colonial global project where indigenous epistemologies, values, and cultural practices are sacrificed on the altar of "development" and "progress."[5] Such a development agenda is reminiscent of the modernization optimism for Africa a few decades back, in that it is a reinvention of the (development) wheel, which failed so dramatically in the past. While President Salva Kiir now is in the process of establishing a new nation and a South Sudanese identity, there is a danger that the majority of the people who constitute the new nation and who are already severely marginalized, will be left out. The "solution" to counteract such a development is to initiate new conversations about ways to forge a new national identity on the basis of the divergent ethnicities, identities, and knowledge systems in the country. School is one of the locations where such conversations need to take place, and clearing such space to query the global architecture of education is crucial, even though it is an uphill battle.

6   The Educational Discourse of Cuba
An Epistemological Alternative for Other Countries in the Global South?

6.1   INTRODUCTION

The Context

Cuba is well known for its education system, which is ranked as one of the best, if not the best, in the global South. Such an evaluation begs the question what "best" means in an education context. The chapter on Cuba explores educational discourse production [1] in a country which, since the socialist revolution in 1959, has been strongly committed to education, both in terms of budgetary prioritization as well as ideological and epistemological considerations.

The education system in Cuba is positioned somewhat ambivalently between being best in the class in the South while at the same time trying to dig out an alternative educational discourse unlike its neighbors in the South.

One concern in this chapter is to explore this almost liminal position by asking first how good the education system in Cuba is, and based on which criteria, and secondly to discuss to what extent Cuban educational discourse is different from what I have called the global architecture of education. The Cuban education system is famous for its focus on inclusion and equality of opportunity, but also for its focus on political and ideological conformity. By tracing the trajectory of the Cuban education system under Fidel Castro from the Year of Education in 1961 to the Battle of Ideas in the late 1990s and to the new transformation in education in the present century, the chapter discusses to what extent the present policy functions as a means of strengthening the government's political goals and its ideological hegemony, and whether this represents an alternative to hegemonic knowledge production in the West. One question here relates to whether the educational discourse transcends its ideological connotations to encompass alternative epistemological principles, for example, indigenous knowledges. When analyzing the Cuban educational discourse there is a need to distinguish between the education system's ideological and epistemological foundation. The Cuban political and educational system is well known for its socialist/communist ideology, but little research has been conducted in terms of its epistemological basis. [2]

Another aspect, and closely related to this issue, concerns the relationship between epistemological foundation, sustainability, and sustainable development. Given Raul Castro's recent economic reform program, I query to what extent Cuba's commitment to an educational policy for sustainable development is viable in the future.

6.2 INDIGENOUS KNOWLEDGES AND SUSTAINABILITY

Cuba is a multi-cultural society with a mix of mainly Spanish and African origins. The composition of the different ethnic groups is, however, hotly disputed. The contentiousness of the issue can be seen by comparing the figures from the CIA Fact Book pre-2002 census with the official 2002 statistics. While the CIA Fact Book reported an ethnic distribution of 51% mulatto, 37% white, 11% black and 1% Chinese, the official statistics gave the following figures: 23% mulatto, 65.05% white, 10.08% black and 1.02% Asian (Afrocubaweb, 2009). The number of Native Americans is small, with perhaps a few hundred families in Oriente. The conflicting figures tell stories of "'blanqueamiento' [whitening] that go back to the 19th century, but have been more pronounced in recent years after the rise of tourism, an enterprise dominated by the Ibero-Spanish" (Afrocubaweb, 2009). The discrepancy may also be due to the reliance on people's self-identification as white, black, or mulatto. Both reasons for over-counting whites and under-counting blacks are due to the preference to being affiliated with the hegemonic ethnic group. We also noted that some informants opted to be classified as white despite their mixed background. As will be discussed in Chapter 7 on Chile and the Mapuche, the same issue of conflicting statistics is a problem there.

Despite the fact that the majority of Native Americans in Cuba were wiped out during the Spanish invasion, their footmark on Cuba is still visible beyond Hatuey beer and some historical artifacts. Cuban peasant culture has a strong indigenous component, and many of the descendants of the Native American population, especially the Taino Indians, the biggest indigenous group in Cuba, live as herbalists. Like other indigenous peoples globally, the Taino people value the interrelatedness between man, the supernatural, and nature. Besides viewing the earth as sacred, the Tainos are particularly known for extracting herbal medicines from plants. Called "green medicine," the herbal plants are highly valued by the Cuban government and are used as an alternative to "classical" or pharmaceutical medicine. The authorities' interest in this alternative is not primarily due to their indigenous origin, but due to the plants' potential in reducing Cuba's dependence on medicines from abroad, a sheer necessity in times of economic hardships.

As a matter of fact, Cuba has developed a diverse biotechnology industry, which focuses primarily on medicines used for prevention rather than cure.

What is of particular interest in our context is that Cuba's biotechnological approach poses an alternative to health issues globally. The domestication or indigenization of medicine shows how a poor country in the margins can develop viable and affordable medicine and can, in many instances, compete with multi-national pharmaceutical corporations. Over the past 25 years, Cuba has established an advanced agricultural biotechnology as well as a biopharmaceutical industry and " has independently developed agricultural products, biopharmaceuticals and biovaccines while retaining the entire intellectual property rights. These can earn 100 million US dollars for Cuba every year" (CTV, 2011).

When the Soviet Union collapsed in the early 1990s, Cuba was forced to rethink its agricultural policy by using agroecological techniques with low-cost, environmentally friendly inputs since the country lost 80% of its pesticide, fertilizer, and oil imports. In 1999, the Swedish Parliament awarded the Right Livelihood Award, or "Alternative Nobel Prize," to the Cuban Organic Farming Association because the Association showed "that organic agriculture is a key to both food security and environmental sustainability" (Mansata, 2010). This policy has not only significantly reduced the country's need for fuel and fertilizers, but has also reduced contamination of land and waters significantly. Moreover, Cuba's agroecology also plays a role in reducing global warming. According to Peter Rosset, Director of Food First at the Institute for Food & Development Policy in the US, "Cuba offers the very first large-scale test of sustainable alternatives . . . before environmental realities mandate the rest of the world embark on a sudden, wholesale switch to organic agriculture " (Mansata, 2010).

According to the *Living Planet Report* issued by the World Wildlife Fund (WWF) in 2006, Cuba was the only country in the world which met the criteria for sustainable development (the sustainability index), that is, meeting the criteria for a globally sustainable society (WWF, 2006, p. 19), based on the data it reports to the UN. The assessment refers to the two internationally established criteria of sustainability, viz. the ecological footprint and high human development (the UNDP Human Development Index). Unsustainability on the other hand is defined as countries "going into what we call 'overshoot'—using far more resources than the planet can sustain" (WWF, 2006, p. 1).

In the 2010 report Cuba fell just outside the sustainability box, but is still among the very best in the world in terms of sustainability (measured as the improvement of the quality of human life while living within the carrying capacity of its ecosystem (WWF, 2010, p. 35). Cuba's high ranking on the sustainability index is impressive, but is nevertheless ambiguous; while positive in terms of the sustainability of the planet, it is problematic in terms of food production. During our field-work period, for example, the farmers' markets in Havana never showed the abundance of fruit and vegetables that one would expect from an island in the Caribbean.

There is considerable debate and controversy over Cuba's current food dependency. While Dennis Avery claims (Avery 2009) that Cuba needs to import more than 80 % of its foodstuff, Miguel A. Altieri and Fernando R. Funes-Monzote in a recent article (2012) claim a 16% dependency. The authors admit, however, that when Cuba was hit by the destructive hurricanes in 2008, "Cuba satisfied national needs by importing 55 percent of its total food, equivalent to approximately $2.8 billion (Altieri and Funes- Monzote, 2012). This food-suffiency controversy notwithstanding it is important to underline that Cuba has been- generally speaking- able to feed its people with either domestic or imported food even though the variety of food stuff is often very limited. The strict government control of farming has until recently allowed very little private entrepreneurship, and it is hoped that the agricultural reforms under Raul Castro (discussed later in the chapter) will eventually reduce import dependency.

6.3   THE EDUCATIONAL DISCOURSE: SOCIAL AND CULTURAL CAPITAL

Given the focus of our research and the methodological challenges in the field, the relationship between discourse and discursive practices and power and control is particularly important for our purposes in this chapter. While previous chapters have been concerned with alternative educational discourses, particularly related to indigenous knowledge systems, the focus in this chapter on Cuba is somewhat different because the indigenous population in Cuba has more or less been annihilated. Still, it is interesting that Cuba is one of the most sustainable societies on earth (according to their own data), partly by using local and sometimes indigenous solutions to meet their challenges. What is important in this context is to explore to what extent Cubans experience the imposition of an alien educational discourse like that witnessed in South Africa and Sudan, or whether Fidel Castro has managed to impress a Cuban, if not indigenous, imprint on the educational discourse in the country. Also in the case of Cuba, the relationship between power and knowledges and the importance of controlling educational discourse production informs my discussion of Cuban educational policy from its inception in 1959 till the new transformation in education in the 21st century.

The Cuban education system's reputation for quality education and equality of opportunity impels the question: how is this possible in a nation with huge economic problems? Cuba's apparent success story seems to undermine the conventional wisdom that only well-functioning countries in the North can provide quality education for the majority of their students. Moreover, the role of cultural capital as defined by Pierre Bourdieu and Jean-Claude Passeron (1990) as an important factor in explaining a student's success (how the values of the intellectual and bureaucratic elite—the hegemonic class—are reproduced in school, thus favoring the children of the same elite), cannot adequately explain why students do well, even though they do not belong to the elite.

Martin Carnoy, Amber K. Gove, Jeffery H. Marshall (2007) admit that, "there are as many suggestions for increasing student learning as there are educational analysts, socially involved business executives, and politicians" (p. 5). While this chapter does not pretend to give an exhaustive explanation of Cuba's apparent success story, it explores how Cuba attempts to neutralize, or at least reduce, the importance of what is traditionally understood by cultural capital.

Carnoy et al. attempt to explain the Cuban situation in terms of what they call state-generated social capital. Taken from Coleman et al. (1966), the concept of social capital is, "unlike other kinds of capital, which is tangible and benefits primarily its owner . . . embedded in *relationships among individuals or among institutions* and benefits all individuals or institutions involved in those relationships by making their work more productive" (Carnoy et al., 2007 p. 11).

Social capital related to family and community makes a difference in school performance. As Carnoy (2007) states, "if a family is particularly cohesive and supportive, and has high expectations for each of its members . . . that type of family structure can be defined as social capital" (p. 11).

Carnoy extends Coleman's social capital theory to include nation-states that systematically support the education system over time and focus on creating a climate of learning for children of the middle and lower socioeconomic classes, hence the concept of "state-generated social capital." While the concept cannot capture the complexity of reasons for Cuba's leading educational role, it underlines the significance of the historical and contemporary as well as the ideological commitment of the Cuban government to education. It is to this role the chapter now turns.

6.4   THE GENESIS OF THE CUBAN EDUCATIONAL SYSTEM

While Cuba is a Latin-American country structured by a common history of colonialism and resistance, neo-colonialism and poverty, it has been noted that Cuba's educational system is reputed to be among the best in the region, if not in the Southern hemisphere. Not even the most ardent critics of the Cuban political system can deny its impressive record since the inception of the revolution. As James Wolfensohn, the former president of the World Bank, stated in 2001:

> Cuba has done a great job in education and health . . . I have no hesitation in acknowledging that they've done a good job, and it doesn't

embarrass me to do it . . . We just have nothing to do with them in the present sense, and they should be congratulated on what they've done (Red Feather Institute, 2001)

Wolfensohn was right, neither the World Bank nor the IMF has given a cent to Cuba since the revolution in 1959.

What is less well known is that before the 1959 revolution the majority of Cubans were in fact literate. In 1899, 43.2% of the population over 10 years of age was literate; in 1953 76% was able to read and write. This figure was only surpassed by Argentina (87%), Chile (81%), and Costa Rica (79%) (Chepe, 2002). What these statistics do not show is the fundamentally unequal distribution of this basic social service. Education did not reach the poor and marginalized, not only because of school fees but because corruption in the education system was pervasive. Cuba's so-called post-independent period from 1902 to 1959 was viewed by the revolutionaries as a period of degeneration, and rampant corruption in education was one important reason for the revolution itself in 1959.

FIDEL CASTRO'S RADICAL REVOLUTION

The all-pervasive corruption of the various regimes before 1959, the greed of the elite, the brutality of the police and the army, the fragility of democracy, and the neglect of the poor and the marginalized all signaled a moral degeneration.

Morality became a focal point for the dissenting forces, especially in the party Fidel Castro belonged to, the Ortodoxo party. In one sense, then, the Cuban revolution was a moral revolution, followed up later by Ernesto Che Guevara, who wanted to shape the new man of Cuba (Guevara, 1988; Beckford, 1986) based on moral and idealistic rather than on economic principles. (Note the description of the Islamist political system in Sudan for comparison.) While the moral imperative was an important impetus to throw Fulgencio Batista out, the outcome of the revolution transcended a mere moral agenda. It was one of the most profound revolutions in Latin American history, "in many ways more profound than the nineteenth century wars for independence which . . . did not overturn the structures of Latin American society" (Chomsky et al., 2004, p. 333; Fagen, 1969). Politics, economics, and society were completely transformed, and education was thought to be the spearhead of the Cuban revolution.

"The Year of Education"

The new revolutionary government (1959) had education and health as their priorities. Here is Fidel Castro's view of the role of education and the role of the teacher in his famous "History will absolve me" speech, six years before the revolution succeeded:

> The happiest country is the one which has best educated its sons, both in the instruction of thought and the direction of their feelings . . . The soul of education is the teacher . . . no one is more dedicated than the Cuban teacher. Who among us has not learned his ABC in the little public schoolhouse. It is time we stop paying pittances to these young men and women who are entrusted the sacred task of teaching our youth (Castro, 2004, p. 313).

"The Year of Education" was 1961 and it aimed to eradicate illiteracy on the island. The literacy campaign transcended mere educational objectives. It was the intention of the revolutionary government to use education in the struggle against neo-colonialism and imperialism. The literacy campaign coincided with the Bay of Pigs invasion and the breaking off of diplomatic relations between Cuba and the US. As Fidel Castro stated, "The battle to be won against ignorance will give our country more glory than the military battles already fought or still to be fought" (Castro, 2004, p. 386). The literacy campaign mobilized more than 200,000 "facilitators," both young and old, and the campaign crossed the rural-urban divide in the sense that the countryside was particularly targeted. The literacy campaign was not without opposition, however, and some brigadistas were even killed during the campaign by counter-revolutionary forces.

The Inclusiveness of the Literacy Campaign.

The literacy campaign was, nevertheless, a tremendous success; after one year, the whole country was declared a "territory free from illiteracy" by UNESCO.

The literacy campaign and the establishment of universal and free education and health care were factors that contributed positively to the improvement of the lives of those people who had been oppressed by the Batista regime. Undoubtedly, not only blacks, who figured on the lowest level of the socio-economic ladder, benefited from these reforms. A 1962 survey found that 80% of Afro-Cubans and the mixed population were unreservedly in favor of the revolution as opposed to 67% among the whites (Saney, 2004, p. 100). Clearly, the targeting of the marginalized and the ending of any kind of discrimination in terms of gender and race—which was rampant in Cuba since colonial days and was still pervasive during Batista's regime—was an important objective of the campaign.

Both Fidel Castro and Che Guevara addressed discrimination against blacks in their speeches. Che Guevara discussed on December 28, 1959, the role of universities in this respect:

> I have to say it [the university] should paint itself black, it should paint itself mulatto, not only its students, but also its professors; that it paint itself people, because the university is the heritage of none, it belongs to the Cuban people . . . the university must be flexible and paint itself black, mulatto, worker and peasant, or it will have no doors, the people will break them down and paint the university the colours they want (quoted in Saney, 2004, p. 101).

Until the end of the 1980s the Cuban government injected huge financial resources into the Cuban education system, and it was reinforced by massive assistance from the Eastern bloc and the Soviet Union in particular. According to the Latin-American and Caribbean Economic Committee (CEPAL), 1989 was the peak funding year for education in Cuba (Chepe, 2002). Fidel Castro's commitment to education was indisputable. Ideologically the Cuban system was heavily entrenched in Marxism, with a focus on materialism and empiricism. This faith in science as the objective truth of reality and the source of knowledges is reflected in Vladimir Lenin's (1927) statement, "The fundamental characteristic of materialism arises from the objectivity of science, from the recognition of objective reality, reflected by science" (p. 252). Therefore, not breaking from hegemonic Western knowledge production, Marxist epistemology took root on the Caribbean island and was introduced in the school system. While the epistemic foundation of the educational discourse was part of Western hegemonic knowledge, its ideological foundation was clearly anti-capitalist and anti-Western, similar to what one found in the Eastern bloc at the time. Its epistemic and ideological foundation notwithstanding, Cubans experienced dramatic progress in terms of basic reading and writing skills, which was noted internationally and compared favorably with most countries in the Third World.

The Tough 1990s: Socialism and Capitalism Hand in Hand

Soon after, with the fall of the Soviet Union in the early 1990s, the economic situation of the Cuban state changed dramatically for the worse. Fidel Castro responded to the crisis by calling for 'a special period in peacetime,' which still has not been called off. The 'special period' meant that Cuba to a much larger extent had to rely on its own resources for survival. The state of economic problems had an immediate effect on all spheres of life.

The regime's introduction of tourism dollars to compensate for economic losses meant a stronger integration into the capitalist world economy and an exodus of teachers from the teaching profession to tourism where salaries were much higher. The education system thus regressed into a state of emergency, if not crisis, where teachers suddenly were in short supply. The budget for education in 1998 decreased by 45% compared to 1989

(Chepe, 2002). While the official statistics also confirm that the government's expenditures on education declined during the next decade in terms of pesos, Fidel Castro "prided himself in speeches for not closing a single school, day-care center or hospital, and for not leaving a single person destitute" (Eckstein, in Chomsky et al., 2004, p. 610).

Not unexpectedly, the introduction of a capitalist economy in a socialist state led to a gradual lack of commitment to the revolution and to the values accompanying the revolution like solidarity, equality, and internationalism. For the regime this alarming development had to be stopped.

The Battle of Ideas

The regime "rediscovered" that youth could be used in the ideological struggle and in December 1999 the authorities launched a campaign called "The Battle of Ideas" to mobilize the new generation for the defense of the revolution. This campaign was primarily directed towards youth in and out of school and followed in the wake of the Elián González affair.[3] The Elián story had mobilized young people, "most of those mobilized and protesting were young Cubans, and youth organizations—notably the Young Communists (UJC), university students (FEU) and the secondary students (FEEM)" (Kapica, 2005, p. 400). Fidel Castro capitalized on this mobilization in his attempt to win the youth back to the ideas of the revolution. Paradoxically, Fidel Castro was trying to ride two horses at the same time, retaining the ideological fervor for the revolution and at the same time allowing a capitalist sector to grow. Concomitantly, the school's transformative role was questioned, and "the Battle of Ideas" became an important platform for the transformation of the schools. However, the message was hard to sell in the classroom without qualified teachers.

One step to get teachers back (or retain some of them) was to increase the salary in 1999 by 30% as an acknowledgement of their dedication and endeavors to the education for the new generation.

Unfortunately, the salary hike was not sufficient to compete with the tourist industry. In the academic year 2005–2006 (during our field-work) teacher salaries never exceeded 20 pesos convertibles (500 pesos *nacionales*) per month. This is equivalent to a little more than 20 US dollars. A university full professor could get up to 1000 pesos *nacionales* (40 pesos convertibles) per month, also a hopelessly inadequate amount. With the high cost of living it meant, and still means (2012), that no teacher or doctor can manage to survive on such a salary; additional income is a must, either through an extra job or through less legal means. The incentive measure did not manage to turn the tide. This was confirmed by the many taxi-drivers we talked with. As one stated: "I left the teaching profession because my salary could not feed the family. Driving a tourist taxi is much more profitable due to the tips I get from the foreigners. Being a taxi driver gives me less headache financially. But my education is more or less wasted" (2005).

The New Transformation in Education

Realizing that other measures had to be taken if the schools were not to be stripped of teachers, the authorities introduced a new educational transformation program in 2001 (Ministry of Education, 2001). The official justification for the new transformation in education was a concern with quality per se, but the teacher shortage did not figure prominently in the official rhetoric surrounding the reform. In private conversations with university people involved in the process, however, it was admitted that the dramatic exodus of teachers from the profession and the lack of revolutionary spirit among the youth were major factors behind the restructuring of the system.

While pragmatic and ideological considerations played an important role in the transformation, the new education system introduced a number of measures that were intended to increase quality:

1. A television set in every classroom.
2. The universalization of computer literacy.
3. Electrification of all schools (many rural schools through solar energy).
4. Primary education with 20 students per classroom.
5. Junior secondary schools with 15 students in class.

In addition, the authorities introduced:

6. Universidad para Todos. Broadcasting of degree-level televised classes in selected subjects targeting young and old outside working hours.
7. Micro-universities. Spreading university provision beyond the few existing centers to all of Cuba's *municipios*. The principle underlying the micro-universities is education for all and local participation.
8. The creation of special schools for unemployed workers to make up for lost schooling. This was done due to the 2003 decision to close half of Cuba's sugar mills, creating thousands of unemployed workers.

In the ordinary education system the impact of the new transformation was particularly felt in the primary and junior secondary school. Primary school classes with more than 20 students were given two teachers. As before, the teacher was responsible for the whole portfolio of subjects but was aided in a much more comprehensive way with this technological equipment.

The New Junior Secondary School: The Idea of Social and Academic Inclusion

Besides the reduction in class size (which developing country can boast similar small numbers?), the changes were felt even more in the junior secondary school (covering Grades 7, 8, and 9) where a new concept, the comprehensive junior secondary teacher, *profesor integral general*, was introduced. In contrast with the earlier system for these grades, where the teachers taught their specialized subject, the teachers were now expected to teach all subjects with the exception of foreign languages, computing, and arts. The specialization in subjects was replaced by more attention to teaching and teaching methods (including TV, video, and computers) and general knowledge in the various subjects. The focus was on interdisciplinary teaching, thus hoping to avoid the earlier fragmentation of school subjects. Much attention was also paid to the social aspect of learning where the idea of inclusion played an important role in the rhetoric around the new reform. The aim was that the *profesor integral general* would be able to cater to the whole student group and their individual needs to a larger extent than previously when the teaching was fragmented by different specialized teachers. Since the upper limit of students in the junior secondary classes is 15, a much more active interaction between the students and teacher was secured. This was confirmed in our discussions with several teachers, and from observations in the classrooms we witnessed a very active student population. While the teacher will be able to follow up closely the development of each individual student there is also an aspect of ideological "control" here that fits well with the Battle of Ideas campaign.

The reduction of the teacher-to-student ratio at a time of teacher shortage necessitated a complete overhaul of the teacher training system both for primary and junior secondary schools.

While the student teachers previously spent their whole training at the university (four to five years), the students in the new system only spent one year at the university. An intensive first-year introduction to the university degree focused, as the Cuban Minister of Education put it in 2004, "on personal development and class participation, thus ensuring that the students are well prepared for the rest of the course and allow[ing] them to improve their learning skills" (Gutierrez, 2004, p. 9).

From the second to the fifth year the students are taught through a system combining study and work in schools transformed into municipal (micro-) universities. The students teach an ordinary class and have an experienced teacher as supervisor and personal tutor. In addition, they attend municipal university branches once a week where assistant professors guide them in their studies.

This change in training had several consequences, and was particularly dramatic for junior secondary school teachers. One issue was the age factor, as it means, for example, that the student teacher often is only 19 when s/he starts teaching 17-year-olds. There is concern, especially among Cuban educators, that the teachers might be too inexperienced to teach their peers. As one professor of education put it: "I am worried about the young age of many student teachers. I often ask myself if they are mature enough to handle the classroom situation" (2005). Also, parents expressed skepticism regarding the young teachers. Another factor is knowledge. Do the student teachers have sufficient knowledge to teach in the junior secondary school when they have only been at the university for one year? Moreover, what kind of values does the teacher convey when s/he is so young? What kind of life experience can s/he bring into the classroom? Is the teacher able to ask critical questions when s/he is so young? The last question may be of greater concern to researchers than to the Cuban authorities.

The transformation meant that the workload for junior secondary school teachers and for teachers with extensive experience increased since they now had to teach multiple subjects. One consequence was that many experienced teachers either refused to teach according to the new transformation program or they quit. This meant that it was not possible to staff all schools with the number of teachers the new system required.

An important principle for Cuba is education for all. It was acknowledged, even by some top-ranking people in the education system, that the concern with quality, one of the official reasons for embarking on the new transformation, had not been prioritized sufficiently due the great quantitative demands. One thing was the problem with a generalist teacher; another was that some rural areas might not be able to provide the same quality education as in Havana. Moreover, access was, and still is not, necessarily the same for blacks and whites. Many black families still live in poor housing and working conditions, and despite the political quest for equality and equity, marginality has not been done away with, as it still has a tendency to reproduce itself, albeit to a lesser degree than most countries in the Southern hemisphere.

This said, Cuba has probably succeeded more than any other country in the global South in making quality education available for its rural population (an expressed goal from the early days of the revolution). Moreover, the capital, Havana, has its own problems with the recruitment of good teachers due to the attraction of the tourist industry, making an urban-rural dichotomy in terms of education quality too simplistic.

The generalist idea of the new transformation program has not reached the upper secondary teacher (pre-university) where teachers remain more specialized. Some teachers teach physics, math, and computation while others teach a cluster of chemistry, biology, and geography, or a cluster of subjects in the humanities, that is, Spanish, history, and civic knowledge. Most upper secondary schools are boarding schools in the countryside (*escuelas de campo*) where the students divide time between theoretical work and manual labor on plots of arable land attached to the boarding school, conforming with the ideological hero, the 19th century Cuban nationalist, Jose Martí's slogan: "In the morning the pen, but in the afternoon the plough." Clearly, the idea of collecting nearly all secondary school students in boarding schools away from their parents has social and ideological implications, creating an ideological space relatively undisturbed by other influences and a sense of solidarity among the students.

An impressive feature of the education system is how well organized it is, from the ministry to the classroom level. The reasons may undoubtedly be linked to the need of the regime to have complete ideological control; nevertheless, there is a lesson or two to be learned both by other countries in the global South as well as in the North.

Discourse Production in the Schools

In line with the Battle of Ideas referred to above, there is in Cuba a strong belief in the liberating or even revolutionary power of education. Moreover, there is an equally strong belief in promoting a specific educational discourse at the expense of other discourses. Even though the Cuban educational discourse is based on Cartesian epistemology, the educational discourse is nevertheless situated in a context of Cubanization and nationalism, thus preventing an undifferentiated and uncritical import of educational ideas from the West. "Official" knowledge implies "the decision to define some groups' knowledge as the most legitimate, as official knowledge, while other groups' knowledge hardly sees the light of day, says something extremely important about who has power in society" (Apple, 1993, p. 222). Besides Fidel Castro, the dominant or hegemonic educational discourse in Cuba is influenced in particular by the two heroes and martyrs, Jose Martí, and Che Guevara. Based on Martí's statement that "No social equality is possible without equality of education and culture," education in Cuba reflects the communist and egalitarian orientation of Fidel Castro's regime. Moreover, as Noah W. Sobe and Renee N. Timberlake (2010) assert, Martí's position has risen significantly in the recent years, possibly to reinforce a national and authentic character of Cuban education. Martí's influence may also indicate how "education has been positioned and has navigated betwixt and between local and global pressures since the fall of the Soviet Union" (p. 352). When the children, before the beginning of the school day, pay allegiance to the Cuban flag, they venerate Che Guevara by reciting the following slogan of the Young pioneers: "*Seremos como Che*" ("We will be like Che").

A strong streak of moralism and idealism permeates the schools, with Che Guevara's vision of "the new man" as a focal point. Guevara argued that an embrace of communism required the scrapping of material incentives for the workers. Instead, he underlined the importance of creating a new, radical consciousness among the people and the adoption of moral rather than material incentives. Fidel Castro endorsed this view:

> Che was radically opposed to using and developing capitalist economic laws and categories in building socialism. He advocated something that I have often insisted on: Building socialism and communism is not just a matter of producing and distributing wealth but is also a matter of education and consciousness (2003, p. 39).

Conscientization and consciousness through education were the fundamental principles in Che Guevara's socialist thinking, implying that "consciousness and education were primary in the study of relations of production in the transitional economy, including the construction of communism" (Martínez, 2005). Che Guevara argued for consciousness and awareness raising, "Without this consciousness, which embraces its awareness as a social being, there can be no communism" (Guevara, 1973, p. 124).

Thus, Che Guevara departed from conventional Marxism by insisting on consciousness and education as the primary engine for achieving higher forms of economic organization. As Rafael Martínez (2005) states, "In Guevara's system, socialist economic development is not really the engine of consciousness, but the other way around, consciousness is the source of socialist economic development."[4] While the role given to conscientization and education and his reversion of the role of base and superstructure was a fundamental deviation from Marxism, Che Guevara's focus on solidarity and communitarianism was not.

Rather perceived as a radical departure from the Western ideology of individualism, the communitarian morality promoted in schools emphasized solidarity, self-sacrifice, and honesty coupled with other key words like nationalism and internationalism (for example, international solidarity). At a specific school level there was an attempt to create an atmosphere of commitment, collective effort, and mutual support.

Che Guevara's ideological anti-Western, anti-capitalist stance coupled with his understanding of conscientization and education as the primary agent of change is reminiscent of Freire's ideas of conscientization, but departs in important ways from the philosophy of the Brazilian educationist. Freire suggests that every human being is a repository of knowledges, not an "empty vessel" devoid of knowledges, and he has valuable experiential knowledges to be applied in problem-posing dialogues. Empowerment and critical thinking is possible through dialogue where no "solution" is pre-empted. Freire (1998) argues, "There are no themes or values of which one cannot speak, no areas in which one must be silent. We can talk about everything, and we can give testimony about everything" (p. 58). This implies that not only hegemonic Western knowledge is invited to these dialogues. On the contrary, indigenous and local knowledges are important experiential knowledges that question the Western knowledge hegemony.

Critical thinking means thinking "which discerns an indivisible solidarity between the world and the people and admits of no dichotomy between them—a thinking which perceives reality as process, as transformation" (Freire 1995, p. 73). Such thinking is crucial to challenging hegemonic knowledge production legitimized by colonial pedagogical practices (Freire and Faundez, 1989). As McLaren (2000) correctly states, "Epistemological critique involves more than unpacking representations, but also exploring the how and why of their historical production" (p. 122).

While consciousness is an important word in Che Guevara's political and economic vocabulary there is little, if any, interrogation of Western hegemonic knowledge production. Moreover, Che Guevara suggests ideological closure where the answers are given and no "real" dialogue is needed or permitted.

According to many of our informants, different opinions and views were/ are, at least in theory, accepted in classroom discussions. It was, however, underlined that non-conformist views had to be very well argued, probably giving the teacher an easy task in imposing "consensus," that is, teaching in agreement with official policies. Not only in the classroom was the idea of consensus important; we were told of incidents when students had to leave the university due to frequent harassment by teachers. As one informant stated, "One student left because her hostile opinions against the regime were not tolerated (2005)." Whether the student was expelled or chose to leave remained unclear.

When asked about the ideological diversity in one of the secondary schools in the countryside (*escuela de campo*) we visited, one of the students responded, "Yes, we discuss a diversity of political systems such as socialism, Marxism, and Leninism (2005)." Clearly there was and is, as Tom G. Griffiths (2009) states, a "consistent, overt politicization of schooling, with some key curricular and pedagogical reforms to drive the socialist formation of the new generations" (p. 51).

While the student's response above is not surprising and underlines the bias of the educational discourse, it is nevertheless grounded in historical and contemporary experiences and can be understood, at least partly, in psychological and socio-psychological terms. It suffices here to refer to the embargo imposed by the US and the Bush administration's comprehensive plans for toppling the regime, creating paranoia and an intruder hysteria that are fully exploited.

The twin relationship between the country's educational discourse and hegemonic political discourse is, as I have noted in previous chapters, not a unique Cuban phenomenon. The close link between knowledge and power is underlined by John Fiske (1989):

> Knowledge is never neutral, it never exists in an empiricist, objective relationship to the real. Knowledge is power, and the circulation of knowledge is part of the social distribution of power (pp. 149–150).

Most nations use, either explicitly or implicitly, the educational system as a means to further ideological objectives. Even in so-called democratic countries, hegemonic knowledge circulates more freely and more comprehensively than non-official knowledges. In the US, the market ideology seems to permeate more and more of the education system (Giroux, 2003b; Apple, 1997), and in Norway the hegemonic role of the mono-cultural Norwegian educational system is, despite the heavy influx of immigrants, more or less unrivalled (Pihl, 2001).

The educational system is a hegemonic tool in constructing and solidifying the nation-state; therefore, the existing power relations are well known in most countries. As Sobe and Timberlake (2010) state, "all forms of schooling (qua schooling) inscribe normative principles and regulate modes of reasoning and possibilities for 'rational' and 'acceptable' behavior—regardless of the political persuasion of the regime" (p. 364).

However, one of the most problematic aspects of the Cuban system—not, in principle, unlike the situation in contemporary Sudan—is the forceful imposition of the hegemonic discourse, leaving almost no space for alternative discourses. It has been noted, by reference to Che Guevara's political philosophy, how the official discourse is basically an undisputed non-postmodern discourse where only one truth, one version of history is being conveyed, leaving no room for Freire's pedagogical dialogue and hardly any space for critical thinking outside the anti-capitalist, anti-Western paradigm.

The existence of the Internet illustrates the need for the regime to exercise hegemonic control. While the official explanation why the Internet is not accessible to the common man is because it is too costly, regulations prevent even those with money to get access. The Internet is used in some higher institutions of learning, like universities, etc., and in various other institutions and companies, but regular Internet use from home is basically restricted to foreigners or to Cubans with the right political affiliation. As one informant told us during our recent visit to Cuba: "It is extremely frustrating to know that the world has access to internet, while here the government puts all kinds of restrictions on our access to international news. The situation has not changed to the better since Raul (Castro) came to power" (2012).

Cuba was officially an atheist state from the victory of the revolution in 1959 until 1992 when atheism (and thus Marist-Leninism) as a state creed was abolished. The deletion of Marxist-Leninism from the constitution and the visits of the Pope in 1999 and in 2012 have eased the situation somewhat for religious students and teachers. According to one of our informants, a dissident: " I do not belong to the Catholic church, but it is quite clear that the Catholic church represents the only alternative institution to the current Cuban government, and has on many occasions entered negotiations with the government to release prisoners and ease political oppression. The Catholic church is doing a fabulous job under very difficult circumstances (2012).

Neither Christian religion nor the Santería, a blend of native African religions and Roman Catholicism, is, however, part of the curriculum, but according to some of our informants atheism is not being taught. Religious believers are tolerated in the schools, and Mormons are, for instance, not forced to pay allegiance to the flag as the vast majority of schoolchildren do every morning.

Christians can now become members of the Communist Party and the Santería religion is now being promoted to attract tourists to the island. Revolutionary Cuba clamped-down on Santería at first, but over the last 15 years or so the government tolerated it more and more and now allows it to flourish. Cynics say that this is because Santería brings considerable hard currency to the island, not because indigenous or Afro-Cuban spirituality is part of the government's epistemic repertoire.

6.5   AN ALTERNATIVE DISCOURSE: INDEPENDENCE, INDIGENIZATION, AND INCLUSIVENESS

While educational discourse production in Cuba is in many ways problematic, its merits should not be underrated. The question is, however, whether the educational discourse in Cuba is systemically all that different from educational discourses in capitalist countries.

Instrumentality

Despite the focus on ideas, morals, and solidarity referred to above, the apparent instrumental character of the Cuban education system has been criticized from the outside and internally. One important aspect of Cuban education is the practice of *estudio-trabajo* (study/work), where "the students were to overcome inherited discriminatory and hierarchical attitudes towards the division of mental and manual work" (Griffiths, 2009, p. 52). This ostensibly meant that the rationale behind schooling was to prepare for work at the expense of the ideological and political values referred to above.

For example, Juan Marí Lois, a former Dean of Education, claimed that schooling as preparation for work was nothing unique for Cuba and called instead for an emphasis on the ideological principles referred to above, like solidarity. Another Cuban scholar argued that its instrumental focus did not distinguish the Cuban system from schooling in capitalist societies (excerpted from Griffiths, 2009, p. 62.)

It is debatable, however, whether the "instrumental education system" necessarily places it in the capitalist camp, or whether such labeling is very useful. Is preparing children for the workforce a typically capitalist value? Given the importance of Jose Martí and his pen and plough metaphor referred to earlier, the focus on preparing children for work is logical, even though the balance between pen and plough is contested terrain (and reminiscent of Nyerere's policy of education for self-reliance). Only preparing students for ideas and ideology in a country that spends so much of its national budget on education would be difficult to defend, and is even more unthinkable in view of Raul Castro's economic reforms discussed later in this chapter. It is true, however, that Che's ideas of moral incentives and consciousness-raising have been picked up in waves by the authorities; they largely disappeared, for example, in the 1970s and 1980s when the authorities emphasized "socialist principles" of increased wage differentials based on productivity and material incentives. Che Guevara has often been invoked in times of austerity, and was particularly invoked during the Battle of Ideas campaign. The study/work strategy was an integral part of the intended political formation (see MacDonald, 1996), but the results of this strategy were mixed as students overwhelmingly opted for professional, white-collar careers rather than manual work (Griffiths, 2004). During our visit to the secondary schools (*escuela de campo*) we watched how the students worked on the land with very little enthusiasm. As one of the students said, "I really hate this agricultural work. I do not understand why we do it, and it produces very little for the school" (2005). The students' option for non-manual, theoretical work resulted in an overproduction of professionals (doctors and teachers); the authorities have repeatedly tried to correct this by reducing university places in humanities in favor of places in, for example, agriculture. Nevertheless, over-employment has been acute; people were employed in professions that did not match their educational background, causing frustration and bitterness. The Battle of Ideas was therefore initiated to instill in the youth a revolutionary attitude to serve the country as a whole, not primarily their individual interests. The work-study strategy was intended to prepare students for work that would be directed toward the national good and national development rather than individual's upward mobility. However, even in Cuba, campaigns of altruism and national consciousness face an uphill battle in the face of tough socio-economic realities.

Education in the Capitalist Camp?

Since the 1990s and the fall of the Soviet Union it has been noted how the Cuban government has prioritised economic development to make Cuba more economically independent by focusing on the tourist industry, the sugar industry, and the biotech sector (Reid-Henry, 2007). It has been noted that particularly due to the tourist industry with its dollars, the Cuban economy has developed a two-tier system, attracting people from the teaching profession to tourism. Building on Wallerstein's world-systems analysis, Griffiths (2009) claims that "the Cuban Revolution itself remained a part of the capitalist world-system, sharing its emphases on human capital theory and instrumental educational systems, structures and practices to achieve scientifically determined and rationally planned national economic growth and development" (p. 54). It is therefore an illusion to believe that it is possible to create socialism within the capitalist world economy.

While it is true that part of the Cuban economic system had to submit to dollar capitalism after the collapse of Eastern Europe, both the macro-economic and the educational terrain are complex and do not lend themselves to simple labeling. Sobe and Timberlake (2010) claim, for example, that:

> The long-standing anti-colonial thrust of Cuban national identity projects means that a plausible claim can be made that both socialism and engagement with global capitalism are reconcilable in the Cuban context, in that both can be seen as furthering Cuba's independence and strengthening the Cuban nation (p. 358).

The Battle of Ideas campaign was a conscious reaction to avert the ideas of capitalism from seeping into the education system. Admittedly, there was a theory-practice contradiction here not easily reconciled, since this ideological campaign was hampered by the contradictory economic signals on the ground (dollar tourism and employment vs. pesos employment). Ideologically the educational discourse thus retained *in principle* its counter-hegemonic anti-capitalist profile with a focus on sustainable development, situated on an island surrounded by more pro-capitalist elements.

6.6   INDIGENOUS KNOWLEDGES AND SUSTAINABILITY

Interestingly, indigenous knowledges now seem to creep into the schools. Cuban children in primary schools are trained in herbal remedies, which they can prepare at home as poultices, tinctures, salves, and teas. In school gardens, the focus is on local knowledges and ecological, sustainable farming without the use of fertilizers and insecticides. In the schools, the students are also introduced to solar energy, and many schools in the countryside are powered by solar panels. The new physics syllabus for Grade 8 focuses on energy and renewable energy sources and their relationship to the environment. In the middle school, the students are taught about different renewable energy technologies. Student teachers are also taught to incorporate renewable energy technologies in teaching (Avia and Guevara-Stone, 2010).

A Sustainable Society?

Cuba's incorporation of indigenous and sustainable knowledges in the national curriculum is due to its centering of sustainability in agriculture and environment, as well as the need to increase knowledge and commitment on these issues in the population. It underlines the inextricable link in Cuba among political, ideological, and educational discourses. Raul Castro's takeover in 2008 meant a change in the country's economic policy. Whether or not this will impact on the country's educational discourse is too early to tell. The Cuban government, trying to increase productivity, allows in the new economic reform program (from 2011) more Cubans to work for themselves and hire their own workers. Simultaneously, the government plans to cut more than a million government jobs, or 20% of Cuba's entire work force, over the next three years. Raul Castro's economic reform will force many graduating students into self-employment; thus, preparing for self-employment will also be an important educational task in the future. This is in line with Martí's dictum.

A result of the new economic reforms may mean that the balance between the pen and the plough in schools will tip even more in favor of the latter. As the Cuban authorities very well know, preaching solidarity, communitarianism, and sustainable development in times of economic hardship and job losses is not a simple task. An increased imbalance between ideology and praxis may jeopardize the efforts of the Cuban government to cling to its ideological independent position and to keep consumerist attitudes in check.

Raul Castro's launch of the new agricultural program (Law Decree 259) on July 18, 2008 opened up 100 acres of fallow state land for private farmers to lease in order to increase production (in total 1.69 million hectares, or 4 million acres). Importantly, the program is based on agricultural sustainability "rooted in an ecological rationality" (Penn, 2008), and is thus a continuation of a sustainable agricultural policy of the last decade. According to Melissa Penn (2008) the policy:

> Was directed to the use of organic fertilizers, soil conservation procedures and the creation of local cooperatives, community environmental programs, land redistribution strategies, as well as a decentralization of government control.[5]

Private farmers now control, through leasing, 85% of the total farm acreage; prior to the agricultural reform, the state owned 80% of the land (Penn, 2008). The question is whether Raul Castro's economic reform program can contribute to greater food production efficiency and reduce food imports, and whether such a program is compatible with Cuba's greater reliance on market mechanisms and market-determined prices. The agricultural reforms have been labeled a window-dressing exercise by some skeptics, but according to dissident economists we talked to (2012) the reforms were real, but were hampered by intricate bureaucratic procedures.

In terms of *urban* agriculture impressive achievements have, however, already been made. According to Altieri and Funes-Monzote (2012), "there are 383,000 urban farms, covering 50,000 hectares of otherwise unused land and producing more than 1.5 million tons of vegetables with top urban farms reaching a yield of 20 kg/m2 per year of edible plant material using no synthetic chemicals—equivalent to a hundred tons per hectare."

The discovery of offshore oil deposits will certainly boost Cuban economy (estimates indicate that deposits would make Cuba one of the 20 largest oil powers in the world [Jamison, 2009]). Oil production from these deposits will make Cuba a net exporter of oil, and make Cuba financially independent for the first time since the revolution in 1959. Exciting as this news is for the financially strained government, it may jeopardize Cuba's sustainability policy. It is worth mentioning here that Cuba's change from an industrial petroleum-based society to a sustainable society focusing on organic and semi-organic farming was not a result of a well-planned policy based on sustainability arguments, but a result of the collapse of oil imports from the USSR in the early 1990s. It remains to be seen if Cuba is tempted to return to a more oil-based society when it becomes oil self-sufficient.

Educational Independency?

After the fall of the USSR and the introduction of the Battle of Ideas, the educational discourse emerged as a hybrid discourse navigating a contradictory and complex terrain by striking a course that transcended the dependency and colonial ideology of many other countries in Latin America, Africa, and Asia. While retaining its anti-colonial and anti-imperialist nature, the educational discourse also articulated a new supplementary epistemological orientation that deviated dramatically from the days of Soviet influence, and which seriously addressed issues of sustainability that the present global architecture of education does not.

In terms of ideological foundation, historical legacy, and medium of instruction the Cuban educational system rests to a large extent on domestic principles. The textbooks in all subjects for primary schools are produced in Cuba and are distributed to all students in all schools in the country. The history and social science books have a clear anti-colonial bias, but they attempt to explore the history of various peoples in the country, and they are all developed to shape a sense of Cuban historical identity and culture. This indigenization of the discourse is a far cry from Western educational discourses in most Sub-Saharan African countries, which are often devoid of any link to the cultures and context of the students in schools. This indigenization is, of course, linked to the nationalist discourse referred to above as well as to the anti-capitalist focus of the curriculum, thus serving the political and ideological interests of the regime. However, it is also a public educational discourse that to a large extent encompasses all peoples of Cuba irrespective of race, gender, or geographical location.

Inclusiveness: We and the Other

The inclusiveness of Cuba's education system is underlined by the fact that education is free from kindergarten to university, implying that success in the system is not wholly dependent on the parents' background. It means that students in the Cuban system are not disadvantaged because "of present forms of racism, present forms of structural inequalities" (Gundara, 2000, p. 53). As Jagdish S. Gundara (2000) states in reference to Western societies, "Until institutional forms of inequality are removed, the education of those who are considered disadvantaged will not improve" (p. 53). Undoubtedly the Cuban system has done away with many forms of institutional inequality compared to most countries in the First and Third Worlds. The Cuban authorities have attempted to eradicate "cultural deprivation" and the "poverty of culture," making the environmental deficit of previously deprived groups less important. In English-speaking countries, considerable research to support the thesis of functional inferiority of black and working-class children has been conducted, but, to my knowledge, not much research has been done in Cuba on this issue. It would probably be difficult to publish research in Cuba if functional inferiority was discovered to be an important aspect of Cuban schooling. Officially, the Cuban system fosters a community spirit in the sense that no group is dramatically alienated in the school system, even though it has been noted that blacks' access to schooling is not as easy as that of whites.Nevertheless many blacks have climbed the social ladder due to the education system under Fidel Castro. One black university lecturer put it bluntly: " Without the present government I as a black man and with my very humble background would never have received the education and the position I now have" (2012). The inclusiveness of the system is, apart from its important social merit, also a means for soaking up unemployment and filling a skills gap. Moreover, by tapping the youth reserve, the regime tries to put a lid on potential discontent among the new generation. This may change, however, with the new economic program.

Such inclusiveness is in any case never complete. The imposition of a hegemonic discourse leaves people out, primarily on ideological grounds. Ideological repression means that everybody who questions the regime in a fundamental way is basically left out in the dark. There is a creation of boundaries between Self and Other that leaves very little room for fundamental critique. Thus, the model of inclusiveness is contradictory or conflicting: its social inclusiveness is counteracted by an ideological exclusiveness that is painful to those who are affected. This creation of boundaries between the Self and the Other is seen by the authorities in Havana as more than a way of solidifying national solidarity premised on one discourse. It is as much based on the external world, grounded in historical and contemporary experiences signified by the big enemy next door, the US. Exclusiveness at home can therefore be understood in psychological and socio-psychological terms, where the focus is on "attitudes and opinions that groups involved may have about one another" (Smith, 1988, p. 199).

There is a Self/intruder dichotomy here, which emphasizes nationhood at the expense of the foreigner/intruder, but the concept of nationhood and solidarity is seldom open to discussion. The basic question is: is the material implementation of the distinction made here between social inclusion and ideological exclusion a unique phenomenon attached to so-called non-democratic countries like Cuba? Clearly, there is a difference in the sense that in countries where there is freedom of expression, at least in principle, divergent views are not being penalized outright, and political repression is not as blatant. However, in so-called Western democracies counter-hegemonic opinions are often controlled, excluded, or toned down by the hegemonic discourse. As Raymond Williams stated about British education:

> However, always selectivity is the point; the way in which from a whole possible area of past and present, certain meanings and practices are neglected and excluded. Even more crucially, some of the meanings are reinterpreted, diluted, or put into form which support or at least do not contradict other elements within the effective dominant culture (in Sarup, 1996, p. 53).

No Assistance from the World Bank or the IMF

The problematic, ideological aspects notwithstanding, the merits of the education system seem to be quite well documented, even though obtaining reliable data is challenging (see endnote 1). This has led to some disagreement among the researchers about the education system's contemporary success (see Cruz-Taura, 2003 and Carnoy, 2007 for conflicting views). However, Cuba has resisted the globalized drive for privatization[6], and its merits have been accomplished—as noted—with no assistance from the World Bank or the IMF. This has only been possible because of the regime's comprehensive commitment to education for all, keeping the education budget at a high level despite the critical situation of the state economy. Below (fig. 6.1) are the resources for educational spending in Cuba in 2009.

All the expenditures for education, either current or capital (investments in construction works or equipment for education, etc.) are paid with state funds, and education is free throughout the system. It has been noted that Cuba has, compared to most countries, an extremely well-organized system both in terms of training, teaching, and school administration, as well as high research competence, which particularly focuses on the country's educational reforms.

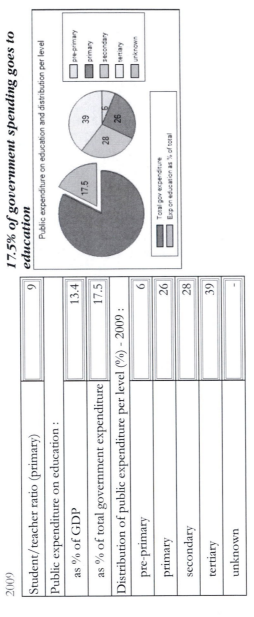

Figure 6.1   Educational spending in Cuba (UNESCO Institute of Statistics, 2009).

In contrast to most countries in the global South, the millennium development goals of universal primary education to be reached by 2015 have already been reached, and Cuba's competence in literacy work and its international collaboration in the field of literacy is unrivalled. Cuba's commitment to education, whatever its current problems, resonates with a population who might be at odds with the Cuban government on many issues, but feels proud about Cuba's achievements and reputation in education.

6.7 WHAT OTHERS SAY ABOUT THE EDUCATION SYSTEM IN CUBA

Many observers from the outside have explored the quality of education in Cuba, even though the new transformation has not yet been comprehensively evaluated due to the short time span from its inception.

Cuba participated in a survey conducted by OREALC, the UNESCO regional office for Latin America and the Caribbean in 1998 and 2001, which ranked Cuba top in the region (UNESCO, 2005, p. 51). The average performance levels of its students were remarkably high compared to those of other countries in the region. According to Saney (2004), the results were very impressive, "The average educational level achieved by Cubans is 10th grade surpassing the 5th grade regional average" (p. 36).

The EFA Global Monitoring Reports

In the EFA Global Monitoring Report 2005 called "The Quality Imperative," Cuba is one of four countries mentioned which "have achieved high standards of education quality." (UNESCO, 2005, p. 49). The report goes on to state, "Cuba and the Republic of Korea have achieved high standards in the past two or three decades, the former inspired by a strong belief that education helps to achieve the objectives of its 1959 revolution . . ." (UNESCO, 2005b, p. 49).

The report describes the Cuban education system fairly enthusiastically:

> At an earlier stage than the Republic of Korea, Cuba was emphasizing education's role in developing the whole individual (including physical education, sports, recreation and artistic education) while explicitly linking education with life, work and production . . . Following the Cuban revolution, education and health care were strongly prioritized . . . to support human development. They were both seen as desirable ends in themselves and as a means of assuring the country's economic and political independence (UNESCO, 2005b, pp. 50–51).

The report furthermore states how Cuba reduced its literacy from 40 pecent to zero in ten years and cites an OREALC/UNESCO study showing that

> "the average performance of the bottom quartile of its tested students was higher than the average of the top quartile of any other country in the survey" (UNESCO, 2005b, p. 51).

In light of these impressive achievements the report also asks if other countries can emulate Cuba's policies. By way of an answer it suggests that the unique and probably catalytic component may be the revolutionary spirit" "that inspired teachers, students and parents to make great efforts for the benefit of the schools may prove to be unique" (UNESCO, 2005b, p. 51). In addition the high esteem of the teaching profession might be an important factor for its success. The report admits, however, that the introduction of tourism might make the teaching profession less popular, a statement confirmed by our research in Cuba in 2005.

Comparing four successful countries (Canada, Cuba, Finland and the Republic of Korea), three common characteristics emerge: (1) high esteem for the teaching profession, (2) continuity of policy, and (3) high level of public commitment to education. Another characteristic for Korea and Cuba "is an extremely high level of energy among learners, teachers, and parents. In both countries it is associated with an atmosphere of competition, albeit from very different standpoints and in very different forms. Whether and how this can be mirrored in other contexts in the global South is an open question" (UNESCO, 2005b, p. 52). In the 2011 Global Monitoring Report, under the section Learning Achievement, it is noted that "Over half of grade 3 students in Cuba performed at level 4—more than three times the share in Argentina and Chile, for example. Cuba registered by far the highest proportion of students scoring at the highest benchmark and by far the smallest proportion scoring at level 1 or below" (UNESCO, 2011a, p. 85).

State-Generated Social Capital: Solving the Code?

Carnoy et al. (2007) use the concept of state-generated social capital, referred to in the beginning of this chapter, to explain why Cuba does better educationally than the two other countries in his comparative study (Brazil and Chile). The Cuban state is much more pro-active in trying to create a good learning environment for all, irrespective of ethnicity and class, compared to the two other countries. The government's massive material, ideological, and psychological investment in education, that is, free education for all, a ban on private schools (with the exception of international schools), and a conscious attempt and (at least partial) success to bridge the rural-urban educational gap are only a few of the factors that give credence to the theory that state-generated social capital (or collective social capital) seems to reduce the importance of what is traditionally perceived as cultural capital. Cuba is a good example of the merits of social capital, where families from disadvantaged environments can accumulate social capital through a benign learning environment. Moreover, since generations of Cubans have been socialized into understanding the merits of education through general literacy and schooling up to a certain level, they have internalized an attitude to schooling that, to some extent, bridges the potential cultural gap between home and school.

Carnoy et al. (2007) emphasize that Coleman's notion of social capital contrasts sharply with the concept of cultural capital, since social capital, in contrast to cultural capital, is independent of class (p. 12). Carnoy's sharp distinction between the two types of capital is somewhat misleading in Cuba's case. There is a sense that cultural capital, so rooted in the hegemonic class in capitalist countries, has been delinked from the socioeconomic background of Cubans. The social capital injected into the communities over generations has paved the way for the possession of cultural capital, not only for the small elite, but also for the majority of the population. If such an analysis is correct, Bourdieu and Passerdon's (1990) concept of cultural capital takes on a new meaning in socialist Cuba. The challenge in Cuba has been and still is the discrepancy between this democratically distributed cultural/social capital on the one hand and the lack of economic incentives and rewards for the well-educated population on the other. The results from a Gallup poll in 2006 show that while the population was very satisfied with access to education (98%) and the quality of schools in their communities (78%), the respondents' job satisfaction was considerably lower than in other Latin American countries, but still relatively high (68%) (Rios and Crabtree, 2006).

6.8 CONCLUSION

These predominantly positive reports on Cuba reflect, in many ways, the findings of our own research (also with research on sites of our own choosing). Only the latest EFA report (UNESCO, 2011) has managed to incorporate some data after the introduction of the new transformation in education of 2001. Carnoy's study does not address at length the serious problems now facing Cuba in terms of education, even though his study was published in 2007. Both the UNESCO 2005 and Carnoy reports refer to tourism as a potential threat to the education system. However, its serious, negative consequences are not addressed. UNESCO's first characteristic of Cuban education as "high esteem for the teaching profession" is also implied in Carnoy's (2007) statement that "Cuba has a distinct advantage over Brazil and Chile in being able to recruit higher-achieving secondary school graduates into teacher education" (p. 91). This does not reflect the contemporary situation on the ground. The teaching profession, and to a lesser extent the medical profession, have declined dramatically in esteem after the fall of the Soviet Union. The exodus of teachers attests to this decline and is closely related to what has been discussed above, the extremely low pay compared to the wages in the tourist industry (see also the film *Suite Habana,* which focuses on the Cuban economic crisis with its daily life implications [Pérez, 2003]). The competition from the tourist industry means that the recruitment of high-caliber students for the teaching profession is not as easy as it once was.

The new student teachers we interviewed seemed, however, to be very committed to Che Guevara's vision of the new man and to the defense of the revolution. One female student said, "The teaching profession is the most important profession in Cuba, and I want to make a difference" (2005). If this commitment is still there when faced with the tough realities of everyday teacher life remains to be seen. Moreover, their academic and pedagogical skills in the new dispensation are, as mentioned, a matter of some concern.

While the reports are unanimous in crediting Cuba's achievements and high level of public commitment (Carnoy's collective social capital is important here), it is essential to query whether Cuba's hybrid educational discourse is sustainable in the long run in a situation where the capitalist sector within Cuba competes for the hearts and minds of the manpower needed in education (as well as in health). It is too early to tell whether the government's response to this dilemma by the introduction of the new transformation in education will succeed. The dilemmas of being a so-called socialist island following a different course in the neighborhood of a hostile foe are multiple. Compromises are necessary but hard to find by a fairly dogmatic ruling class. The Cuban government has probably few compromises to offer in terms of the main principles of the educational discourse. Its uniqueness in a global perspective, its more or less universally distributed cultural capital, and its focus on sustainability represents an alternative educational, and to some extent a different epistemological route. Whether Raul Castro's economic reform program will change this situation in the future is difficult to predict. Despite the current difficulties in the education system, Cuba's educational trajectory ought to be of interest to other countries in the region, as well to countries in Africa and Asia (and the North), but as long as political stigma is attached to Cuba, the country is isolated from the major international arenas of educational debate, with the exception of UNESCO.

Cuba's economic and education policy for sustainable development is reminiscent of indigenous peoples' focus on the sacredness of land and sustainable land management. However, even though Cuba makes use of indigenous plants from the Taino Indians in their alternative pharmaceutical industry, the nexus between Cuban policy and indigenous knowledges is apparently tenuous. The reasons for this situation are multiple. One is the fact that the indigenous population in Cuba, the Taino Indians, is such a tiny minority that epistemological visibility is difficult. Another is that even though Cuba's literacy campaigns to indigenous peoples are implemented in many countries in the global South, the literacy method of "Yes I can" and "Yes I can continue" is so basic that epistemological considerations are not very prominent. Third, the communist regime is skeptical of everything that smacks of spirituality ("the general Latin American preference for more traditional, fatalistic, and mystical ways of knowing" [Paulston, 1973, p. 168]). Since the very ideological basis of the Cuban state is "rational" and non-spiritual in nature, there is a sense that the strong streak of dogmatic Marxism mixed with a nationalistic Martian philosophy provides little space for so-called non-scientific belief systems.

Still there is this affinity *in practice* between the Cuban policy and indigenous knowledges in terms of sustainability. In a sense the Cuban government has "understood the need for new images of nature in post-modern civilization . . . [and] the need for a new social contract which is concerned not only with social justice of the relations between humans, but the relations between humans and the nonhuman world" (Devall, 1990, p. 27).

Cuban history after 1959 is a history of resistance and a struggle for sovereignty and political and educational independence, as well as a history of heavy domestic repression (which has not been substantially softened during Raul Castro's regime).

In the last two decades resistance has taken an additional direction: The creation of a model of sustainable development that challenges, in a fundamental way, the European epistemic exploitation of Mother Earth. Whatever the model's pragmatic and/or epistemological rationale (and despite resistance among some cadres in the Communist party), such a challenge cannot go unheeded in a world of ecological unsustainability. At the 1992 Earth Summit, Fidel Castro warned in a speech that "Tomorrow will be too late." According to the International Energy Agency's (IEA) 2011 World Energy Outlook report, the year 2017 is the point of no return if we want to limit global warming to below two degrees Celsius ("so as not to risk the most dangerous and unpredictable impacts") (IEA, 2011). The fear is that tomorrow is already here.

7 Cognitive Violence Against Minority Groups
The Case of the Mapuche in Chile

7.1 INTRODUCTION

> They wrenched off our fruits, they ripped off our branches, they burned our trunk, but they could not kill our roots.
>
> —An old Indian saying

The Context

A comparative study of the education systems of Cuba, Chile, and Brazil (Carnoy et al. 2007) found that Cuba performed much better than the two other countries based on a number of criteria, from elementary school students' results and teaching material to the quality of the performance of the teachers. On Chile, Carnoy et al. (2007) state, "our classroom videos and interviews showed why: when left to their own devices, schools, whether public or private, can't overcome low standards and expectations, inadequate teacher training and their students' social environment" (p. 40).

This is the education situation in a country that prides itself on being one of the richest in Latin America (ranked as the richest in 2009 and the second richest in 2010 [*Latin Business Chronicle*, 2010]). While the quality of education in Chile in general terms is inadequate, the argument of this chapter is that the education situation of the Mapuche, the largest Indian group in the country, is even more problematic in terms of quality, content, and epistemological orientation.

The Mapuche were the only indigenous group in Latin America to successfully resist the Spanish invasion in the 19th century and their territorial rights were recognized by the Spanish. Besides having a proud history of resistance, the Mapuche are even today engaged in disputes and sometimes violent confrontations with the majority society by resisting the impositions of the Chilean authorities in a variety of ways. 'Mapuche' means people of the land. The Mapuche's profound attachment to the land and their view of the land as sacred is the underlying cause of many of their conflicts with the Chilean state. Like that of the Xhosa in South Africa, the Mapuche cosmovision and epistemological orientation are inextricably linked to the holistic relationship between man, nature, and the supernatural.[1] Since the Mapuche cosmovision and epistemology are markedly different from those of Chilean mainstream society, there is a concern among the Mapuche that the education system should be inclusive of indigenous knowledges and worldviews. For the purposes of this book, a discussion about the Mapuche as a minority people fighting for epistemological and educational justice and sustainable development is meant to contribute to a more comprehensive understanding of how indigenous peoples position themselves in the global village and how they, in many ways, are essential partners in new conversations about the future of our planet.

By first situating the Mapuche demographically, judicially, politically, and culturally, the chapter proceeds to analyze how the education system in Chile addresses indigenous knowledges and epistemologies. The chapter discusses both the ideological and epistemological content of the country's main curriculum *Marco Curricular* (MINEDUC, 2001 a) as well as the supplementary curriculum *Programa Educación Intercultural Bilingüe*, EIB (MINEDUC, n.d.), which is particularly designed to suit the needs of the various Indian groups in the country. Given the fact that the Chilean government has given space to a supplementary curriculum for minority groups, the pivotal point in the chapter is whether such a supplementary curriculum addresses the fundamental issues of the Mapuche, both in terms of identity construction, cognition, and multi-culturality, but also in terms of the wider issues related to the land issue and sustainable development.[2]

7.2   THE SITUATION OF THE MAPUCHE

The Number Game

Even though the indigenous population in Chile is clearly a minority, the question of the actual number of indigenous peoples will be discussed in this subsection because there is clearly a correlation between political leverage and population size. The actual number, particularly of the Mapuche, does not, however, seem easy to estimate; the two censuses in 1992 and 2002 published very different figures about the Mapuche population.

According to the 1992 census, the Mapuche constituted 928,060 people whereas the 2002 census stipulates the number to be 604,349, a dramatic decline of 30% (Instituto National de Estadísticas, 1993, 2003). This apparent decline in the 2002 census was denounced by several organizations as "statistical genocide" since the questions asked in the two censuses were different.[3]

Whether this was a deliberate attempt of the Chilean government to reduce the number of indigenous peoples is not known, but the two censuses are quite unhelpful if one wants to compare the population groups from 1992 to 2002.

What blurs the number situation even more is that the census in 2006 by CASEN (Characterizacion Socioeconomica Nacional) found that 1,060,786 people identified themselves as belonging to native groups, equivalent to 6.6% of the Chilean population, with the Mapuche making up 87.2% of the country's indigenous peoples (CASEN, 2006a, 2006b). These figures are close to the figures of the 1992 census.

Traditionally the Mapuche lived in rural areas, but the 1992 census revealed that around 400,000 Mapuche (44% of the 930,000 persons 14 years old or older who identified themselves as Mapuche) lived in Santiago (see Jara, 1997). Despite the urbanization of the Mapuche, the Mapuche question is traditionally related to the rural Mapuche in the Araucanía region, where land and water resources are contested issues. However, as Gustavo Quilaqueo states:

> There is not a Mapuche family living in the countryside who does not have any relative in the city and vice-versa. The ties with those who migrate are strong and people in the cities mobilize and fight alongside the rural communities (in Morrisey, 2010).

The Socio-Economic and Legal Situation of the Mapuche

According to the latest statistics, poverty in Chile comprises 22.7% of the population while among indigenous peoples the poverty level is 35.6%. Indigenous families earn nearly half the income of non-indigenous families. Infant mortality rates in some indigenous municipalities are 50% higher than the national average (Calbucura and Le Bonniec, 2009). Social and economic conditions in the Araucanía, where Mapuche unrest has been most acute, are among the worst in the country. Of all Chile's regions, it scores lowest on the Human Development Index (UNDP, 2004). Mapuche women from the region, who are often in the front line of protests, score lowest of all (Institute of Indigenous Studies, 2003, pp. 265–274).

One central issue in the discussion about indigenous peoples in Chile—and in our case, the majority group, the Mapuche, in particular—is related to whether indigenous peoples can be said to be protected by the rights afforded to citizens of Chile and whether measures beyond these rights to protect them are legitimate. In many other Latin America countries, it is acknowledged that some form of cultural difference can only be accommodated through special constitutional measures, above and beyond the common rights of citizenship (Kymlicka, 1995, p. 26).

In the following sections, I will discuss to what extent the Mapuche special rights should be recognized, or whether "universal individual rights can be said to accommodate cultural differences" (Kymlicka, 1995, p. 107).

Even though the Chilean state seems to under-communicate the multi-ethnicity/culturality of the country, the very fact that there are various ethnic groups who occupy specific territories means that Chile can be defined as a multi-national and multi-cultural country. According to Will Kymlicka (1995) a 'nation' in "this sociological sense is closely related to the idea of a 'people' or a 'culture'—indeed these concepts are often defined in terms of each other" (p. 11). However, as we shall see later in this subsection, the concept of 'people' has not, until recently, been accepted as a term to define the indigenous peoples in Chile.

It is a historical fact that the indigenous peoples in Chile have had their territories invaded and that much of the land has been taken away from them. The agrarian reform under Allende, where much of the land had been returned to the Mapuche, was reversed under Pinochet: the Mapuche retained only 16% of the land returned to them between 1962 and 1973 (Correra, Molina, and Yáñes, 2003). Since the indigenous population is relatively small, the very existence of these indigenous groups has often been ignored and any question of self-government has been denied them.

The discourse of "benign neglect" (García-Alix and Hitchcock, 2009) perceives that an ethnic minority group is adequately taken care of by being citizens of the country, and that there is no need of special rights to protect them, that is, universal individual rights accommodate cultural differences. The view of strictly separating state and ethnic origin does not necessarily mean an underestimation of the ethnic cultures. Rather it is suggested that "the members of the culture will sustain it through their own choice. If the culture is decaying, it must be because some people no longer find it worthy of their allegiance" (Kymlicka, 1995, p. 108). This idea of "benign neglect" is by no means a dominant discourse in Chile, nor is it a view supported by the world community through the UN. In Chile the indigenous population is viewed as needing special treatment, manifested through various legal measures.

There are basically three laws or provisions that define the indigenous peoples' position in Chile, viz. the Constitution, the indigenous law and the ILO convention. The Chilean Constitution does not recognize the distinct political and cultural identities of indigenous peoples within Chile, insisting on Chile as a mono-cultural and mono-ethnic nation.

The indigenous law was passed in 1993[4] to recognize, protect, and support indigenous peoples. Focusing on five aspects (political participation, education, land rights, cultural rights, and development rights), the law is meant to address the rights and freedoms of indigenous peoples in accordance with the ILO Convention No. 169.[5] The law established CONADI (the National Corporation for Indigenous Development) which was meant to advise and direct government programmes to assist the cultural and economic development of indigenous people. According to the first CONADI leader (a Mapuche) CONADI has good ideas, but it was weak from the very beginning because " the government has never given it necessary resources and CONADI has never had proper political support. When I as the first leader of CONADI asked for resources, the government did not listen.

CONADI warned the government that if it didn't give them resources, they (CONADI) would be confrontational. It is common practice that CONADI leaders are fired when there is a conflict" (2008).

While the law definitely was a step in the right direction, the Mapuche leaders were skeptical. This is what a leader, José Santos Millao, from a Lafkenche Mapuche community said when the law was proclaimed:

> We must be absolutely clear and responsible to our people, the Chilean society and history, that the Law that today has been approved by Congress is not in accordance with the indigenous peoples of this country, for the simple reason that it is not conducive to our fundamental historical demands, which according to us, include constitutional recognition as a nation and a people with a territorial space and autonomy . . . this is a law which does not recognize our political participation in our own affairs (in Ortiz, 2007, pp. 43–44).

Since the law recognizes indigenous populations as 'ethnicities' and not as 'peoples', the Mapuche (and other indigenous peoples in Chile) did not have easy access to the UN or the Organization of American States (OAU), since declarations of indigenous rights by the UN or the OAU only refer to 'peoples,' not ethnic groups. Moreover, the problem is that there was no governmental body in Chile assigned to control the enforcement of indigenous rights.[6] Additionally, other laws like the Law of Energy of 2008 and the Decree Law on electricity of 1982 have more prestige and leverage.

International pressure mounted for Chile to ratify the International Labour Organization's (ILO) Convention 169 on tribal peoples' rights. The Senate was the stumbling block, but finally the Senate yielded and ratified the ILO convention on March 4, 2008. On September 15, 2008, the ILO announced that ratification was complete. Chile is the latest country to sign the key international law on tribal peoples' rights (ILO, 2008).

The ILO convention includes a series of rights in favor of indigenous peoples that were not reflected in the indigenous law. One example is that the word 'people' is recognized. Another is the use of the term 'territory' to refer to where the indigenous peoples live. Convention No. 169 also presumes that indigenous and tribal peoples are able to speak for themselves as well as have a *right* to take part in this decision-making process in their own country. However, the implementation of the ILO convention has been a long, drawn-out process, even though Chile's courts have started taking the convention's stipulations into considerations in some of their rulings.

According to our informants, the various governments after Pinochet, whether left or right, have all refrained from seriously addressing the indigenous challenges when it comes to praxis: "It does not matter if the government is socialist or conservative, the indigenous question is very low on the political agenda. The Chilean government is immoral because they do not respect their own laws" (former CONADI leader, 2008).

There seems to have always been a rhetoric/reality discrepancy, or an ambiguity towards the Mapuche and other indigenous groups, which makes enforcement of the legal rights for the Mapuche difficult or half-hearted. On the one hand Chile has not adopted multi-cultural institutionalism in the constitution; on the other hand, they have signed the ILO treaty which accepts ethnic groups as indigenous peoples.

The Land Issue

It has been noted that the land question is one of the contentious issues in many conflicts between indigenous groups and the majority society in many parts of the world. It is probably fair to say that if indigenous cultures are to survive, their land base needs to be protected. According to Kymlicka, indigenous struggles over land are the single largest cause of ethnic conflict in the world (Kymlicka, 1995; Muehlebach, 2003). This is also the case in Chile. Applying compensatory justice, that is, that all land taken from the original owners should be given back to them, is not a feasible solution. It would mean that the Chileans of non-indigenous origin would have to leave the country, and this would in turn cause another injustice. Kymlicka states, "Suffering historical injustice is neither necessary nor sufficient for claiming self-government rights. It implies that all land taken from indigenous peoples in the Americas should be returned to them. This would create massive unfairness" (Kymlicka, 1995, p. 220).

While dismissing the concept of compensatory justice as both unfeasible and unfair, the concept of distributive justice navigates between compensatory justice and benign neglect. The concept, which is inherently based on an equality argument, aims to provide sufficient territory for indigenous groups to sustain a viable living. While the equality argument seems more appropriate than the compensatory justice argument in addressing minority rights, the latter is also somewhat problematic since the argument is quite vague and open for interpretation. What is meant by equality? Is their low standard of life due to the fact that the Mapuche refuse to accept a modern way of life? How much should be compensated? What are the practical implications of the equality argument? These questions are central in the contentious issues pertaining to the territory in the Araucanía region where the Mapuche are claiming territory that was originally theirs. Much of the territory that the Mapuche are claiming is now owned by national and transnational corporations (these corporations own three times more land than the Mapuche [HRW and ODPI, 2004]). The corporations have been subsidized heavily by the various governments, and the Mapuche fight for land rights and the right to decide on Mapuche territory is perceived as an obstacle to capitalist territorial expansion and access to resources that is so important to capitalist globalization.

The Mapuche response to globalization is fierce. The Mapuche Forum (2004) states:

Contrary to the claims made by governments, businesses and transnational corporations about economic globalization, we do NOT understand globalization as a world of opportunity. We understand it as a world of exclusion, marginalization, oppression, ex-appropriation; a world where indigenous peoples are displaced and their land and natural resources over-exploited; a world in which big corporations use their instruments the World Bank, the IMF, the WTO, the FTAA, Free Trade Agreements and APEC to exercise imperialist power—a power which in many cases transcends that of government and the state to control markets and trade. The current globalization of free trade promotes a neo-colonialism, which, in contrast to the colonialism of yesterday, affects not only indigenous peoples and nations but vast sectors of the world's population.

After the indigenous law was passed in 1993, the Chilean government through CONADI has bought the land back for the Mapuche, but to a limited extent due to ideological considerations and due to lack of financial capacity to do it. As the first leader of CONADI put it: "CONADI has been very slow in terms of buying back the land, but some land is not "legally" theirs, but belong to the companies. In reality it is the land of the Mapuche" (2008).

Moreover, to regain more land the Mapuche must show that title was granted to them in the late 19th century (*Economist*, 2009) at a time when they were conquered by the independent Chilean government after a war of extermination in 1883 (the "Pacificación de la Araucanía"). To what extent such an arrangement can be said to comply with the principles of redistributive justice is contentious since titles were also given to people who had robbed the Mapuche of their land. While there is no space to enter a comprehensive discussion of the land issue here, the contentiousness of the issue has forced the government to undertake a study on the issue of land ownership in Araucanía. Some critics would say that this is long overdue.

It may seem as though increased globalization has sharpened government opposition to indigenous rights and has given transnational corporations more or less free rein to exploit natural resources on Indian land. Transnational corporations such as the Angelini and Matte-Larrain family conglomerates construct dams, engage in logging activities, and export timber at the expense of Mapuche rights and sacred land (Motaung, 2009). Moreover, these conglomerates will not give away their lands for free nor sell them for less than the current market price.

What makes the situation even more complicated is that a return to the land does not necessarily make the Mapuche more prosperous. The return of the land is often more a matter of cultural and religious identification rather than a matter of getting a better life. The distributive justice argument is therefore problematic since the reclaiming of land is more related to cosmological/epistemological issues than a matter of material gain.[7]

Ratification of the ILO convention means, however, that the international community will keep its eyes on Chile's implementation policies, meaning that the Chilean state has to take the indigenous peoples' territorial claims much more seriously than in the past.

The Cosmology and Epistemology of the Mapuche

As has been noted, one of the most important reasons for claiming back territory stolen from them is the cosmology and epistemology of the Mapuche. The Mapuche are, and historically have been a very religious people with a set of well-defined beliefs and ceremonial practices linked to specific sites. Their cosmological beliefs focus on the sacredness of land, the natural elements, and spirituality. It has been noted how both the non-exploitative attitude to Mother Earth and the emphasis on spirituality of indigenous peoples ran counter to Western forms of secularism in the era of imperialism and colonialism (see also Barker, 2000). The whole struggle for territorial rights is linked to the respect for land and place and to the location of the ancestors. The concept *communalidad* (community) sums up this cosmology as "a collective . . . that includes the world beyond the humans, that is, nature and deities" (Vasquez, 2010, p. 277). It is the epistemic dislocation of indigenous beliefs that is being countered by the Mapuche in their struggle for land and epistemic legitimacy. Reclaiming spirituality means very explicitly the re-establishment of indigenous identities and evocation of agency to resist or fight back repression from the hegemonic society with its secular underpinnings. As Andrea Muehlebach (2003) states, "the notion of indigenous cultural identity has become intimately intertwined with what . . . is called a 'distinctive' spiritual and material relationship to the land" (p. 251).

The divergent epistemological positions encompassed by Mapuche *Kimün* (indigenous knowledges) and secular Western worldviews have important political, philosophical, psychological, and pedagogical consequences, the discrepancy between, in Grimaldo Rengifo Vasquez's (2010) words, "the 'living world' of the indigenous in which everything is experienced as alive and imbued with personhood and a 'mechanical world,' a world of objects which is the one lived and projected by modernity" (p. 280). Whereas Western knowledge has been compartmentalized into clearly defined subjects (for example, math, science, music, or languages) that are considered to have a logic of their own, there is a holistic interrelatedness in all aspects of Mapuche *Kimün*. Such an understanding is similar to the cosmology of the Xhosa discussed in Chapter 4.

Mapuche cosmology is delimited geographically and culturally in the sense that the emphasis is on place and territory, which in the Mapuche conflict cannot be overestimated. It is, I argue, impossible in the case of the Mapuche to talk of self-determination as a deterritorialized right. The Mapuche fight for reclaiming the land is therefore a fight for Mapuche identity and the demand to be recognized as a people with a specific cosmology and epistemology (see also Bammer, 1994) The importance of the ILO convention is its recognition that indigenous peoples have a right to speak for themselves and that they have a *right* to take part in the decision-making process that has an impact on the indigenous peoples. It is in this perspective of cultural and epistemological identification that the struggle over education must be seen.

7.3   EDUCATION IN CHILE: *MARCO CURRICULAR*

While education in some circles in Chile is perceived as a social equalizer (Carnoy et al., 2007, p. 35), statistical data does not seem to support such an optimistic scenario. On the contrary, education in Chile seems to reproduce inequality. Moreover, as will be shown from the data below, the Mapuche do not have the same educational level as non-minority Chileans.

Even though the Mandatory Primary Education Law of 1926 required all children to attend school up to Grade 8, a study by Berlung in 1977 indicates that most Mapuche did not complete more than three or four years of schooling, especially in the rural areas of the Araucanía (Ortiz, 2007, p. 101).

A new law of compulsory schooling was passed by Congress in 2004, in which Grade 12 has become mandatory. Primary education in Chile is from Grades 1–8. Chile's education system is a mixed system with private (not receiving stately economic support), publicly subsidized (privately owned but receiving economic support from the Chilean state), and municipal-owned schools (public schools) (Carnoy, 2007).

According to the last national census (INE, 2002) the Mapuche population older than 10 years of age has a 91.8% literacy rate, as opposed to the non-Mapuche population, which has 96%. Education among indigenous peoples is 2.2 years less than the national average of 9.5 years, and only 3% of the *rural* Mapuche population has received any secondary education by 15 years of age. There is a noticeable difference between Mapuche men and women, especially in the rural areas where women are clearly less schooled than men. There is also a generational difference; Mapuche between 16 and 29 years old have an average of 11 years of schooling versus Mapuche above the age of 50, who have an average of only 7 years of schooling.

The quality of schools in areas of high Mapuche concentration remains, however, very low, measured by a yearly standardized test, *Sistema de Evaluación de la Calidad de la Educación* (SIMCE) (Ortiz, 2007, p. 105).

While one issue is this apparent low quality in the Mapuche schools, the most contested issue is the content of the primary school curriculum. The reason is the pervasive mono-cultural educational discourse in the *Marco Curricular* (basic curriculum), resulting in the marginalization of the indigenous history and cultures. The hegemonic, mono-cultural nature of the education system is in line with the constitution's lack of recognition of Chile as a multi-ethnic and multi-cultural society. Clearly, school has played a crucial role in the national policy of mono-culturality by means of, as Benjamín Maldonado Alvarado (2010) states, an interventionist army of "teachers and curricula" (p. 375).

While the Chilean education system has a decentralized curriculum where each school draws up a detailed plan for its school using the *Marco Curricular* as the basis, the *Marco Curricular* does little more than pay lip service to the history and situation of indigenous peoples. It is worth noting that until recently textbooks on Chilean history discussed the war of extermination against the Mapuche (Pacíficacón) as a victory of civilization over the uncivilized and barbarous (Bengoa, 1985).

There are, however, pockets/sections where indigenous traditions are referred to, for instance under Lenguaje y Comunicación, Octavo Año Basico/Nivel Basico 6: Las multiples tradiciones culturales de Chile ('The many/numerous cultural traditions of Chile"), with a focus on ethnic and cultural diversity. The aim is to:

- Promote awareness of cultures, discovering evidence of them. Develop respect for the uniqueness of them; make contact with their customs, beliefs and vocabulary.
- Rescue and preserve their values, spreading what they learn and know.
- Sharing their world and their ways of expression.

(MINEDUC, 2004, p. 107)

In another section in *Marco Curricular* the music and literature of indigenous groups are mentioned, as well as indigenous peoples in pre- and post-Columbian times. Moreover, the plan suggests that the students organize a forum to discuss the importance and validity of Chile's indigenous groups.

These references notwithstanding, the Mapuche were never satisfied with these inclusions due to their folkloristic nature and their superficial treatment. The hegemonic discourse in *Marco Curricular* is never questioned in a comprehensive and fundamental way. Neither the deep-rooted causes for the socio-economic marginalization of the indigenous groups nor their epistemological assumptions is properly addressed. On the contrary, the indigenous knowledges of the communities are questioned on a daily basis in the classrooms, consciously or not, as "obsolete, backwards, and without a rational base" (Alvarado, 2010, p. 376). It may create, like in South Africa, alienation and cultural and epistemological disillusionment among the children of indigenous origin.

This curricular policy can be understood as a natural step by the government to try to assimilate indigenous groups into the mainstream Chilean society. The disagreement between those who think that individual universal rights are sufficient, presumably a minority opinion, and those who favor distributive justice in varying degrees is related to whether a predominantly mono-cultural curriculum and the marginalization of indigenous knowledges and local cultural practices have major implications for the Mapuche, and whether such implications matter in the national context and in terms of development. Clearly, the prioritization of non-indigenous knowledges means an under-utilization of indigenous resources and knowledges in the development of a given society. However, this may be viewed as a necessary step towards modernization of the Chilean society.

The Mapuche who are politically active, however, consider *Marco Curricular* to be counterproductive to their struggle to regain Mapuche language, culture, and identity. Claiming that it is insufficient to channel enough resources into the Mapuche schools to make them on par with non-indigenous schools, Mapuche activists argue that the contents of the curriculum must be changed. They demand a *Marco Curricular* for all students that also represents indigenous epistemologies and cultures and accommodates cultural difference.

According to one representative from Origenes " the Chilean population is ready to incorporate aspects of indigeneous cultures in the curriculum. I receive many messages from teachers who want to know more about indigenous peoples. There are some aspects of indigenous culture in the curriculum already, but not enough- it is important to make the students aware of the fact that Chile is a multi-cultural narion" (2008).

Basically, the demand for a different curriculum is a request for proper recognition, partly because recognition is closely linked to identity construction, where, as Charles Taylor (1992) suggests, the latter term designates something like a person's understanding of who they are, of their fundamental defining characteristics a human being (p. 25). If recognition from significant others is withheld, it can, as Taylor (1992) states, "inflict damage on those who are denied it" (p. 36). This is in line with Ngũgĩ's concept of colonizing the mind and Fanon's perception of the subaltern as the "wretched of the earth" without a history. As Fanon (1963) states:

> Colonialism is not content to impose its rule upon the present and the future of a dominated country. Colonialism is not satisfied with holding a people in the grip and emptying the native's brain of all form and content. By a kind of perverted logic, it turns to the past of the oppressed people, and distorts, disfigures and destroys it. The work of devaluing colonial history takes on a dialectical significance today (p. 210.)

The very fact that the language, the cultures, and the worldviews of the Mapuche are only sporadically touched upon in *Marco Curricular* does something to the self-confidence and self-esteem of the Mapuche in addition to the potential learning challenges it creates in school. Since the *Marco Curricular* basically seems to suggest that everything worth narrating is of European heritage, the dislocation of indigenous knowledges and cultures represents a kind of identicide.

It is therefore a question of decolonizing the mind, which encompasses "resistance to domination of the past, contamination of the present and the stealing of a people's future" (Dei, 2006, p. 11). What politically active Mapuche are asking for is a politics of difference where the majority society is "asked to recognize . . . the unique identity of the individual and the groups, their distinctiveness from everyone else" (Taylor, 1992, p. 38).

7.4 EDUCACIÓN INTERCULTURAL BILINGÜE (EIB)

It can be argued that this lack of indigenous recognition and referencing in the *Marco Curricular* has to some extent been acknowledged by the Chilean government since the educational reform in the 1990s, when it attempted to address indigenous issues. In particular, the introduction of the concept of equity implied that everybody should get the same quality education, but that groups with special needs should be assisted with special programs (Brunner and Cox, 1995). Special groups here meant particularly indigenous groups. Facilitated by the *Ley Orgánica Constitutional de Enseñanza* (1990) and *Ley Indigena* (1993), EIB was introduced to selected primary schools in 1995 While the introduction of EIB was a significant educational step in Chilean educational history, it must be noted that EIB is a supplementary curriculum to the national curriculum, *Marco Curricular.*

In an unusually strong statement from the first director of EIB in the Ministry of Education, Guillermo Williamson, the failure of the national curriculum to accommodate indigenous peoples is underlined:

> For us it is very clear that the hegemonic setting of schooling for indigenous peoples has never worked and what remains of it today is still not working. No matter how many millions in resources and time you invest in the current model, it will not work, because there are factors of values, of learning approaches, of social and community patterns of interaction and links to local development that are fundamental to the indigenous cultures, that are just not present in the current European centered modern schooling that is dominant today in this country (in Ortiz, 2007, p. 106).

It is the cognitive violence of indigenous epistemologies that the new curriculum, according to Williamson, wanted to address. According to this view, securing the basic property rights of the Mapuche is inadequate as long as the knowledge base is not protected.

Underlining the basic ideological underpinnings of the Chilean curriculum as being mono-cultural, mono-national, and assimilationist, Williamson proposed a totally new school model that deviated from the hegemonic occidental, assimilating educational discourse. The question is as to what extent Williamson's call for a change to a new schooling model has been materialized in EIB.

What is Educación Intercultural Bilingüe (EIB)?

Despite skeptical ideological opinions from various groups within the Mapuche community and the ambivalence of the Concertación government (the center-left coalition government), EIB was launched and was based on the laws (1990, 1993) referred to above and *Programa Orígenes*. The law, passed during the presidency of Patricio Aylwin, the first president after the Pinochet's dictatorship ended, stated that:

> CONADI (the National Indigenous Development Corporation), in areas with high density of indigenous population and in coordination with the state departments or agencies concerned, should develop an intercultural bilingual education system in order to prepare indigenous learners to function in an appropriate manner, both in the home society and in the society at large . . .The law . . . [also provides] a scholarship program for indigenous students and students called *Becas*. . . . the selection of beneficiaries should be considered by the CONADI (*Ley indigena*, 1993).

The EIB program is limited to a relatively small selection of schools because few schools sign up for *Programa Orígenes*, which is the umbrella program for EIB. *Programa Orígenes* addresses urgent indigenous needs in the three areas of education, health, and community development (*Programa Orígenes*, 2006). Statistics made by the government show that there are 160 EIB schools in five regions (Huenchullán and Millacura, 2007) whereas the Ministry of Education claims seven regions: 1st, 2nd, Metropolitan, 8th, 9th, 10th, and 12th regions (Jakobsen, 2009). According to Carolina Huenchullán and Claudia Millacura (2007) the 9th region, Araucanía, has the majority of EIB schools (100 schools out of 160 schools in total).

It is important to reiterate that EIB is not a completely new curriculum; it is a supplement to the national curriculum to address issues of cultures, cosmologies, histories, and worldviews among the indigenous peoples. As one principal with an EIB program explained, "We all follow the occidental program and Mapuche activities are sometimes added to the ordinary curriculum activities" (2008).

Today, EIB programs remain as *Proyectos Educativos Institucionales* (PEI) and *Proyectos Curriculares* (PC) (Huenchullán and Millacura, 2007), that is, curricular projects that provide an opportunity for schools or communities to incorporate part of their cultural and linguistic heritage into the school programs of their children. These are not part of the mandatory curriculum, do not have the credits of a regular course, and generally do not have grades or evaluations.

Since EIB caters only for schools with an indigenous population, one would expect the teaching to be in the indigenous peoples' language. However, not even this supplementary program manages to provide indigenous language teaching, primarily due to the lack of bilingual teachers. The term EIB is therefore misleading since it does not cater to the bilingual aspect of the program.[8]

While EIB is a peripheral curriculum compared to the Basic National Curriculum, its focus is *per definitionem* different by emphasizing the language, cultural customs, and the identity of the Mapuche. EIB is supposed to help the children reach their potential with the indigenous worldview and the indigenous language playing an important part.

The objectives of EIB are quite impressive (excerpts below):

- To design, implement, and evaluate a pedagogical alternative for the improvement in access to, and quality of, the learning.
- To advance significantly in the acquisition of knowledge, comprehension, discerning capacity, values, disposition for social coexistence. In this way, indigenous children would reach their maximum personal development in the context of their culture of origin.
- To have the participation of indigenous communities in the processes of elaboration of curricular activities of the schools [so that] they can integrate the traditional knowledge, techniques, and visions of the world, to the curriculum and school administration.
- To facilitate access and favor retention in basic, secondary, and tertiary education.
- To prepare qualified human resources that promote the valuing and development of indigenous cultures and languages in all instances of national life (EIB, n.d..)

EIB in Chile is partly funded by the Banco Interamericano de Desarollo (Inter-American Development Bank), but does not have the resources to make this a viable alternative for the Mapuche or other indigenous peoples since the EIB curriculum is not accredited within the Chilean state educational policy. After the minimum requirements of the national curriculum have been taught, the *Origenes* schools can include EIB, but until today EIB courses in Chilean schools remain primarily in the category of 'workshops," often held once a week by a cultural advisor as optional enrichment hours outside the main core-curriculum courses. When asked how they seek to promote Mapuche identity, one principal said, "Through Mapuche food, interviews with elderly Mapuche as well as storytelling. On Fridays a Mapuche visits the school for a workshop and Mapundugun is spoken" (2008). Another teacher: "The facilitator works together with the teacher in the classroom. The facilitator comes three times a week. It is a person from the community, elected by the community. In the beginning of the year there is a meeting, and a person is elected. It is a person who is respected, responsible and have clear values. He takes care of the Mapuche ceremonies and he represents the machi (but he is not himself a machi). On a special date the machi comes.

He plays the kultrun, and the students make instruments that everybody can play" (2008)..

Another principal responded about the role of the facilitator, in that, "He engages the students in Mapuche ceremonies and he tries to teach respect for the nature. For example if the students need special branches from trees in their school work—they will have to ask for permission" (2008).

In another school where approximately 50% of the students are Mapuche the principal teachers stated: "We celebrate the Mapuche new year, a celebration which lasts for 24 hours and the Mapuche Student Day in commemoration of a student who was killed by the police some years ago" (2008).

Indigenous Language

While teaching in EIB is primarily in the colonial language, Spanish, EIB focuses on the value of the indigenous language with its oral traditions and cultures as a personal and social enrichment for the indigenous child. It is also supposed to promote cultural diversity. While the intention is good, there are at least two issues here, transcribing the oral tradition to text, and translating orality from Mapudungun to Spanish. The oral traditions are, as Marcela Tovar Gómez (2010) states:

> "Rescued" (that is, written down) in school work assigned to indigenous children ... often, when these are written down in Spanish, their narrative structure is "adjusted" to that of Spanish. These stories, decontextualized from their cultural meaning or significance, are accepted as testimonies that reveal the thinking or worldview of indigenous peoples ... interpreted based on cultural schemes and structures foreign to those that authentically organize both their content and their profound significance (p. 183).

The ambitions for indigenous language teaching are not impressive. According to the curriculum, the students are to learn vocabulary and read texts in an indigenous language and reproduce greetings in the indigenous language, for example, Mapudungun. In the social science subject it is suggested that students "Exhibit a figure of the human body (for example a poster), locate the different organs, senses (smell, touch, etcetera) [. . .] parts (eyes, arm, hand, leg, and so on) [. . .] and write them down in both Spanish and the indigenous language [Mapudungun]" (MINEDUC. *Estudio y Comprensión de la Sociedad* (Social science), 2001, p. 210).

Indigenous Social and Economic History: Indigenous Epistemologies

In EIB, the importance of indigenous social and economic history and cultural practices is also stressed. Moreover, traditional ways of life should be included in the teaching. The curriculum presents elements of indigenous epistemologies related to life, death, health, and nature as well as traditions, fables, stories, legends, music, and poetry while underlining at the same time that indigenous culture should not be taught like a piece of an artifact in a museum. (MINEDUC, 2005. *Orientaciones para la Contextualización de Planes y Programas para la Educación Intercultural Bilingüe*). According to the curriculum, successful EIB can only come about by close co-operation with families and the community, for example, through cultural events (MINEDUC, 2004, *Lenguaje y Comunicación* ['Language and Communication']).

In social science subjects, the students are to be introduced to the topic of indigenous medicine, preferably by a *machi* since she functions as an indigenous doctor in the Mapuche community.

Indigenous Identity Construction

EIB is concerned with the indigenous child's identity construction. Fundamental concepts here are respect, knowledge, and consideration. Furthermore, characteristics the curriculum hopes to develop in students are generosity, compassion, respect for the human body, cognitive and intellectual development, and the ability to express their own thoughts. Moreover, the importance of the social and spiritual position of the family is underlined as well as the development of a personal and national identity. The importance of acquiring intercultural competence (ICC) by taking part in the society at large as well as reinforcing their identity and cultural background is emphasized.

While students are asked to compare the lives of indigenous communities in the past and the present and also to analyze the consequences for future life in these communities, there is little information about how EIB can be used as a tool to develop and liberate indigenous peoples from domination, discrimination, and poverty.

The importance of many of the EIB objectives discussed above is indisputable for self-recognition and cultural renaissance among the Mapuche. The point is underlined by Patricio Rodolfo Ortiz (2007), who states that:

> Giving recognition to Mapuche indigenous knowledge (*Kimün*), as a legitimate philosophical, political, religious and scientific interpretation of the world, giving it a place among other respected disciplines in the school dialogue, is of great importance for the self-esteem of Mapuche children, who as indigenous youngsters, see the validation of their ancestral backgrounds as something that is respecting and giving consideration to a fundamental part of who they are (p. 206).

The question that begs itself is, however, to what extent indigenous identity construction is possible when the major thrust of the *Macro*

Curricular, the focus at school every day, is assimilationist in nature and consolidates the epistemologically determined objective of the hegemonic epistemology. Even though the intention behind EIB is clearly to provide more relevant knowledges about Mapuche culture, the question asked during the field research was related to whether such a supplementary educational track really is a good tool, not only to preserve, but also to develop Mapuche identity and culture, to foster intercultural understanding, and to improve Mapuche status as ordinary, not second- class, citizens. Or is EIB, as some skeptics claim, solely meant as a tranquilizing pill for those groups who are worried about the potential cultural, linguistic, and epistemological extinction of the Mapuche? One Mapuche teacher in a Catholic school was worried about the future for the Mapuche people: "The future will be difficult, because Intercultural and Bilingual Education has focused only on Mapuches, not on the rest of Chile (2008)".

EIB in the Schools

Interrogating the meaning of indigenous cultures and knowledges in EIB is not only related to how EIB is perceived in policy documents by politicians and by indigenous leaders, but also how EIB is being practiced in school settings. According to the information we got from our field-work in Araucanía, the problems in implementing EIB were multiple; besides lacking language teachers in Mapundugun (according to one representative of Origenes: "Not even many of the facilitators know the indigenous language" (2008)), there were not sufficient facilitators, teaching material was inadequate, funding was insufficient, and there was also often disagreement among the teachers about the role of EIB. Clearly, EIB plays a marginal role in Mapuche students' daily life at school. This does not necessarily mean that EIB is superfluous, since it touches on Mapuche life and culture. What is not easy to gauge, however, is whether its marginality and the small space it occupies in school contributes to underlining the exoticism of Mapuche culture rather than its uniqueness and fundamental characteristics in terms of worldview and epistemologies. Our field-work seems to give multiple answers depending on how well and systematically EIB is run and the multi-cultural climate in the school. Some students expressed pride in their Mapuche heritage and were eager to learn Mapundugun. The EIB learning space enabled some students to reflect on their indigenous background and to appreciate cultural and religious indigenous ceremonies of the community taught by the Kimches (a Mapuche sage). Other students did not want to expose their Mapuche origin in a school context, ashamed as they were of their ethnic background.

If EIB is to function as a radical boost to Mapuche self-recognition and identity construction, the government needs, as Ortiz (2007) states:

To give to IBE programs in the Mapuche context a more serious consideration and a more recognized status as important subject matters,
which addresses important cultural and linguistic issues of a traditional culture and people in need of cultural and linguistic survival.
The state needs to recognize that IBE programs in schools should go
beyond being alternative cultural awareness workshops held as non-
graded school activities, to become serious curriculum based courses,
organized systematically and which count in the academic load of the
students that take them (p. 207).

The responses from the majority of the informants, mainly principals and
the teachers, signaled that it was difficult to envisage how EIB in its current
shape could manage to go beyond the exotic to relate to the dynamism and
change in indigenous knowledges and the cultural diversity between indigenous groups. The importance of this is related to the need to transcend a
static model of past and present and to provide a conceptual framework for
social, cultural, epistemological, and linguistic diversity. There is a need
(which EIB could hardly be expected to fulfill) "to situate cultural heritage
in a historical perspective and to overcome the tendency . . . to treat culture
as a static and bounded phenomenon . . ." (Aikman, 1999, p. 165).

Even though some teachers and students appreciate the EIB program, its
extra-curricular and marginal nature, except in rare cases, does not seem
to give the Mapuche the cultural and epistemological substance needed for
self-recognition and for indigenous identity construction. Moreover, EIB's
exclusive focus on Mapuche schools means that the necessary interaction
with the majority society is precluded. The *Origenes* program (where EIB is
included) is therefore acknowledged among indigenous leaders as a strategy
to reduce conflicts by throwing money at the indigenous communities. As
Patricia Richards states: "Even the program's motto: *Mira el futuro desde to
origin* ('Look towards the future from your origins') seems to encourage the
indigenous to keep their traditions but forget their ancestral claims" (Richards, 2010, p. 70). EIB does not, therefore, provide a third space referred
to in earlier chapters where negotiations between Western and indigenous
knowledge systems can take place or where indigenous knowledges are
excavated from the state of oblivion in a meaningful way. On the contrary,
instead of providing the possibility of generating cultural centered knowledges in the third space, EIB seems in most cases to only cement the dislocation of indigenous knowledges in the Chilean educational discourse.

One representative from the Ministry of Education and leader of the *Origenes* program was quite explicit about the need to integrate indigenous cultures and epistemologies more comprehensively in the *Marco Curricular*:

Marco Curricular has some aspects of indigenous culture, but not
enough. It is necessary to strengthen the indigenous part of the
curriculum to make the students aware of the fact that Chile is a

multicultural country. Many teachers are interested, but resources are not sufficient (2008).

The comments above are interesting for their radical departure from the government's traditional educational policies since Pinochet. While the mono-cultural profile of the *Marco Curricular* had little to offer indigenous groups, the introduction of EIB in the late 1990s was only, as has been noted, a half-hearted boost to indigenous self-recognition, since EIB's supplementary status satisfied only a few and could not remedy past wrongs. Moreover, EIB's lack of a multi-cultural profile meant in reality that the "intercultural" discourse of EIB was mainly assimilationist in its effect.

As a matter of fact, Chile did not adopt multi-culturality and a multi-cultural policy until 2008, when President Bachelet proposed a new social and political agreement with indigenous peoples:

> It is time that we assume us as diverse and that this diversity should have the political representation it is due. I want to see indigenous representation in Congress . . . But let's call things by their name; it has not been easy to leave behind old racist prejudices and the lack of understanding of the indigenous world by some sections of Chilean society (in Grant and Portera, 2011, p. 327).

However, even President Bachelet's embrace of multi-culturalism was clouded in ambiguity and contradictions. While proclaiming recognition of the Mapuche in a multi-cultural nation, the Concertación government simultaneously used anti-terrorist laws against Mapuche activists who wanted territorial and cognitive justice.[9] Having constructed images of the Mapuche as either integrationists or terrorists, the various governments have maintained social control by supporting the integrationists and clamping down with punitive measures on those who did not consent to what the government had to offer. There is therefore a sense that Bachelet's "multi-culturalism" was more symbolic and rhetorical than substantive and had little redistributive and territorial clout. Her adoption of multi-culturalism is "tantamount to recognizing diversity without doing anything about the power inequalities that racial structures entail" (Richards, 2010, p. 65).

The extra-curricular status of EIB in the education system and the marginalization of indigenous issues in *Marco Curricular* seem to be due to the fact that acknowledging epistemologies that transcend or contradict the Western hegemony might have, from a majority point of view, unforeseen political and cultural consequences. The Chilean government's ambiguous attitude towards the indigenous population must be understood within this scenario. Obviously the question of a more balanced *Marco Curricular* in terms of ethnic representation transcends mere educational considerations. What is at stake is an understanding of Chile as a nation and the foundation on which the Chilean state has been based. Strengthening the indigenous part and the epistemological diversity of the *Marco Curricular* would mean a translation of the government's rhetorical multi-culturalism into praxis and invoke political controversy and strife.[10] As Santos (2007) states: "The recognition of epistemological diversity is a highly contested terrain because in it converge not only contradictory epistemological and cultural conceptions but also contradictory political and economic interests" (p. xli).

The battle in the schools is clearly a social struggle about the whole fabric of society. While school is an important contact point in any conflict between the dominant and indigenous cultures and epistemologies, school cannot play the role of a redeemer in a system that promotes inequality. On the contrary, school often perpetuates inequality by sanctioning the cultural capital that is transmitted from one generation to the next. Under a relatively static political and social order (whether the left/center or the right is in power), the education system has up till now been very resistant to change. One of the accusations against the Piñera government is that the contemporary school system in Chile sustains culturally sanctioned beliefs by defending pre-established social, cultural, ethnic, economic, and political privileges.

Therefore, the struggle for epistemic justice cannot only take place on the cultural and educational playing fields; the struggle for epistemic justice takes us to the stronghold of economic and political hegemony, and it is doubtful, due to the intimacy and inextricable link between political and educational discourses, whether a subversion of the education system is possible without political transformation.

A transformation of the education system in Chile is premised on the space entrusted by the political authorities or appropriated (most likely forcefully) by counter-hegemonic forces. Since an educational discourse with a multi-cultural perspective must interrogate asymmetrical power relations as well as identify and acknowledge the existence of various knowledge systems in the Chilean society, there is a sense that such a discourse is too much of a challenge for the very power structure on which the Chilean government is built. This is why the struggle for epistemic justice is not only a struggle for conscientization by those who are marginalized (Freire, 1970); it is a struggle to deconstruct the current power structures in education and the society at large. The hegemonic position of Western knowledge expressed in the *Macro Curricular* reflects the position of the governing elite in all spheres of life and any *proper* inclusion of contesting epistemologies in school or society is, by the elite, viewed as inappropriate and seen as a deviation from Chile's path to modernization and modernity. Despite pressure from the international community, the various governments have been dragging their feet in recognizing epistemic and cultural diversity. Chile lags behind most Latin American countries, as Richards (2010) correctly observes, "in formal recognition of indigenous rights" (pp. 70–71). The repeated failure to include indigenous rights in the Constitution is a telling case in point as is the belated signing of ILO Convention 169. It is too early to tell whether the massive student protests in Chile throughout

2011 (which have also attracted several other segments of the Chilean society, including the Mapuche) will result in a more comprehensive and stable resistance against the hegemonic power structures in the country.

The Mapuche Are Split

When Dei (2006) claims that the "dominated/colonized subject survives despite attempts to deny her existence" (p. 11) it is, in the case of the Mapuche, a subject under siege in the face of colossal economic, political, and cultural forces, both nationally and globally. This is illustrated in the split in the Mapuche community, both on the question of EIB as well as on other issues, a reflection of the division among the Mapuche on the question of identity and re-ethnification. As the first leader of CONADI stated: "There are a lot of political organizations (among the Mapuche). The Mapuche people are politically and culturally divided. The most important thing now is to unite the Mapuche people" (2008).

The divisions make the situation difficult for the Mapuche activists and easier for the reluctant authorities. In a statement from the 1990s the CONADI states:

> The impression remains that the Mapuche communities do not believe that an education that gives value to their language and their culture can change the depression within the Mapuche society. Some parents have said: "the Mapuche language and the culture have no future. They are agonizing. It is already too late . . . a sector of the community even opposes IBE, seeing it as a step backwards, a useless education, since it has no value for interacting within the Winka world [mainstream Chilean society]. It is seen by some as an education, which in the long term, impedes the good acquisition of Spanish language skills, of calculus and science (in Ortiz 2007, p. 13).

To the dismay of Mapuche activists, the ambiguity in Mapuche communities also to-day toward including Mapuche values in the school curriculum (whether in EIB or in *Marco Curricular*) indirectly supports the laissez-faire policy of the government and solidifies a position of epistemic hegemony and assimilationist objectives. It is this ambiguity that Mapuche activists hope to change.

Undoubtedly there are complex socio-political reasons why many Mapuche communities have not supported re-ethnification projects that were proposed by the Mapuche intellectual leadership. While one should be careful not to over-interpret the reason for the skepticism of many Mapuche, it is not too much to suggest that the low estimation that many Mapuche hold of their own language and culture can be traced back to the historical context of colonialism and the very long history of oppression to which the Mapuche people have been subjected. Mapuche leaders attribute this attitude to the very fierce assimilation policy that permeated Chilean education policy for decades, As Wane (2006) states, "Most indigenous peoples who have been subjected to Western education have become a commodity of Western ideology" (p. 98). The situation in Chile is quite similar to the situation in Africa, where illiterate parents defy their own traditions in order to "help" their children succeed in school. Moreover, many in the Mapuche communities themselves question whether the teaching of indigenous knowledges in schools is the right forum, and they query whether Kimches have the appropriate education and background to teach their children at school.

Many Mapuche have read the writing on the wall and perceived that the only way to succeed in the Chilean society is to discard their indigenous identity, take Spanish names, and sweep their ancestral roots under the carpet. Since the Chilean government has only half-heartedly supported the cultural renaissance of the Mapuche and other indigenous groups, the perception among many Mapuche has been that an assimilationist strategy might be professionally and economically more rewarding. The various governments' divide and rule strategy on indigenous issues (embracing and supporting the integrationists and assimilationists and marginalizing the Mapuche who insist on redistributive, territorial, and cognitive justice) has made the terrain difficult for resistance politics.

In terms of schooling, the government policy has therefore meant that many Mapuche want the same education as the majority society in order to succeed in society, believing that the introduction of indigenous cultures and language will impede their children's success in Chilean society. They think that it is only by internalizing the values of the dominant culture that they can eliminate their marginalization, or as Fanon (1967) states, their "jungle status":

> Every people in whose soul an inferiority complex has been created by the death and burial of its cultural originality finds itself face to face . . . with the culture of the (dominant) mother country. The colonized is elevated above his jungle status in proportion to his adoption of the mother country's cultural standards (p. 18).

The construction of a conscious, Mapuche identity has thus been hampered by the majority society and has been facilitated by the contemporary bleak socio-economic situation among the Mapuche. It is a colonization of the minds, which the school system has systematically backed. Freire (1970) states that, "Education as the exercise of domination stimulates the credulity of students, with the ideological intent (often not perceived by educators) of indoctrinating them to adapt to the world of oppression" (p. 78).

7.5   THE MAPUCHE STRUGGLE FOR TERRITORIAL AND COGNITIVE RIGHTS

The Mapuche struggle for territorial and cognitive/epistemic rights must be understood as a struggle to reclaim their indigenous identities in confrontation with the enormous powers of national and international corporations, and most often backed by the Chilean government. Such a struggle is the *sine qua non* in the Mapuche understanding of who they are.

SN Power

The case of Norwegian SN Power development on Mapuche land is of interest here. SN Power is a hydropower development company, operating exclusively in emerging markets. SN Power was planning to build four hydroelectric plants in *Coñaripe* in the southern region of Araucanía, the middle of traditional Mapuche land. When we visited the region in 2008, we were met with great hostility among the Mapuche due to the fact that we were from Norway. Many Mapuche declined to talk to us and posters opposing the project hung along the roads in the area.

Our discussions with the SN Power director in the area and with the Mapuche confirmed a conflict over the right of SN Power to build hydroelectric plants on ancestral lands and make use of Mapuche rivers and streams. Interestingly, the management of SN Power project (in *Coñaripe* called Hidroelectrica Trayenko), insisted that they would not go ahead with their plans until a negotiated settlement with the Mapuche had taken place. As the director of Trayenko, a Chilean, stated: "It is important for us to have a good dialogue with the Mapuche. We hope we can agree with the Mapuche on our plans. We do not think it will affect the Mapuche territory very much" (2008).

In an article I wrote after returning from Chile I said:

> Better than many other foreign companies SN Power has entered a comprehensive dialogue with the Mapuche. In a conversation with the leader of the SN Power project (Trayenko) we were told that Trayenko would not proceed with the building of power plants until they reached a certain degree of agreement with the Mapuche. The problem is, however, that irrespective of the time spent in negotiations with the identity-conscious Mapuche, there is little reason to believe that they will achieve consensus. The reason is that the Mapuche perception of the world is totally different from a Western rationality (Breidlid, 2009).

I also wrote that the dialogue with the Mapuche was a recognition that the world can be viewed through different epistemological lenses, and that the worldview of the Mapuche is worth listening to. The dilemma of SN Power was, however, that it was difficult both to take the Mapuche resistance seriously and at the same time proceed with the building of plants according to the wishes of the hegemonic Chilean society.

Unfortunately, my predictions of a deadlock between the two parties seem to have been confirmed. In the beginning of 2011, Norway's SN

Power sold its 80% stake in Trayenko to its partner Centinela, which owned the rest of Trayenko. The reason for this "reorganization" was clouded in newspeak ("SN Power reorganizes its portfolio"), but there is reason to believe that the negotiations had not reached a successful conclusion. This raises the question of whether another strategy relating to Bhabha's third space might have resolved the deadlock. While differences between the knowledge systems were certainly mobilized, there is reason to believe that it was impossible to agree on a framework for decolonizing the knowledge traditions that hegemonize Western epistemology. There is a sense that the generation of a common framework is almost inconceivable when advanced technological interests with big profit-generating potential are at stake, or at least inconceivable until the clock is past twelve and there is no tomorrow. Admittedly, there is a difference between combating HIV/AIDS in Zambia (Carm, forthcoming 2012) referred to earlier, where collaboration between knowledge systems is fruitful and where the end result is agreed upon, and the Trayenko situation with no such agreement. While the Trayenko project may be sustainable in terms of H_2O emissions, the project is nevertheless part of a long history of the grabbing of Mapuche land by both national and international companies. The resistance against Trayenko and SN Power is therefore a continuation of Mapuche resistance against hegemonic and colonial imposition.

Protests against Hydroelectric Plants in Patagonia

A recent development in Chile is the controversy related to the HidroAysén hydroelectric power project that intended to construct and operate five hydroelectric power plants in the Chilean Patagonia region. The construction of the project will have an impact on "six national parks, eleven national reserves, twenty-six conservation priority sites, sixteen wetland areas and thirty-two privately owned protected conservation areas" (Futurechallenges, 2011). Moreover, six tribal communities of the Mapuche people will be affected. Demonstrations in 2011 against the approval of the project were massive and soon merged with huge student protests all over the country over the costs, profits, and fairness of higher education and gained massive public support. The Mapuche Student Federation (Federación Mapuche de Estudiantes) took active part in the demonstrations. The Chile demonstrations (which spread to different sectors of the Chilean society) clearly represent a profound dissatisfaction with the social and economic consequences of the neo-liberal capitalist policies that Chilean governments have pursued after Salvador Allende. What these demonstrations will mean in the long run is difficult to predict, but they suggest the possibility of a real political transformation of the power structures in Chile. Clearly, the demonstrations in 2011 against the authorities' oppressive policies have widened the counter-hegemonic struggle base of which the Mapuche have long been a part.

Indigenous Medicine and Biopiracy: Another Neo-colonial Imposition

The recovery of indigenous medicine based on indigenous plants referred to in Chapter 3 is a tremendous boost to Mapuche self-recognition and identity since the medicine is used among the majority population and as an alternative or supplement to classical medicine. The downside of this medicinal recovery is, however, that interest in indigenous plants, for both medical and agricultural use, has been aroused not only among Chilean citizens, but among the huge pharmaceutical and agricultural multi-corporations as well. The issue of biopiracy discussed in Chapter 3 is now becoming a concern among indigenous groups in the country. The Senate adopted the International Convention for the Protection of New Plant Varieties (UPOV 91) in 2011. This "Monsanto Law"[11] gives patent rights over new plants to those who have discovered, developed, or modified them (UPOV 91). The Mapuche and environmental organizations are mobilizing against the law and what they term the "legal theft" of the genetic heritage of the indigenous peoples. They warn that the law allows multi-national corporations to appropriate indigenous plants for agricultural and medical purposes and to introduce transgenic crops with their negative impact on biodiversity.[12] The Mapuche are concerned that the law might prevent them from saving seeds, and they will have to purchase expensive genetically engineered seeds as well as medicine from corporations like Monsanto, thus resulting in increased poverty among the indigenous communities. The Mapuche Health Network states that UPOV 91:

> Seriously attacks our rights and ancestral heritage, particularly on our cultural system of health, as well as also our food sovereignty, which has traditionally been the basis of our comprehensive health, holistic and territorial . . . This Convention seriously is against our Mapuche health agents, our practice of healing, our sacred spaces, our *lawen* (medicine), making a "legal theft" to usurp the genetic patrimony that our people has been developed for millennia (Mapuche Health Network, 2011).

The support of UPOV 91 by the conservative Piñera only underlines the systematic oppression and exploitation of indigenous knowledges in the Chilean society. It perpetuates, as Mapuche Health Network (2011) states, our "exclusion and marginalization."

History repeats itself: only when indigenous knowledges can be exploited for profit is it interesting to the North. The fundamental difference from the colonial days is that the contemporary theft, while continuing to appropriate territory (also in Mapuche land), colonizes creation and life itself. The problem here is not only the theft of "genetic patrimony," but also the new ability to read and manipulate the genetic code. While there are different opinions in the Western scientific community about genetically engineered seeds, there is a general concern about the environmental hazards, human health risks, and economic consequences of genetically engineered seeds. For the Mapuche, with their spiritual outlook on life, the issue is less complicated: plants and seeds are not to be manipulated and exploited. The issue is clearly related to the sustainability of the planet and to two colliding worldviews. The concern here is again the asymmetry of the North/South relations, and the North's power to impose its hegemonic view. While the Mapuche are mobilizing against grabbing of land, GE seeds, and GE tree mono-culture on their ancestral territory (Pnyv, 2006), confrontations with the authorities are at times violent, resulting in killings, terrorist charges, and long prison terms.

7.6 CONCLUSION

The Mapuche, like many indigenous and marginalized groups globally, have become vocal opponents of the global architecture of education by exposing "dominant practices that negate the power of spirituality and local indigenousness . . ." (Dei, 2006, p. 15), as well as those aspects of globalization that impose homogeneity on a heterogeneous political and ideological landscape.

From the perspective of the Mapuche, physical and epistemological colonization are two sides of the same coin, and the urgency of reclaiming the future can be seen in the activists' demands for cognitive recognition in a school system, which denies the self-identity of the Mapuche and the idea of reclaiming the Mapuche land.[13]

An important step towards conscientization is to know Mapuche history as well as the colonial history of oppression and subjugation. Since neither the *Marco Curricular* nor the EIB interrogate the colonial onslaught on the Mapuche and other indigenous peoples in a non-exotic and non-hegemonic way, the space in school for an understanding of how the Mapuche have been exposed to territorial and epistemic violence and conquest is, to this day, more or less closed. The exposure of the hidden narratives on nation-building where difference is camouflaged is a prerequisite if resistance consciousness is to extend beyond the handful activists. Moreover, the pretense and rhetoric of multi-culturality in nation-building must be unraveled and interrogated since it, in effect, rejects recognition of people outside the mainstream society who are not towing the line. It only serves the interests of the hegemonic society. The massive demonstrations for educational justice and equality in 2011 (with participation from Mapuche students) may open up an educational space where anti-colonial knowledges are given legitimate space and where indigenous and non-indigenous students alike enter negotiations to establish a common ground of understanding and interest in fighting epistemic and societal injustice. It has repeatedly been noted that the importance of indigenous knowledges in sustainable development should not be underrated and should be given additional weight in times of ecological uncertainty.

The current economic crisis in the West may accelerate a hegemonic decline and affect relations between the hegemonic power structures and indigenous and other marginalized peoples. In other words, marginalized groups like the Mapuche may emerge in a different position following hegemonic decline, bringing comprehensive changes to the core-periphery relationship. However, there is another scenario, even if we accept the analysis of hegemonic decline, where oppression of indigenous peoples may accelerate, as Stephanie Teixeira-Poit and Keri Iyall Smith (2008) suggest: "Although the hegemonic decline of nation-states provides opportunities for indigenous peoples, nation-states may further oppress indigenous peoples if they take advantage of these opportunities" (p. 42).

It is in this uncertain terrain that the Mapuche struggle for sustainable development and for political and epistemic sovereignty and autonomy. Cognitive justice is important for the identity and self-recognition of the Mapuche and other indigenous peoples. The struggle for a more inclusive and epistemologically diverse education system is not, however, only an educational issue; it is part of a larger struggle for indigenous rights and a more sustainable future.

8   Protest and Beyond
A Case for Optimism?

"It may seem impossible to imagine that a technologically advanced society could choose, in essence, to destroy itself, but that is what we are now in the process of doing."

—Elizabeth Kolbert, *Field Notes from a Catastrophe: Man, Nature and Climate Change*, 2006, p. 189

The book has called for *alternative knowledge systems* to supplement Western hegemonic knowledge that drives education systems, cultural expressions and economic thinking down an ideological and epistemological one-way street. There is a need to replace the monological focus on Western knowledge production with what Gregory Bateson calls double or multiple descriptions (Bateson, 1979, p. 142). Such an approach allows for the incorporation of various epistemological discourses, both in the classrooms and in the discussions of a sustainable future.

For students in the South who are marginalized by Western knowledge, it is essential to provide an alternative space that is liberating in terms of history, culture, and epistemological orientation, since curricula and classroom practices that relate to the students' background will maximize learning outcomes and reduce the home-school gap. While it is urgent that education in the 21st century is education for sustainable development, appropriate choices for a sustainable future can only be made on the basis of comprehensive knowledges; therefore, school has a role to play in conscientizing students as well as teachers. Given the global architecture of education, such teaching and learning necessitates the subversion of hegemonic curricula and the conversion of the classroom into a decolonizing space. Bishop's (2007) experiences from the Māori in New Zealand discussed earlier shows how this is possible, but there is no denying that in impoverished education settings like in some of our case countries, this is no simple task; it needs the backing not only of the school leadership, but of the communities around the schools as well of national authorities.

While education for sustainable development needs to reorient its epistemological focus by taking on board alternative epistemologies, it must also navigate a terrain in which the information flow has changed dramatically over the last decade due to advances in information and communications technology (ICT).

Even though there is still a digital divide between the North and the South, people in the South are accessing the Internet and social media much more and in new and creative ways compared to only a few years back. Many students get information from a variety of sources other than school, a fact that makes the role of the school more, not less important. One of the tasks of school in the digital era is to counteract the top-down transmittance of information from the North to the South via ICT, which perpetuates the century-long imposition of Western hegemonic epistemology on the South with a speed that is completely new. The role of the school in such a situation is to provide counter-narratives, and ICT can facilitate such an approach. Like Western knowledge that is often transmitted decontextualized in the textbooks in the South, information from the North via ICT is often alien and out of context, and the school's role is to provide a framework to understand and critically evaluate this information flow. Equally important is the provision of information and knowledges from below (the South), from the bottom up, culturally sensitive, and contextualized. According to Arvind Ranganathan (2004), "A bottom-up approach may provide a more realistic opportunity to capture the ideals of people-centered, need-based sustainable development" (p. 1).

What will be the role of indigenous knowledge production in the future with the invasion of the Internet and the social media? Will ICT homogenize a previously heterogeneous knowledge terrain? The digital revolution eliminates in one sense the difference between place and space as ICT makes it possible to communicate and interact with people who are geographically in another part of the world. What will be the consequences of, for example, Xhosa identity construction and its linkage to place discussed in Chapter 4? Does the suspension of the place-space dichotomy mean a farewell to indigenous knowledges?

There are no simple answers here, but there are a few points to be considered. First, the suspension of place-space is only a virtual, not a geographical suspension. Indigenous communities are, as Ranganathan (2004) states, "largely concerned with local issues that are geographically determined, such as health, agriculture, water, and land management" (p. 6). This probably means that knowledges from similar contexts, most likely geographically close contexts, are of greater interest and utility than contexts far away. Second, experiences from other counter-hegemonic environments seem to suggest that while modern technology is employed to communicate across borders, it does not mean that identities necessarily are watered down. The Mapuche Indians in Chile and the Xhosa in South Africa are cases in point. Nevertheless, indigenous knowledges are and have been in a liminal position that has been accelerated by the ICT revolution. While local knowledges and local identities in certain contexts are being sustained, they are also under siege and are, as stated earlier, subalternized, Orientalized, and Othered. For many indigenous people the strategy is to succumb to the pressure from the hegemonic discourse and to adopt hegemonic identities in order to succeed in society. There is a push-pull situation here where indigenous knowledges are being pushed under the carpet as irrational, useless, and unproductive. At the same time, they are being pulled back by environmentalists who value the conservationist and sustainable profile of indigenous knowledges and by multi-nationals that value the potentiality of indigenous knowledges to maximize profits. There is a fear that the wealth of indigenous knowledges from the South could be transmitted in such a way that it could easily be hijacked by governments and multi-national corporations residing in the North. The discussion of intellectual property rights and patents in earlier chapters has shown how indigenous knowledges have become attractive to commercial Western interests and that online information about these knowledges may be the subject of biopiracy.[1] There is an inherent conflict of interests here. On the one hand, it is vital to spread information about specific types of indigenous knowledges related to, for example, issues of land conservation, farming, and indigenous medicines. On the other hand, it is important for communities in the South to protect their ownership of such knowledges. If not, the same communities may later have to buy products based on these knowledges via patent regimes in the North, examples of which we have discussed in the cases of both South Africa and Chile. Clearly, biopiracy practiced by the big pharmaceutical corporations and governments may threaten indigenous knowledges. What is needed is a system of ownership that prevents monopolies and encourages the sharing and utilization of indigenous knowledges. In the present capitalist global context such an open system is difficult to envisage, but the current economic and ecological crises may open up spaces for an alternative world order and more democratic ownership practices.

One important difference between the knowledge systems discussed in this book is that indigenous epistemologies are not premised on a clear line of demarcation between human beings and nature, and that human beings are not set to dominate and exploit nature. By contrast, hegemonic Western epistemology accompanied by capitalism is human-centered and relates to nature in an exploitative and non-sustainable way. There is, therefore, a need to transcend the dichotomized relationship of man and nature and a need for a "a new social contract which is concerned not only with social justice of the relations between humans, but the relations between humans and the nonhuman world" (Devall, 1990, p. 17). It has already been noted how the different perceptions of the man-nature relationship primarily stems from the indigenous emphasis on the spiritual aspects of existence, and there is a sense that the lacking spiritual dimension of hegemonic Western epistemology is a major stumbling block in any potential rapprochement between the knowledge systems. Western hegemonic knowledge needs to examine critically not only its own epistemological basis, but also critique its projection of indigenous knowledges into the domain of myth, irrationality, and superstition.

The problematic aspects of Western knowledge production is exposed in the present economic crisis in the US and Europe where the only "solution" to the crisis seems to be to stimulate more economic growth irrespective of its fatal consequences for the environment. Against the backdrop of the current economic crisis it was not possible, during the COP 17 conference in Durban, to arrive at an agreement with the US and the emerging industrialized countries India and China, the worst polluters globally. The seriousness of the situation is underlined by the continuing "rises in annual global CO_2 emissions—up six per cent, to 33.51bn tons, in 2010. The levels of greenhouse gases are higher than the worst-case scenario outlined by climate experts just four years ago" (*The Independent*, 2011). Even though the emission of greenhouse gases in Africa is small, the effects of global warming on Africa will be huge. A 2% rise in temperatures will cause a sharp decline in crop yields in tropical areas (5 to 10% in Africa) and will lead to an increase in people affected by hunger and malnutrition.

Likewise global warming in Latin America, besides leading to the melting of the Andean glaciers, the death of portions of the Amazonian rainforests, and rising sea levels, could devastate agricultural production, thus contributing to a global food crisis (Inside Climate News, 2009). While there is no doubt that the exploitation of the earth's resources at an unprecedented level has contributed to the present crisis, with the old and the newly emerging industrial nations as the biggest polluters and culprits, issues related to sustainable development are complex and no "easy" solutions are at hand. There is therefore also a need to critically explore the counter-discursive terrain of indigenous knowledge systems in the future more comprehensively in order to assess their viability as a major vehicle of sustainable development and their proper role in the curriculum and in the classrooms in the global South.

While the potential of indigenous knowledges has been grossly underutilized in the past, the contributions of indigenous knowledge systems in relation to sustainability and sustainable development should not lead to the temptation, as Paulin J. Hountondji (2002) reminds us, "to overvalue our heritage" (p. 25). This is in line with Sillitoe's (1998) warning that "we need to guard against any romantic tendency to idealise it" (p. 227).

Given the current situation globally, I have underlined in the preceding chapters the need for new conversations and questions about knowledges, how they are acquired, and the sources of knowledges. Questions of what kind of knowledges exist in schools are seldom asked and problematized, even though there is common knowledge that the indigenous knowledges of millions of students are dislocated and rubbished. Questions related to the kind of knowledges for combating the ecological crisis seldom transcend the Western knowledge universe and the faith in super-technological "solutions." Therefore, there is a need for a third space which generates new possibilities and even "solutions" by transcending the entrenched positions of knowledge systems and opening up alternative ways of knowledge production. There is, however, a danger of conceiving an encounter in the third space between different knowledge systems "as consisting of two discrete worlds facing each other rather than of social worlds that are part of each other yet constituted differently" (Tucker, 1999, p. 16). Creating a third space means overcoming these antagonisms by generating new possibilities on the basis of interactions between the existing knowledge systems and where there is an attempt to suspend asymmetrical power relations. Such an encounter necessitates not only the creation of decolonizing sites, but modifications and adjustments of previously held positions in order to generate new possibilities. It has therefore been suggested that St. Francis of Assisi's alternative vision of the relationship between man and nature represents a viable Western, non-hegemonic response to indigenous knowledges, which might provide the basis for negotiations in the third space.

There is a sense that ICT and the social media may play a pivotal role in conversations for a sustainable future. While we have seen that the leaders of the most powerful nations of the world have been dragging their feet in terms of implementing crucial measures to avoid the steady increase of greenhouse gases, grassroots movements as well as scholars in the North and the South are getting impatient. Since the expense of telling stories via text, sound, and picture have plummeted over the last years, the Internet and social media are also within reach for the unprivileged and subaltern. During the Arab Spring, Occupy Wall Street, as well as events in Russia, and in Chile, social media mobilized people from all spheres of life to take to the streets. Powerful institutions that firmly hold on to "old" solutions see their power base eroding. In Santiago, a student leader, Camilla Vallejo, needed only "to tweet to marshal thousands of her 320,000 followers to the streets in protest of the steep costs of education" (Manning, 2011), and President Piñera was under siege. The events of 2011 have challenged the hegemonic core in new ways. They may open up for new political, cultural, and epistemic relationships between marginalized people globally and bring comprehensive changes to the core/periphery relationship. With a streak of irony, the new conversations about the planet's future and the challenge to hegemonic epistemology may take place via the social media/Internet—the epitome of Western technology. Such conversations need to address the hubris inherent in the position of Western knowledge without romanticizing and idealizing indigenous knowledges, and it must accept multiple ways of thinking. There is a need to deconstruct Western science's obsession with controlling and exploiting nature. Given the limits to growth, it should instead focus on how mankind can live in harmony with nature and the world we have inherited. It is here that indigenous knowledges can and should play a part in exchanging ideas about sustainable practices without sweeping contradictions within indigenous knowledges under the carpet. Since the world's leaders seem unwilling to educate the public about the potential prospects of an ecological collapse, the role of education in the widest sense of the word is more important than ever. What is needed is a new alternative global architecture of education for sustainable development. Moreover, the problematic nexus between capitalism and the ecological crisis necessitates discussions and more comprehensive research on economically viable alternatives to the present hegemonic economic system before it is too late. The mobilization of a conscientized population[2] (via, for example, social media or the Internet) about the threat to our planet is perhaps the only way to enforce a paradigmatic shift in the power structures that are not willing or able to come to grips with the situation facing our common earth.

Notes

NOTES TO CHAPTER 1

1. As I discuss later in the book, Western epistemology is not as monolithic as is suggested here, but for the purposes of this book it is important to underline the role of a specific Western epistemology in terms of global hegemony.
2. The term South is used here invariably to denote nations that fall below a certain line of GNP, formerly called the developing countries. This qualification notwithstanding, the variations among the nations in the South are huge. The East, as used in Said's *Orientalism* (1979), is encompassed in the notion of South, but countries like India and China, both in the process of becoming the new economic superpowers, are liminal countries in this context. The focus of this book is however on Africa and Latin America, since the case studies are from countries on these two continents. The North is defined as countries previously defined as developed countries. It is more a socio-economic and political division rather than a geographical description. Countries like Australia, New Zealand, and Japan are also defined to belong to the North regardless of their geographical location. However, the terms 'developed' and 'developing' are contentious and there is no established convention for the terms of 'developed' and 'developing' countries in the United Nations.
3. The term 'global architecture of education' should not be confused with "the new architecture of international cooperation: innovative financing and creative multipartite partnerships" which is a mechanism for partnerships in implementing the Education for All goals (UNESCO, 2010).
4. Discourse is here understood as "a whole field of domain within which language is used in a particular way" (Loomba, 1998, p. 38), and is rooted in human practices, institutions, and actions. It is a group of statements belonging to a single system of formation (Foucault, 1995). A hegemonic discourse is a discourse which makes a particular way of interpreting "a whole field of domain" hegemonic.
5. The research was done when Sudan was one country.

NOTES TO CHAPTER 2

1. This statement appeared in a footnote in a revised edition of "Of National Character," not in the original from 1748.
2. Tucker rejects the polarities of tradition and modernity altogether: "These temporal metaphors used to conceptualize otherness and distance in historical time are transposed on to spatial realities and used to designate a

normative development trajectory. Societies that deviate from the European techno-economic standards and designated as 'traditional' or 'primitive' despite the fact that they are contemporaneous with those who label them as such" (1999, p. 8)

3. For example, the world is more globalized financially with the explosion of international and global financial markets and the expansion of multi-national corporations, and may be interpreted as a further expansion of capitalism.

4. At the time of the submission of this manuscript researchers at CERN, the European Organization for Nuclear Research outside Geneva (one of the world's foremost laboratories), wrote about a "startling find that a subatomic particle seemed to move faster than the speed of light has scientists around the world rethinking Albert Einstein and one of the foundations of physics. Now they are planning to put the finding to further high-speed tests to see if a revolutionary shift in explaining the workings of the universe is needed—or if the European scientists made a mistake" (france24.com). In February 2012 the team of researchers acknowledged that they had found problems with the test that might have affected the test results. Further tests will be conducted from May 2012 to find out to what extent these problems affect measured speed.

5. The "Frankfurt School" refers to a group of German academicians (such as Max Horkheimer, T.W. Adorno, Herbert Marcuse, Leo Lowenthal, and Erich Fromm) who worked at the Institut für Sozialforschung in Frankfurt, Germany in the late 1920s and early 1930s. The Frankfurt School developed' critical theory' which criticized economism and materialism, and they were percveived as 'revisionsits' by orthodox Marxists.

NOTES TO CHAPTER 3

1. Appiah refers to Durkheim who " cannot allow that religious beliefs are false, because he thinks that false beliefs could not survive. Since if they are false they would not have survived, it follows that they must be true: and since they are not literally true, they must be symbolically true (p.116)."

2. This does of course not imply that all Western natural scientists are non-religious or completely secular. There are many renowned scientists, Nobel laureates among them, who profess a religious or Christian faith. The point I am trying to make though, is that their religious faith never spills over in their research as natural scientists. In their scientific work, they try to describe, unveil, and discover the laws of nature but never proceed to explain why nature behaves so and so. God is not in the scientific equation. What Christian scientists will claim is that there is obviously a God behind the laws of nature, that there is purpose in the universe, and that there is a personal Creator responsible for the universe. (Collins, 2006; Davies, 1992).

3. There is also another side to this: In cases where land has been "purchased" by big international corporations indigenous peoples sometimes demand royalties from international corporations that are exploiting their land, thus "profiting" from land that otherwise might have been "unutilized."

4. The withdrawal of the case by pharmaceutical corporations against South Africa, and the withdrawal of the US dispute against Brazil in the case of producing affordable medicines.

5. The thoughts and ideas of deep ecologists are reminiscent of St. Francis' view of the man-nature relationship without necessarily agreeing on the spiritual aspects of this relationship (see Næss, 1973).

6. See Botha, 2011, for a more detailed discussion of the cultural-historical activity theory.

7. Reminiscent of the epistemological orientation of St. Francis, inclusive humanism may also be a partner in such a dialogue. Perceived to be humanism with "an inclusive sensibility for our species, planet and lives" (Jones, 2012) inclusive humanism thus extends its focus beyond *homo sapiens* where non-human life and nature (environment) have value independent of mankind.

8. In what is now South Sudan, the Christian elite is governing the country. Many people in the South, however, are believers in indigenous religions.

9. A notable exception to the global educational discourse is to be found in Muslim countries, for example in Sudan, one of the case countries in this book.

10. This lack of recognition is not something that only relates to minority or oppressed groups—everybody is dependent on recognition in terms of identity formation, a point to bear in mind when discussing minority politics. Our identity construction is always shaped through a dialogue with others, and if the significant others, like the role models in the textbooks, are alien to the student's home environment, it does something to their self-esteem and image of themselves, as well as being detrimental to the learning process.

11. According to a report published by the Organisation for Economic Co-operation and Development (OECD), "income inequality in South Africa increased between 1993 and 2008, making inequality levels in the country among the highest in the world" (OECD, 2010). While data for the new nation South Sudan is uncertain, it is ranked among the poorest countries in Africa. In particular, the gap between rural and urban areas is huge. Chile is one of the richest countries in Latin America (per capita GDP), but the gap between rich and poor is one of the widest in Latin America. Chile ranks as the world's sixteenth most-unequal country, along with El Salvador and Panama (Peoples Assemblies Network, 2011). Cuba is poor, but is one of the most sustainable countries on earth (WWF, 2006; see also Chapter 6).

12. UNESCO is also responsible for the *Local and Indigenous Knowledge Systems* (LINKS) project (2002). On their website UNESCO argues for the importance of LINKS: "The environmental knowledge of local and indigenous peoples is now widely recognised as an essential building block for sustainable development and the conservation of biological and cultural diversity . . . The LINKS project acknowledges the crucial role that the environmental knowledge of local people must play in the thrust for sustainable development" (UNESCO, 2003). Moreover, LINKS has an on-line discussion forum whose ultimate goal is to help reinforce indigenous knowledges in the global climate change debate.

13. An independent internal review of the World Bank's sustainability impacts between 1990 and 2007 "found that the bank's private-sector funding arm, the International Finance Corporation, was still promoting the expansion of livestock herds, soybean fields and palm oil plantations—all which accelerated deforestation in the tropics, hastening the pace of climate change . . ." (Business Ethics, 2011).

14. The Norwegian government set up the Norwegian Education Trust Fund (NETF) in January 1998 after a World Bank initiative to assist Sub-Saharan African countries to prioritize basic education and to increase the efficiency of the World Bank. (Avenstrup et al, 2003, p. 11).

NOTES TO CHAPTER 4

1. Qualitative data collection techniques were used in analyzing the Xhosa world views and epistemologies. Community leaders, teachers, parents, and students in the communities in Cape Town and Eastern Cape were

interviewed on the basis of interview guides with open-ended and semi-structured questions. The interviews were conducted in English as well as in Xhosa. A Xhosa research assistant translated the Xhosa interviews into English and the interviews were audio-taped and transcribed. Observations in the classrooms at both sites were also conducted. The coding of the data was employed in the analysis of the various types of data. The research was funded by the Norwegian Research Council and the lead researchers were David Stephens and the author. Both indigenous and Norwegian field-workers were used to collect data in 2001 and 2002.

Subsequent to the original fieldwork I have visited South Africa several times (most recently in 2010) and been in constant dialogue with South Africans from a variety of backgrounds on the themes raised by my research. These interactions indicate that the research findings in this chapter to a large extent resonate with current Xhosa world views and experiences of knowledge production, despite the dynamic nature of these communities and the changes taking place within the broader contexts.

2. There are approximately eight million Xhosa people in South Africa. The Xhosa language is closely related the Zulu language. Xhosa history is one of oppression and subjugation. The Xhosa were denied South African citizenship and the apartheid regime attempted to confine them to "homelands" before 1994.

3. After having visited Langa several times since the original research took place (last time in 2010), I have observed that socio-economic changes have taken place, but not as quickly as the residents had hoped after the ANC came to power.

4. While changes in Xhosa religion have taken place (and is still taking place) after the advent of Christianity the indigenous religion was not in a state of stasis before the coming of the Christian religion. Clearly, as Appiah states, "African historians can trace changes in religious and other beliefs in many places long before the advent of Christian missionaries and colonial educators" (Appiah, 1992, 126).

5. The use of mobile phones and the Internet may in the long contribute to even more porous boundaries and weaken the place-rootedness of Xhosa identity construction. It would, however, be premature to project a dramatic change since, as already noted, even in modernity people "continue to construct some sort of boundaries around their places" (Escobar, 2001, p. 47).

6. A revised version came out in 2002 for implementation in January 2004, The Revised National Curriculum Statement for GET (the General Education and Training band (up to Grade 9).

7. The problematic point with Foucault's concept of power and knowledge is its pervasiveness, which means that the imposition of power seems unavoidable and that there is nothing outside of power. This pervasiveness is due to the transformation of power to knowledge, which is being transmitted in the net-like fashion mentioned above, meaning that Foucault's theory seems to leave no room for opposition or resistance from the outside (not very dissimilar to Althussser's focus on dominant ideology). By picking up the issue of subaltern resistance, which he neglected in *Orientalism*, Said critiques, in a fundamental way, Foucault's concepts of power and knowledge. Said insists that there is no system of domination that is so all-pervasive that there are no spaces outside its control. Said leans on Gramsci's theorizing of hegemony to underline that ideology in general works to maintain social cohesion and dominant interests, but that there are also particular ideologies that express the protest of those being exploited (Said, 1984, p. 246).

8. The lack of coordination may be due to the fact that the IK Policy Paper was issued by the Department of Science and Technology whereas the Revised National Curriculum Statement was published by the Department of Education and that the two documents appeared in different years (2002 and 2004). It is also noteworthy that the DoE Task Team referred to earlier never discusses indigenous knowledges in their report.

NOTES TO CHAPTER 5

1. 'Islamism' is a somewhat contentious term, and some experts favor the terms 'political Islam' or 'militant Islam' instead. 'Islamism' in this book is used to denote a belief system, which holds that Islam is not only a religion but a political system. It is characterized by moral conservativism and argues for the enforcement of Sharia (Islamic law) as well as Islamic values throughout society. Islamism is described in some more detail in this chapter.

2. In this note, I describe the research process in more detail than in the other chapters because of the long research period and also because of the challenges to do research in a conflict situation are multiple. This chapter is based on fieldwork done during the civil war in Yei River County, Eastern Equatoria, Southern Sudan in 2002, 2003, and 2004. It is also based on field-work done in camps for displaced Southern Sudanese people in Uganda, and in and around the IDP camps in Khartoum and in Khartoum City, where the Ministries were located in 2002 and 2003 (three months every year). The field-work during the civil war in the South was conducted by two well-trained Sudanese field-workers, three Norwegian research assistants, and me. In the North, one Sudanese field-worker and two Norwegian research assistants helped out. As a member of the Joint Assessment Mission (JAM), I collected data on my own for the JAM report in 2004. Data was also collected during 2006–2011 (after the CPA was signed and also after the referendum), but the data collection process was not as comprehensive as that which was done prior to the CPA, and it was undertaken by the author without the help of the research team. Conducting field-work in the so-called liberated areas of the then Southern Sudan areas controlled by the Sudanese People's Liberation Army (SPLA) was challenging, and our plans also had to be dramatically changed due to the volatile situation. Originally, the field-work in the refugee camps in Uganda was not part of our plan but came about as we were suddenly evacuated from Yei in Southern Sudan due to military events as a result of the civil war. On a positive note, research permits and access to important informants were quickly obtained. The challenges in the South were almost exclusively linked to the war situation. Doing research in and around Khartoum was challenging in a different way. Data and information from official sources in Khartoum were on the whole difficult to obtain, and the ideological jargon was hard to penetrate despite my long history with the country and despite the extensive use of Sudanese field-workers.

   The research team collected data from more than 100 informants in the North and from the South during the Civil War. Informants were picked using a purposive sampling approach to collect data from people of different ethnic groups and involved in different roles. In the South, Bari, Kakwa, and Dinka informants residing in Yei were interviewed. In the North, Southern migrants from these tribes and the members of the Lotuka tribe were interviewed, as were Muslim teachers and Muslim leaders in the NCP. Researchers also requested meetings to conduct interviews with officials in order to gain additional information about the research topic. Interviews were conducted in English or in one of the indigenous languages. Local translators were then being used. We conducted *formal interviews* with individuals oriented by interview guides containing open-ended and semi-structured questions and using an approach that emphasized "openness and flexibility" and "on-the-spot" confirmation or disconfirmation of the interviewer's understanding or interpretation of what an interviewee stated (Kvale, 1996, pp. 84, 189). All formal interviews were audio taped and transcribed. In addition, the research team also conducted *informal interviews* as well as observations in the class-rooms. The data was coded according to a set of categories and we employed these codes in our analyses of various types of data.

   Doing Research after the CPA. I also undertook shorter visits to Sudan after the CPA: Khartoum in 2006, 2008, and 2009; Juba (Southern Sudan) in 2007, 2009, and 2011; and Malakal (Southern Sudan) in 2006 and 2008. Each of these visits lasted from one week to one month. Because I was the coordinator of an extensive academic program involving both Southern and Northern universities from 2007 (still on-going), I was able to arrange meet-ings and interview a variety of actors like ministers from the Government of National Unity in Khartoum, the deputy SPLM leader (a Northern Sudanese) in Northern Sudan, and the deputy speaker of the general assembly in Khar-toum (a Southern Sudanese), as well as obtain informal interviews with vice-chancellors and staff members from three different Northern universities, all of North Sudanese origin. In the South, I conducted informal interviews with the Minister of Education, Science and Technology in the Government in Southern Sudan. Informants were from various ministries in Juba, South-ern Sudan; they included one vice chancellor and staff members from South-ern universities (all Southern Sudanese). Additionally, I interviewed different people not linked to the political hierarchy in Khartoum, Juba, and Malakal. For a more comprehensive discussion of the research, see Breidlid, 2010.

3. Around a third of the humanitarian funds tracked within the United Nations (UN) humanitarian work-plan (consolidated appeal) are channeled to South Sudan each year (Global Humanitarian Assistance, 2011). According to Save the Children (2011) the funding outlook for the new country is, however, somewhat unclear. The global economic meltdown may mean a decrease of aid to the country, and there is a sense that the funding situation may remain even more unclear if the government goes ahead with its plans to channel large portions of aid to the construction of a new capital.

4. See Save the Children's "Agenda for Action in a Post-independent South Sudan" (Save the Children, 2011) and UNESCO's "Building a Better Future: Education for an Independent South Sudan" (UNESCO, 2011b). Since the education situation in South Sudan is very fragile, it is natural that the inter-national donors focus on access and equity aspects of education. It is, how-ever, striking that not even UNESCO, often perceived to be one of most progressive UN organizations, refers to indigenous, local, or traditional knowledge in its policy paper on South Sudan.

5. Deng is right when claiming "the government has no environmental laws, policies and regulations that would put pressure on oil companies to observe compliance with environmental sustainability principles" (Deng, 2009). This lack of compliance poses great threats to the environment in South Sudan.

NOTES TO CHAPTER 6

1. The chapter is based on field data gathered during a research visit to Cuba in 2005 and from literature in the field. Conducting field-work in Cuba is not without problems, and in many ways more difficult than field-work that I have conducted in African countries like South Africa and Sudan. The reason for this

is the tight ideological control that the Cuban government wants to keep over its visiting researchers. The institute we were attached to, *Instituto Pedagógico Latinoamericano y Caribeño* in Havana, gave us, besides all the necessary policy documents on education used in our documentary analysis, a list of schools in which we could do research and visit. To a certain extent, this restricted our movements and the variety of schools examined, but we also managed to visit schools not planned for in advance. The impressions from those schools did not, however, deviate much from the schools visited in the official program. In-depth interviews were conducted among a nucleus of key informants and stakeholders (students, teachers, professors, government officials, and informed citizens). The interviews were primarily conducted in Spanish, but in rare cases (with university professors) English was used. Besides interviews (formal and informal), participant observation was employed in the schools as a complimentary method (providing triangulation). One problem recurred during the formal interviews: the informants were mainly quite loyal to the official education policy, and were careful about criticizing the government. To interpret 'between the lines' became a challenging task. Moreover, teachers who we identified on our own (and outside the official program) often did not turn up for the interview. We learned that many of them were worried about the consequences of participating in interviews with foreign researchers. Fortunately, it was possible to identify well-informed citizens who were critical of the political system, including the education system, and who were very outspoken. In addition, many informal interviews with taxi drivers with a teacher background were conducted. They had left the school for greener pastures and were not afraid to voice their often very critical opinions. During a brief visit in early 2012 we were given the opportunity to discuss the current political situation with both party members and dissidents.

2. Rolland G. Paulston, for one, refers to Cuba's epistemological revolution by contrasting Cuba's use of scientific method with "the general Latin American preference for more traditional, fatalistic, and mystical ways of knowing" (Paulston, 1973, p. 168).

3. The Elián González affair was a boost to the Castro regime in the sense that Elián, after having lost his mother, who drowned attempting to flee from Cuba, was returned by the US courts to his father in Cuba despite the resistance of Elián's relatives in the exiled Cuban community in Florida.

4. Lenin claimed the opposite. "Further, to be 'materialist' in a philosophical sense means that consciousness or ideas spring from and are a reflection of our interaction with an actually existing material world, and not vice versa—that is, the material world emerging from consciousness alone" (Lenin, 1927).

5. However, the policy of ecological agriculture is not without its adversaries in the Cuban government, and there are government programmes—with the pronounced aim of securing food security and reducing food imports—which focus on monoculture methods depending "on synthetic chemical inputs, large scale machinery, and irrigation—despite proven energy inefficiency and technological fragility" (Altieri and Funes-Mpnzote (2012).

6. During our most recent visit to Cuba (2012) it was reported that underground, illegal private schools had mushroomed in Havana recently, primarily due to the decreasing quality in the public schools.

NOTES TO CHAPTER 7

1. Like other indigenous or non-European groups in the South, the Mapuche were also Othered, Orientalized and described as irrational, barbarous, and

uncivilized. A prominent newspaper wrote in 1859 that "nature had spent everything on the development of [the Mapuche's] body, while his intelligence has remained at the level of scavenging animals and that [the Mapuche] are nothing more than a wild horde, whom it is urgent to chain or destroy in the interest of humanity and for the good of society" (in Pinto, 2003).

2. The chapter is based on field-work in the Araucanía region in 2008 and on literature in the field. The data was primarily collected through formal interviews based on interview guides containing open-ended and semi-structured questions.The informants were: students, teachers, and headmasters in Mapuche and public schools; a former Mapuche leader of the CONADI; several Mapuche leaders with a variety of political affiliations; a leader of the *Origenes* program and other government officials; the dean of education at Universidad Católica in Santiago as well as professors at the Villarica branch of Universidad Católica; professors at Universidad Católica de Temuco; the director of the Institute of Aboriginal Studies of the Universidad de la Frontera, Temuco; a prominent human rights lawyer; and a director of a hydro-electric plant on Mapuche territory. In addition, several informal interviews were conducted. The data was coded according to a set of thematic areas and we employed these codes in our analyses of the different types of data relevant to our research focus. The interviews were conducted in Spanish.

3. In 1992 those 14 years or older were asked: "If you are a Chilean, do you consider yourself belonging to one of the following cultures: Mapuche, Aymara, Rapa Nui, or none of the previous?" The 2002 census asked, "Do you belong to some of the following or indigenous peoples: Alacalufe (Kawashar), Atacameño, Aymara, Colla, Mapuche, Quechua, Rapa Nui, Yāmana (Yagán), or none of the previous?" One problematic aspect here is the fact that in the 1992 census the implication was that you are Chilean, and in addition you might belong to an ethnic group, whereas the 2002 census did not query about national identity before the question of ethnic identity was asked. Since the stigmatization of the indigenous peoples has been rampant in Chilean society, many indigenous individuals might have been reluctant to expose their indigenous identity if their Chilean indigenous identity was not taken for granted (*Instituto National de Estadísticas*, 1993, 2003). Note that the same tendency of "blanqueamiento" (whitening) was also seen in the different Cuban censuses in the previous chapter.

4. Law 19.253 for the Protection, Promotion and Development of Indigenous peoples. The law is a modified version of the original draft and the linguistic and cultural rights have been toned down.

5. The Indigenous and Tribal Peoples Convention (see ILO, 1989)

6. En su artículo 1°: "El Estado reconoce que los indígenas de Chile son los descendientes de las agrupaciones humanas que existen en el territorio nacional desde tiempos precolombinos, que conservan manifestaciones étnicas y culturales propias, siendo para ellos la tierra el fundamento principal de su existencia y cultura." A su vez, el Estado de Chile asume el deber de respetar, proteger y apoyar el desarrollo de las personas y comunidades indígenas (Ley Indígena 1993). English translation: "The state recognizes that Chile's indigenous peoples are the descendants of the human groups which have existed on the national territory since pre-Colombian times and which conserve their own ethnic and cultural manifestations, the land being for them the principal foundation of their existence and their culture." At the same time the Chilean state is committed to respect, protect and support the development of individuals and the indigenous communities (Indigenous Law, 1993).

7. Mapuche resistance against the exploitation of Mapuche lands has been met with severe repression from various governments. The anti-terrorism law

dates back to the Pinochet dictatorship (1973–1990). The law was reintroduced during the presidency of Ricardo Lagos when Mapuche groups carried out attacks on property and lands originally belonging to the Mapuche. According to Human Rights Watch (HRW), the anti-terrorism law is the "harshest" of all Chilean statutes (Latin America Press, 2008). Also during the regime of Verónica Michelle Bachelet (2006–2010) the anti-terrorist law was employed, leading to hunger strikes by some of the activists, among them the former professor of theology Patricia Troncoso. She ended the longest hunger strike in Chilean history after 111 days as a response to certain concessions granted by the Chilean government. During the regimes of Bachelet and Miguel Juan Sebastián Piñera (2010–), there have been violent clashes between the authorities and militant Mapuche.

8. It is also in fact doubtful if EIB can be termed intercultural if intercultural is interpreted as an "interactive process of mutual influence among bearers of cultural and especially linguistic difference" (Postero, 2007, p. 13) since EIB is offered in Mapuche schools only.

9. The resort to arms by some Mapuche activists is reminiscent of Fanon's call for violence to purge oneself of self-depreciating self-images. Instead of more comprehensively addressing the grievances of the Mapuche, the government responded by resorting to state violence. Both policy brutality and human rights abuses have been verified (Richards, 2010).

10. Referring to Chile as a neo-liberal multi-cultural nation, Patricia Richards defines Chile's version of neo-liberal multi-culturalism as "the indigenous policies and accompanying discourses that have been expanding since the return to democracy" (Richards, 2010, p. 67). Undoubtedly, Chile has for long adhered to the principles of neo-liberalism, but as I have tried to argue in this chapter, the various Chilean governments have, at best, pursued an ambiguous multicultural policy, which has not addressed the grievances of the indigenous minorities in a comprehensive way. There is therefore a need to distinguish between Chile as a multi-cultural society (multiple cultures living within the borders of the Chilean state) and a policy of multi-culturalism, which means "recognition and respect of numerous cultures" (Postero, 2007, p. 13). It is to the latter point that the Chilean state has a long way to go (see also Haughney, 2006).

11. The Monsanto Company is a US-based multi-national biotechnological and agricultural corporation. It is the world's leading producer of herbicides (weedkillers) as well as genetically engineered (GE) seed. The assumption is that UPOV 91 serves the interest of the Monsanto Company.

12. In a North/South perspective, it is interesting to note that Norway has turned down UPOV 91 in order to uphold the rights of the farmers.

13. Interestingly, the Mapuche claims are not without their supporters in the mainstream Chilean society. In a poll by the Instituto de Estudios Politicos, Encuesta (IDEP) in June 2003, Mapuche claims were mainly endorsed by people living outside the Araucanía region (IDEP, 2003). Other polls indicate a more negative attitude toward the Mapuche, particularly toward the militant activists.

NOTES TO CHAPTER 8

1. Google has been accused of being the biggest threat to biopiracy for its alleged plan to establish an online database of genetic information (ZDNet 2006).

2. Interestingly *Time*'s Person of the Year 2011 is the Protester.

Bibliography

Abdi, A. A. (2006). Culture of education, social development, and globalization: Historical and current analyses of Africa. In A. A. Abdi, K. P. Puplampu, & G. J. S. Dei (Eds.). *African Education and Globalization: Critical Perspectives.* Lanham, MD: Lexington Books, 13–30.

Abdullah, A. R. S. (1982). *Educational Theory: A Qur'anic Outlook.* Makkah, Saudi Arabia: Umm Al Quara University.

African Young Scientists and Youth Initiative on Climate Change and Indigenous Knowledge Systems (AYSICCIKS). (2011). Retrieved from http://mbarara. academia. edu/anke/Papers/1228709/COP17_IKS_Communique_AYSICCIKS on December 15, 2011.

Africa Progress Panel. (2011). *The Transformative Power of Partnerships. Africa Progress Report 2011. Geneva, Africa Progress Panel.* Retrieved from http://www.africaprogresspanel.org/files/7713/0441/3939/APP_APR2011_FINAL.pdf on January 5, 2012.

Afrocubaweb. (2009). Cuba's 2002 Census. Retrieved from http://afrocubaweb.com/census2002.htm on November 5, 2011.

Agence France-Presse April 5, 1998. Retrieved from http://www.vitrade.com/sudan_-risk/terrorism/980405b.htm, on November 5, 2003.

Agrawal, A. (1995). Dismantling the divide between indigenous and scientific knowledge. *Development and Change,* 26(39), 413–439.

Agrawal, A. (2005). Indigenous knowledge and the politics of classification. In N. Stehr and R. Grundmann (Eds.). *Knowledge: Critical concepts,* Vol. 2. London: Routledge, 370–384.

Ahmad, A. (1992). *In Theory: Classes, Nations, Literatures.* London: Verso.

Aikman, S. (1999). *Intercultural Education and Literacy.* Amsterdam, Philadelphia: John Benjamins.

Akinnaso, F. N. (1993). Policy and Experiment in Mother-Tongue Literacy. *Nigeria International Review of Education,* 39, 255–285.

Al-Bashir, M. (2004). Basic education: The concept, its characteristics and aims. *Educational Studies Journal of the National Council Curricula and Educational Research,* 5(7) (June), 43–57 [in Arabic].

Alexander, N. (2000). *English Unassailable but Unattainable: The Dilemma of Language Policy in South African Education.* Cape Town: PRAESA.

Alexandre, P. (1972). *An Introduction to Languages and Language in Africa.* London: Heinemann.

Alidou, H., Diallo, Y. S., Heugh, K., Wolff, H. E., Brock-Utne, B., Boly, A. (Eds). (2006). *Optimizing Learning and Education in Africa—the Language Factor: A Stock-taking Research on Mother Tongue and Bilingual Education in Sub-Saharan Africa.* Paris: Association for the Development of Education in Africa (ADEA).

Allen, T. (1994). Ethnicity and tribalism on the Sudan-Uganda border. In F. Fukui & J. Markakis (Eds.). *Ethnicity & Conflict in the Horn of Africa*. London: James Curry and Ohio University Press, 112–139.

Althusser, L. (1969). *Essays in Self-Criticism*. London: NLB.

Altieri, M.A. and Funes-Monzote, F.R. (2012). The Paradox of Cuba Agriculture. Monthly Review, 63(8). Retrieved from http://monthlyreview.org/2012/01/01/the-paradox-of-cuban-agriculturehttp://monthlyreview.org/2012/01/01/the-paradox-of-cuban-agriculture on April 29, 2012.

Alvarado, B. M. (2010). Communalidad and the education of indigenous peoples. In L. Meyer & B. M. Alvarado (Eds.). *New World of Indgenous Resistance*. San Francisco: City Lights Books, 367–383.

Alvares, C. (1992). Science. In W. Sachs (Ed.). *The Development Dictionary: A Guide to Knowledge as Power*. London: Zed Books.

Amadiume, I. (1997). *Reinventing Africa: Matriarchy, Religion, and Culture*. London: Zed Books.

Appel, R., & Muysken, P. (1987). *Language Contact and Bilingualism*. London: Edward Arnold.

Appiah, K. A. (1992). *In My Father's House: Africa in the Philosophy of Culture*. London: Methuen.

Apple, M. W. (1993). The Politics of Official Knowledge: Does a National Curriculum Make Sense? *Teachers College Record 95*(2) (Winter), 222–241.

Apple, M. W. (1997). Consuming the Other: Whiteness, education, and cheap French fries. In M. Fine, L. Weis, L. C. Powell, & M. Wong (Eds.). *Off White: Readings on Race, Power, and Society*. New York: Routledge, 121–128.

Arneil, B. (1996). *John Locke and America: The Defence of English Colonialism*. New York: Clarendon Press of Oxford University Press.

Arnot, M., & Fennell, S. (2008). (Re)visiting education and development agendas: Contemporary gender research. In S. Fennel & M. Arnot (Eds.). *Gender Education and Equality in a Global Context*. London and New York: Routledge, 1–16.

Arnove, R., & Torres, C. A. (Eds.). (2007). *Comparative Education: The Dialectic of the Global and the Local*. Lanham, MD: Rowman & Littlefield.

Association for the Development of Education in Africa (ADEA). (2006). Biennial Meeting, ADEA, GTZ, UNESCO, Gabon.

Avenstrup, R., with Nottelman, A., Ojanperä, S., Uusihakala, J., Kalyalya, J., Nkata, J., and Sidibe, H. (2003). *Evaluation of the Norwegian Education Trust Fund for Africa in the World Bank*. Oslo: Det norske Utenriksdepartement.

Avery, D. T. (2009, April 2). "Cubans Starve on Diet of Lies." Retrieved from http://cgfi.org. on March 26, 2012.

Avia, M. A. A., & Guevara-Stone, L. (2010). *Renewable Education: Key for Sustainable Development. Cuban Experience*. SOLAR 2010 Conference Proceedings. American Solar Energy Society. Retrieved from http://www.ases.org/papers/189.pdf on January 18, 2012.

Bakan, J. (2004). *The Corporation*. London: Constable.

Bammer, A. (1994). *Displacements: Cultural Identities in Question*. Bloomington and Indianapolis: Indiana University Press..

Barker, I. (2000). Disenchanted rights: The persistence of secularism and geopolitical inequalities in articulations of women's rights. *Critical Sense 103*, 103–134.

Bateson, G. (1979). *Mind in Nature: A Necessary Unity*. New York: E. P. Dutton.

Battiste, M., & Barman, J. (1995). *First Nation Education in Canada: The Circle Unfolds*. Vancouver: University of British Columbia Press.

Battiste, M., & Youngblood Henderson, J. (2000). *Protecting Indigenous Knowledge and Heritage*. Saskatoon, Canada: Purich Publishing.

Bauman, Z. (1989). *Modernity and the Holocaust*. Ithaca, NY: Cornell University Press.

Beattie, J. (1999). *Other Cultures: Aims, Methods, and Achievements in Social Anthropology*. London: Routledge. (Original publication 1964).

Beckford, L. S. (1986). *La formación del hombre nuevo en Cuba* (The creation of the new man in Cuba). Havana: Editorial de Ciencias Sociales.

Bengoa, J. (1985). *La historia del pueblo mapuche*. Santiago: Editorial Interamericana Ltda.

Berger, P. L., & Luckmann, T. (1966). *The Social Construction of Reality: A Treatise in the Sociology of Knowledge*. London: Penguin.

Berger, P. L. (1999). The desecularization of the world: A global overview. In P. L. Berger (Ed.). *The Desecularization of the World: Resurgent Religion and World Politics*. Grand Rapids, MI: Wm. B. Eerdmans, 1–18.

Berkes, F., Colding J., & Folke, C. (2000). Rediscovery of traditional ecological knowledge as adaptive management. *Ecological Applications*, 10(5), 1251–1262.

Bernstein, B. (1971). On the classification and framing of educational knowledge. In M. F. D. Young (Ed.). *Knowledge and Control: New Directions for the Sociology of Education*. London: Collier-Macmillan, 47–69.

Bernstein, B. (1990). *Class, Codes, and Control*. Volume 4: *The Structuring of Pedagogic Discourse*. London: Routledge.

Bhabha, H. K. (1990). Interview with Homi Bhabha. In J. Rutherford (Ed.). *Identity, Community, Culture, Difference*. London: Lawrence and Wishart, 207–221.

Bhabha, H. K. (1994). *The Location of Culture*. London: Routledge.

Bhabha, H. K. (1996). Cultures in between: Questions of cultural identity. In S. Hall & P. Du Gay (Eds.). *Questions of Cultural Identity*. London: Sage, 1–17.

Bhola, H. S. (2003). Reclaiming old heritage for proclaiming future history. *Africa Today*, 49(3), 3–21.

Bishop, R. (2007). Te Kotahitanga: Kaupapa Māori in Mainstream Classrooms. In N. K. M. Denzin, Y. S. Lincoln, & L. T. Smith (Eds.). *Handbook of Critical and Indigenous Methodologies*. Los Angeles, London, New Delhi, Singapore: Sage, 439–458.

Boddy-Evans, A. (2011). *Apartheid Legislation in South Africa*. Retrieved from http://africanhistory.about.com/library/bl/blsalaws.htm on January 23, 2012.

Botha, L. (2011). *Incorporating Indigenous Knowledges into Our Knowledge Making: Experiences from a South African Context*. (PhD thesis). Oslo: Oslo University College.

Bourdieu, P., & Passeron, J. (1990). *Reproduction in Education, Society, and Culture* (Theory, Culture and Society Series). Thousand Oaks, CA: Sage.

Breidlid, A. (2002). *Resistance and Consciousness in Kenya and South Africa*. Frankfurt am Main, Berlin, New York, and Oxford: Peter Lang.

Breidlid, A. (2003). Ideology, cultural values and education: A critical analysis of Curriculum 2005 in South Africa. *Perspectives in Education*, 2, 83–103.

Breidlid, A. (2005a). Sudanese migrants in the Khartoum area: fighting for educational space. *International Journal of Educational Development*, 25, 253–268.

Breidlid, A. (2005b). Education in the Sudan: The privileging of an Islamic discourse. *Compare*, 35(3), 247–263.

Breidlid, A. (2009). Norsk navigering i ulendt terreng. [Norwegian navigation in troubled waters.] *Dagbladet*, July 23.

Breidlid, A. (2010). Sudanese images of the Other: Education and conflict in Sudan. *Comparative Education Review*, 54(4), 555–579.

Breidlid, A., Breidlid, A. K., & Androga, A. S. (Eds.). (2010). *A Concise History of South Sudan*. Kampala: Fountain Publishers.

Breidlid, A. & Breidlid, H. (forthcoming 2012). Women in South Sudan: Education, empowerment and identity construction. In H. B. Holmarsdottir, V. Nomlomo, A. I. Farag, & Z. Desai (Eds.). *Gendered Voices: Reflections on Gender and Education in South Africa and Sudan*. Rotterdam: Sense Publishers.

Briggs, J. (2005). The use of indigenous knowledge in development: Problems and challenges. *Progress in Development Studies, 5*(2), 99–114.

Brock-Utne, B. (2000). *Whose Education For All? The Recolonization of the African Mind*. New York and London: Falmer.

Brophy, M. (2003). *Progress to Universal Primary Education in Southern Sudan: A Short Country Case*. Paris: UNESCO.

Brunner, J. J., & Cox, C. (1995). Dinámicas de transformación en el sistema educacional de Chile. In J. M. Puryear & J. J. Brunner, (Eds.). *Educación, Equidad y Competitividad Económica*, Vol. II. Washington, DC: Organization of American States, 101–152.

Buchert, L. (1994). *Education in the Development of Tanzania, 1919–90*. London, Dar es Salaam, Mkuki na Nyota, and Athens: James Curry and Ohio University Press.

Business Ethics. (2011). World Bank Confronts Sustainability Criticism. Retrieved from http://business-ethics. com/2011/03/19/1900-world-bank-confronts-sustainability-criticism/ on October 3, 2011.

Bush, K. & Saltarelli, D. (2000). *The Two Faces of Education in Ethnic Conflict: Towards a Peacebuilding Education for Children*. Florence: UNICEF Innocenti Research Centre.

Caballero, J de la L. (2001). *Pastoral Synod of the Episcopal Church of Cuba*. Retrieved from http://www.anglicancommunion.org/acns/news.cfm/2001/1/17/ ACNS2346 on October 6, 2009.

Calbucura, J., & Le Bonniec, F. (2009). Territorio y territorialidad en contexto post-colonial. *Ñuke Mapuföralget Working Papers No. 30*. Chile.

Cape Argus. (2009). South Africa's Education Crisis. Retrieved from http://www. christianaction.org.za/articles/South%20Africas%20Education%20Crisis%20 and%20the%20Biblical%20Solution.htm on March 12, 2011.

Capra, F. (2000). *The Tao of Physics*. 4th ed. Boston: Shambala.

Carm, E. (forthcoming 2012). The role of local leaders in cultural transformation and development. *Compare, 42* (5).

Carnoy, M., Gove, A. K., & Marshall, J. H. (2007). *Cuba's Academic Advantage: Why Students in Cuba Do Better in School*. Stanford, CA: Stanford University Press.

Carnoy, M. (2007). Cuba's academic advantage. *Berkeley Review of Latin American Studies*. Retrieved from http://www.clas.berkeley.edu/Publications/Review/ Fall2007/pdf/BRLAS-Fall2007-Carnoy-standard.pdf on August 5, 2011.

Castro, F. (2004). History will absolve me. In A. Chomsky, B. Carr, & P. M. Smorkaloff (Eds.). *The Cuba Reader: History, Culture, Politics*. Durham, NC and London: Duke University Press, 306–315.

Cesaire, A. (2000). *Discourse on Colonialism*. Joan Pinkham (Trans.). New York: Monthly Review Press.

Chabal, P., & Daloz, J. P. (1999). *Africa Works: Disorder as Political Instrument*. Oxford, Bloomington, and Indianapolis: James Curry and Indiana University Press.

Chakrabarty, D. (1992). Postcoloniality and the artifice of history: Who speaks for "Indian" pasts? *Representations, 37*, 1–26.

Characterizacion Socioeconomica Nacional (CASEN). (2006a). National level (National Socio-economic Survey). Retrieved from http://www.mideplan.cl/ casen/publicaciones/2006/casen2006.pdf on March 5, 2011.

Characterizacion Socioeconomica Nacional (CASEN). (2006b). La Araucanía region level. Retrieved from http://www.mideplan.cl/casen/publicaciones/2006/ CASEN2006-LaAraucania.pdf on March 5 2011.

Chepe, O. E. (2002). S. O. S. education en peligro. Retrieved from http://www.cubanet.org/CNews/y02/sep02/25a7.htm on March 3, 2006.

Chidester, D. (1996). *Savage Systems: Colonialism and Comparative Religion in Southern Africa.* Charlottesville: University Press of Virginia.

Chivaura, V. G. (2006). African indigenous worldviews and ancient wisdom: A conceptual framework for development in Southern Africa. In J. E. Kunnie & N. I Goduka (Eds.). *Indigenous Peoples' Wisdom and Power: Affirming Our Knowledge through Narratives.* Aldershot, Hampshire: Ashgate Publishing., 213–224.

Chomsky, A., Carr, B., & Smorkaloff, P. M. (Eds.). (2004). *The Cuba Reader: History, Culture, Politics.* Durham, NC and London: Duke University Press.

Claxton, M. (2010). Indigenous knowledge and sustainable development. *Third Distinguished Lecture.* St. Augustine, Trinidad and Tobago: The Cropper Foundation UWI.

Coleman, J. S., Campbell, E., Hobson, C., McPartland, J., Mood, A., Weinfeld, F. & York, R. (1966). Equal educational opportunity. Washington, DC: US Govermnent Printing Office.

Collins, F. S. (2006). *The Language of God: A Scientist Presents Evidence for Belief.* New York: Simon and Schuster.

CONADI. Corporación Nacional de Desarrollo Indígena (the Bureau of Indigenous Affairs) (1996). Retrieved from http://www.chileclic.gob.cl/1542/w3-propertyvalue-17243.html on January 6, 2010.

Constantino, R. (1971). Historical truths from biased sources. In J. R. M. Taylor, *The Philippine Insurrection Against the United States: A Compilation of Documents with Notes and Introduction.* Pasay City: Eugenio Lopez Foundation, ix–xii.

COP 17 (2011). The 17th Conference of the Parties to the United Nations Framework Convention on Climate Change (UNFCCC). Retrieved from http://www.cop17-cmp7durban.com/ on January 3, 2012.

Correra,M., Molina, R. and Yáñes, N (2003). *La Reforma Agraria y las tierras mapuches.* Santiago: LOM.

Council on Foreign Relations. (2011). China's Environmental Crisis. Retrieved from http://www.cfr.org/china/chinas-environmental-crisis/p12608 on September 3, 2011.

Crossman, P., & Devisch, R. (2002). Endogenous knowledge in anthropological perspective. In C. A. Odora Hoppers (Ed.). *Indigenous Knowledge and the Integration of Knowledge Systems.* Claremont, Cape Town: New Africa Books, 96–128.

Cruz-Taura, G. (2003) *Rehabilitating Education in Cuba: Assessment of Conditions and Policy Recommendations.* Miami, FL: Institute for Cuban and Cuban-American Studies, University of Miami.

CTV (2011). Cuba Biotechnology. Retrieved from http://202.108.9.138/news.jsp?fileId=110019 on December 3, 2011.

D'Ambrosio, U. (1997). Ethnomathematics and its place in the history and pedagogy of mathematics. In A. Powell & M. Frankenstein (Eds.). *Ethnomathematics: Challenging Eurocentrism in Mathematics Education.* Albany: State University of New York Press, 13–24.

D'Ambrosio, U. (1999). Ethnomathematics and its first international congress. *Zentralblatt für Didaktik der Mathematik, 3*(2), 50–53.

Daily Telegraph (2009). Humans "evolved" to believe in God. September 7. Retrieved from http://www.telegraph.co.uk/journalists/richard-alleyne/6146411/Humans-evolved-to-believe-in-God.html on October 2, 2011.

Darder, A., Baltodano, M., & Torres, R. D. (Eds.). (2003). *The Critical Pedagogy Reader.* New York and London: Routledge Falmer.

Darnell, F., & Hoem, A. (1996). *Taken to Extremes: Education in the Far North.* Oslo, Stockholm, Copenhagen, and Boston: Scandinavian University Press.

Davidson, B. (1978). *Africa in Modern History: The Search for a New Society.* London: Allen Lane.

Davies, L. (2004). *Education and Conflict: Complexity and Chaos.* London and New York: Routledge Falmer.

Davies, P. (1992). *The Mind of God: The Scientific Basis for a Rational World.* New York: Simon and Schuster.

Dei, G. J. S. (1994). Afrocentricity: A cornerstone of pedagogy. *Anthropology & Education Quarterly, 25*(1), 3–28.

Dei, G. J. S. (2006). Introduction: Mapping the terrain—towards a new politics of resistance? In G. J. S. Dei & A. Kempf (Eds.). *Anti-Colonialism and Education: The Politics of Resistance.* Rotterdam: Sense Publishers, 1–24.

Dei, G. J. S., and Kempf, A. (2006).Conclusion: Looking forward—the pedagogical implications of anti-colonialism. In G. J. S. Dei & A. Kempf (Eds.). *Anti-Colonialism and Education: The Politics of Resistance.* Rotterdam: Sense Publishers, 309–314.

Delanty, G. (2000). *Modernity and Postmodernity.* London, New Delhi, and Thousand Oaks, CA: Sage.

Deng, D. K. (2011). The New Frontier: A Baseline Survey of Large-scale and Land-based Investment in Southern Sudan. Report 1/11. Oslo: Norwegian People's Aid (NPA). Retrieved from www.npaid.org on January 3, 2012.

Deng, D. Y. B. (2009). Looming anarchy in South Sudan. *Sudan Tribune.* Retrieved from http://www.sudantribune.com/Looming-anarchy-in-South-Sudan,30989 on April 5, 2011.

Deng, F. M. (1995). *War of Visions: Conflict of Identities in the Sudan.* Washington, DC: The Brookings Institution.

Department of Arts, Culture, Science, and Technology (DACST). (1998). *The South African Publishing Industry Report.* Retrieved from http://www.info.gov.za/view/DownloadFileAction?id=70498 on November 6, 2011.

Department of Education (DoE). (1995). *National Qualifications Framework.* Working Document. Pretoria: Government Printers.

Department of Education (DoE). (1997a). *Policy Document: Foundation Phase.* Western Cape Education Department edition. Pretoria: Government Press.

Department of Education (DoE). (1997b). *Policy Document: Intermediate Phase.* Pretoria: Government Press.

Department of Education (DoE). (2002). *Revised National Curriculum Statement.* Pretoria, Government Press.

Department of Education (DoE) (2009). *Report of the Task Team for the Review of the Implementation of the National Curriculum Statement: Final Report 2009.* Pretoria, Government Press.

Department of Science and Technology (DST). (2004). *Indigenous Knowledge Systems Policy (IKS Policy).* Pretoria: Department of Science and Technology. Retrieved from www.eifl.net/system/files/201101/sa_iks.pdf on November 7, 2011.

Devall, B. (1990). *Simple in Means, Rich in Ends.* London: Green Print.

Diamond, J. (1993). New Guineans and their natural world. In S. R. Kellert & E. O. Wilson (Eds.). *The Biophilia Hypothesis.* Washington, DC: Island Press, 251–271.

Dillabough, J. A., & Kennelly, J. (2010). *Lost Youth in the Global City: Class, Culture, and the Urban Imaginary.* London and New York: Routledge.

Diop, C. A. (1974). *The African Origins of Civilization.* New York: Lawrence Hill Press.

Durban Climate Change Conference. (2011). The Forgotten Planet. Retrieved from http://www. independent. co. uk/environment/climate-change/durban-conference-the-forgotten-planet-6272110.html on January 26, 2012.

Durkheim, E. (1956). *Education and Sociology*. Chicago: Free Press. (Original publication 1922).

East African. (2011). Investors in scramble for South Sudan's fertile land. 10 July. Retrieved from http://allafrica.com/stories/201107111824.html on August 5, 2011.

Economist, The. (2009). The people and the land: A fight over history and poverty. November. Retrieved from http://www.economist.com/node/14816728 on September 18 2011.

Economist, The. (2003). Inequality in Latin America: A stubborn curse. November. Retrieved from http://www.economist.com/node/2193852 on November 15, 2011.

Edwards, A., Daniels, H., Gallagher, T., Leadbetter, J., & Warmington, P. (2009). *Improving Inter-professional Collaborations: Multi-agency Working for Children's Wellbeing*. London: Routledge.

Eidhamar, L. G., & Rian, D. (1995). *Jødedommen og Islam*. Oslo: Høyskoleforlaget.

Elliott, A. (1996). *Subject to Ourselves: Social Theory, Psychoanalysis, and Postmodernity*. Cambridge: Polity Press.

Engeström, Y. (1987). *Learning by Expanding: An Activity-Theoretical Approach to Developmental Research*. Helsinki: Orienta-konsultit.

Engeström, Y. (2001). Expansive learning at work: Toward an activity theoretical reconceptualization. *Journal of Education and Work, 14*(1), 133–156.

Ernest, P. (1998). *Social Constructivism as a Philosophy of Mathematics*. New York: SUNY Press.

Ernest, P. (2007a). Epistemological issues in the internationalization and globalization of mathematics education. In B. Atweh, M. Borba, A. Barton, N. Gough, C. Keitel, C. Vistro-Yu, & R. Vithal (Eds.). *Internationalization and Globalization of Mathematics and Science Education*. Dordrecht, The Netherlands: Springer, 19–38.

Ernest, P. (2007b). Mathematics education ideologies and globalization. *Philosophy of Mathematics Education Journal*, 21 (Special Issue on Social Issues, Part 2). Retrieved from http://people.exeter.ac.uk/PErnest/pome21/index.htm on March 28, 2012.

Escobar, A. (2001). Culture sits in places: reflections on globalism and subaltern strategies of localization. *Political Geography* 20, 139–174.

Escobar, A. (2004). Beyond the Third World: Imperial globality, global coloniality, and anti-globalisation social movements. *Third World Quarterly, (25)*1, 207–230.

Fagen, R. R. (1969). *The Transformation of Political Culture in Cuba*. Stanford, CA: Stanford University Press.

Fakudze, C. G. (2003a). The nature of world views held by Swazi high school students. In M. B. Ogunnyi & K. Rochford (Eds.). *The Pursuit of Excellence in Science and Mathematics Education*. Cape Town: University of Western Cape, 58–63.

Fakudze, C. G. (2003b). The African learner model. In M. B. Ogunnyi, & K. Rochford (Eds.). *The Pursuit of Excellence in Science and Mathematics Education*. Cape Town: University of Western Cape, 132–138.

Fanon, F. (1963). *The Wretched of the Earth*. C. Farrington, Trans. New York: Grove Weidenfeld.

Fanon, F. (1967) *Black Skin, White Masks*. C. Lam, Trans. New York: Grove Press.

Fataar, A. 2005. Discourse, differentiation, and agency: Muslim community schools in postapartheid Cape Town. *Comparative Education Review* 49 (1): 23–43.

Faulstich, P. (2003). Human Ecology Perspectives on Sustainability. Humanities and Sustainability Workshop. Pitzer College, Los Angeles.

Fernandez-Armesto, F. (1995). *Millennium*. New York: Simon and Schuster.

Fiske, J. (1989). *Reading the Popular*. Boston: Unwin and Hyman.

Foster, P. (1965). The vocational school fallacy in development planning. In A. A. Anderson & M. J. Bowman (Eds.). *Education and Economic Development*. Chicago: Aldine, 142–166.

Foucault, M. (1995). *The Archeology of Knowledge*. Bristol: Routledge.

Foucault, M. (1980). *Power/Knowledge: Selected Interviews and Other Writings 1972–77*. Hertfordshire: Harvester Press.

France24.com. (2011). Speedy neutrino has scientists questioning Einstein. 23 September. Retrieved from www.france24.com/en(2011)0923-particle-travel-faster-speed-light-einstein-relative-theory-subatomic-cern-science-neutrono on October 6, 2011.

Frank, A. G. (1969). *Latin America: Underdevelopment or Revolution*. New York: Monthly Review.

Freire, P. (1970 *Pedagogy of the Oppressed*. London: Penguin Group.

Freire, P. (1972). *Cultural Action for Freedom*. Harmondsworth: Penguin.

Freire, P. (1995). *Pedagogy of Hope*. London and New York: Continuum.

Freire, P. (1998). *Pedagogy of Freedom: Ethics, Democracy, and Civic Courage*. Lanham, MD: Rowman & Littlefield.

Freire, P., & Faundez, A. (1989). *Learning to Question: A Pedagogy of Liberation*. New York: Continuum.

Futurechallenges.org. (2011).The energy crunch and popular demand—Chile's quest for balance. Retrieved from http://futurechallenges.org/local/energy-crunch-and-popular-demand-chiles-quest-for-balance/ on November 3, 2011.

García-Alix, L., & Hitchcock, R. K. (2009). A report from the field: The Declaration on the Rights of Indigenous Peoples—implementation and implications. *Genocide Studies and Prevention, 4*(1), 99–109.

Gellner, E.A.(1973). Cause and meaning in the social sciences. London: Routledge and Kegan Paul.

Giddens, A. (1991) *Modernity and Self-Identity: Self and Modernity in the Late Modern Age*. Cambridge: Polity.

Giroux, H. A. (1983). *Theory and Resistance in Education: A Pedagogy for the Opposition*. London: Heinemann.

Giroux, H. A. (2003a). A critical theory and educational practice. In A. Darder, M. Baltodano, & R. D. Torres (Eds.). *The Critical Pedagogy Reader*. New York and London: Routledge Falmer, 27–57.

Giroux, H. A. (2003b). Education Incorporated? In A. Darder, M. Baltodano, & R. D. Torres (Eds.). *The Critical Pedagogy Reader*. New York and London: Routledge Falmer, 119–126.

Global Humanitarian Assistance. (2011). *Aid in Transition: South Sudan*. Retrieved from http://www. globalhumanitarianassistance. org/wp-content/uploads/ (2011)/07/gha-aid-in-transition-South-Sudan.pdf on August 5 2011.

Gómez, M. T. (2010). Political uses of communalidad: Citizenship and education. In L. Meyer & B. M. Alvarado (Eds.). *New World of Indgenous Resistance*. San Francisco: City Lights Books, 179–191.

Grant, C. A., & Portera, A. (2011). *Intercultural and Multicultural Education: Enhancing Global Interconnectedness*. New York: Routledge.

Griffiths, T. G., & Knezevic, L. (2009). World-systems analysis in comparative education: An alternative to cosmopolitanism. *Current Issues in Comparative Education, 12*(1), 66–76.

Griffiths, T. G. (2004). Learning "to be somebody": Cuban youth in the special period. *International Journal of Learning, 11*, 1267–1274.

Griffiths, T. G. (2009). Fifty years of socialist education in revolutionary Cuba: A world-systems perspective. *JILAR—Journal of Iberian and Latin American Research, 15*(2), 45–64.

Gross, L., & Lewis, M. W. (1997). *The Flight from Science and Reason.* New York: New York Academy of Science.

Gruenewald, D. A., & Smith, G. A. (Eds.). (2008). *Place-Based Education in the Global Age: Local Diversity.* New York: Lawrence Erlbaum.

Guardian, The. (2011). Fears grow for minorities in north Sudan if south votes to secede. 8 January. Retrieved from http://www.guardian.co.uk/global-development/poverty-matters/(2011)/jan/08/south-sudan-referendum-bashir-sharia-law on February 2, 2011.

Guevara, E. (1973). On the budgetary finance system. In E. Guevara. *Man and Socialism in Cuba.* Atheneum: New York.

Guevara, E. (1988). *El socialismo y el hombre en Cuba* [Socialism and man in Cuba]. Havana: Editora Politica.

Gundara, J. S. (2000). *Interculturalism, Education, and Exclusion.* London: PCP Publishing.

Gyekye, K. (1997). *Tradition and Modernity in Africa.* New York and Oxford: Oxford University Press.

Gutierrez, L. G. (2004). Cuba: the Profound Educational Revolution. Inaugural Address, XII World Congress on Comparative Education. Havana, October 25–29.

Habermas, J. (2001). *The Postnational Constellation: Political Essays.* M. Pensky, Trans. & Ed. Cambridge, MA: MIT Press.

Hamel, J. L. (2005). *Unleashing the Power of Knowledge for Sustainable Development in Africa: Fundamental Issues for Governance and Meeting MDGs.* Economic Commission for Africa, Addis Ababa, Ethiopia. Retrieved from http://www.uneca.org/estnet/Ecadocuments/Knowledge_for_Sustainable_Development.doc on November 6, 2011.

Hamilton, R. J. (2001). The role of indigenous knowledge in depleting a natural resource: A case study of the bumphead parrotfish (*Bolbometopon Muricatum*). Artisanal fishery in Roviana Lagoon, Western Province, Solomon Islands. Putting fishers' knowledge to work. *Conference Proceedings, Fisheries Centre Research Reports.* Vancouver: University of British Columbia (Canada), 68–77.

Haneef, S. (1985). *What Everyone Should Know about Islam and Muslims.* Lahore: Kazi.

Haughney, D. (2006). *Neoliberal Economics, Democratic Transition, and Mapuche Demands for Rights in Chile.* Gainesville: University Press of Florida.

Head, B. (1971). *Maru.* London: Heinemann.

Heelas, P., Lash, S., & Morris, P. (Eds.). (1996). *Detraditionalization.* Oxford: Blackwell.

Heider, F. (1958). *The Psychology of Interpersonal Relations.* New York: John Wiley & Sons.

helplinelaw (2000) . Sudan Constitution (1998). Retrieved from http://www.helplinelaw.com/law/sudan/constitution/constitution02.php on March 12, 2005

Heradstveit, D. (1979). *The Arab-Israeli Conflict: Psychological Obstacles to Peace.* Oslo, Bergen, and Tromsø: Universitetsforlaget.

Heradstveit, D., & Bonham, G. M. (1996). *Attribution theory and Arab images of the Gulf War. Political Psychology* 17(2) (June), 271–292.

Heugh, K. (2000). *The Case against Bilingual and Multilingual Education in South Africa.* Cape Town: PRAESA.

Higgs, P. (2000). *African Voices in Education.* Cape Town: Juta Publishers.

Hobson, J. M. (2004). *The Eastern Origins of Western Civilisation.* Cambridge: Cambridge University Press.

Hofstede, G. (1991). *Culture and Organizations: Software of the Mind.* London: McGraw Hill.

Horsthemke, K. (2004). Indigenous knowledge—conceptions and misconceptions. *Journal of Education, 32,* 31–48.

Horsthemke, K. (2009). The South African higher education transformation debate: Culture, identity and "African ways of knowing." *London Review Education*, 7(1), 3–15.

Hountondji, P. J. (Ed.). (1997). *Endogenous Knowledge: Research Trails*. Dakar: CODESIRA.

Hountondji, P.J. (2002) "Knowledge production in a post-colonial context." In C.A. Odora Hoppers (Ed.) *Indigenous Knowledge and the Integration of Knowledge Systems*. Claremont, Cape Town: New Africa Books, 23–39.

Hourani, A. (1983). *Arabic Thought in the Liberal Age*. Cambridge: Cambridge University Press.

Huenchullán, C. & Millacura, C. (2007). Nación, ciudadanía y el otro. Retrieved from http://books.google.no/books/about/Naci%C3%B3n_ciudadan%C3%ADa_y_el_otro.html?id=8AkzOAAACAAJ&redir_esc=y on January 6 2008.

Human Rights Watch and Observatorio de Derechos de los Pueblos Indigenas (HRW and ODPI). (2004). *Undue Process: Terrorism Trials, Military Courts, and the Mapuche in Southern Chile*. Retrieved from http://www.hrw.org/en/reports/(2004)/10/26/undue-process on October 3, 2011.

Hume, D. (1753–1754). Of national character. In *Essays and Treatises on Several Subjects*. Footnote 10. In *The Philosophical Works of David Hume*, Volume III, Bristol: Thoemmes Press, 1996.

Hunter, M. (1979). *Reaction to Conquest. Effects of Contact with Europeans on the Pondo of South Africa*. Cape Town: David Philip. Abridged paperback edition.

Iaccarino, M. (2003). Science and culture. *EMBO reports 4*, 220–223.

Idowu, E. B. (1982). *African Traditional Religion*. London: SCM.

Independent, The. (2011). Durban Conference: The forgotten planet. Retrieved from http://www.independent.co.uk/environment/climate-change/durban-conference-the-forgotten-planet-6272110.html on January 19, 2012.

Inside Climate News. (2009). Climate Change Could Devastate Latin America's Agriculture. Retrieved from http://insideclimatenews.org/news/(2009)0306/climate-change-could-devastate-latin-americas-agriculture on October 4, 2011.

International Energy Agency (IEA). (2011). *World Energy Outlook*. Retrieved from http://www.iea.org/weo/docs/weo(2011)/WEO(2011)TOC.pdf on December 8, 2011.

International Labour Organization (ILO). (1989). C169 Indigenous and Tribal Peoples Convention. Retrieved from http://www.ilo.org/ilolex/cgi-lex/convde.pl?C169 on April 5, 2011.

International Labour Organization (ILO). (2008). Convention C169. Retrieved from http://www.ilo.org/ilolex/cgi-lex/ratifce.pl?C169 on January 8, 2012.

Instituto National de Estadisticas (INE), (1993 and 2003). Censo de Poblacion y Vivienda (1992) and (2002). Santiago: INE. Retrieved from http://www.ine.cl/canales/chile_estadistico/estadisticas_sociales_culturales/etnias/etnias.php?lang=eng on September 14, 2011.

Instituto de Estudios Politicos (IDEP). (2003). Encuesta IDEP. Retrieved from www.unab.cl/idep on September 5, 2011.

Institute of Indigenous Studies. (2003). *Los Derechos de los Pueblos Indígenas en Chile: Report of the Program of Indigenous Rights*. University of the Frontier. Santiago: LOM.

Intercontinentalcry.org. (2011). Indigenous Peoples of Africa. Retrieved from http://intercontinentalcry.org/regions/africa/ on January 14, 2012.

Irwin, R. G. (2006). *Dangerous Knowledge: Orientalism and Its Discontents*. New York: Overlook Press.

Jakobsen, L. (2009). *The Way in which Mapuche and the Mapuche Culture Is Addressed in Chilean Education Today*. (Masters dissertation). Oslo: Oslo University College.

Jamison, C. (2009). Family tradition: Cuban policy reform as Raul Castro takes the reigns. *Law & Business Review of the Americas, 15*(4), 891–922. Retrieved from http://studentorgs.law.smu.edu/getattachment/International-Law-Review-Association/Resources/LBRA-Archive/15–4/SMB407.pdf.aspx on January 18, 2012.

Jansen, J., & Sayed, Y. (2001). *Implementing Education Policies: The South African Experience*. Cape Town: UCT Press.

Jara, J. A. (1997). Urban Mapuche: Reflections on a modern reality in Chile. *Abya Yala News, 10*(3). Retrieved from http://www.mapuche.info/mapuint/ancan00.htm on September 5, 2011.

Jegede, O. J. (1995). Collateral Learning and the Eco-Cultural Paradigm in Science and Mathematics Education. Paper presented at the Third Southern African Association for Research in Mathematics and Science Education (SAARMSE), Cape Town. January.

Jegede, O. J., & Aikenhead, G. S. (1999) Transcending cultural borders: Implications for science teaching. *Research in Science and Technology Education, 17*, 45–66.

Jervis, R. 1976. *Perception and Misperception in International Politics*. Princeton, NJ: Princeton University Press.

Johnson, D. H. (2007). *The Root Causes of Sudan Civil Wars*. Updated fourth impression. London: International African Institute; Oxford: James Currey; Bloomington: Indiana University Press; Kampala: Fountain Publishers.

Joint Assessment Mission (JAM) (2005a). Volume 1. Retrieved from http://www.internal-displacement.org/8025708F004CE90B/(httpDocuments)/B092967CA3F27A29C12575710068F5AA/$file/JAM-Vol_I.pdf on April 3, 2008. 2011

Joint Assessment Mission (JAM). (2005b). Volume 3. Retrieved from http://postconflict.unep.ch/sudanreport/sudan_website/doccatcher/data/documents/Joint%20Assessment%20Mission%20(JAM)%20Volume%20III.pdf on April 3, 2008.

Jok, J. M. (2001). *War and Slavery in Sudan*. Philadelphia: University of Pennsylvania Press.

Jok, J. M. (2007). *Race, Religion, and Violence*. Oxford: One World.

Jones, D.G. (2012). Humanism. Retrieved from http://humanism.ws/about-3/

Jones, P. W. (2007). Education and world order. *Comparative Education, 43*(3), 325–337.

Joseph, G. G. (1997). Foundations of eurocentrism in mathematics. In A. Powell & M. Frankenstein (Eds.). *Ethnomathematics: Challenging Eurocentrism in Mathematics Education*. New York: SUNY Press, 61–81.

Kapica, A. (2005). Educational revolution and revolutionary morality in Cuba: The "new man," youth, and the new "Battle of Ideas." *Journal of Moral Education* (34)4, 399–412.

Kearney, M. 1984. *Worldview*. Navato, CA: Chandler Sharp.

Kenyi, C. M. (1996). *Report of a Survey of Educational Needs and Services for War Affected South Sudanese*. Nairobi: AACC and Swedish Save the Children.

Kincheloe, J. L. & Steinberg, S. R. (2008). Indigenous knowledges in education: Complexities, dangers, and profound benefits. In N. K. M. Denzin, Y. S. Lincoln, & L. T. Smith (Eds.). *Handbook of Critical and Indigenous Methodologies*. Los Angeles, London, New Delhi, and Singapore: Sage, 135–157.

King, K. (2007). Education, skills, sustainability, and growth: Complex relations. Paper presented at the 9th UKFIET International Conference on Education and Development, Oxford, September 11–13.

Kipling, R. (1889). The ballad of East and West. *Pioneer*, December 2. Collected in *The Sussex Edition* Vol. 32, p. 231.

Klees, S.J. (2008). A quarter century of neoliberal thinking in education: Misleading analyses and failed policies. *Globalisation Societies and Education* 6(4), 311–348.

Klees, S.J., Samoff, J. and Stromquist, N.P. (Eds.) (2012). *The World Bank and Education: Critiques and Alternatives.* Rotterdam: Sense.

Kolbert, E.(2006). *Field Notes from a Catastrophe: Man, Nature, and Climate Change.* London: Bloomsbury.

Kubow, P. K. (2009). Democracy, identity, and citizenship education in South Africa: Defining a nation in a post-colonial and global era. In J. Zajda, H. Daun, & L. J. Saha (Eds.). *Nation-Building, Identity, and Citizenship Education: Cross-Cultural Perspectives.* London: Springer.

Küper, W., & Lopez, L. E. (1999). La educacion intercultural bilingüe en Americas Latina: balance y perspectivas. *Revista Iberoamericana de Educacion, 20,* 17–85.

Kuper, A. (2000). *Culture: The Anthropologists' Account.* Cambridge, MA: Harvard University Press.

Kyle, W. (1999). Critical issues of school and teacher education reform: Transforming science teaching and learning for a new millennium. Paper presented at the Second Sub-Regional Conference of Public Understanding of Science and Technology. Botswana. December 6–9.

Kymlicka, W. (1995). *Multicultural Citizenship.* Oxford: Clarendon Press.

Kvale, S. (1996). *Interviews: An Introduction to Qualitative Research Interviewing.* Thousand Oaks, London, and New Delhi: Sage.

Larson, D. W. (1985). *Origins of Containment: A Psychological Explanation.* Princeton, NJ: Princeton University Press.

Latin Business Chronicle. (2010). Argentina richest in Latin America. Retrieved from http://www.latinbusinesschronicle.com/app/article.aspx?id=4169 on October 7, 2011.

Latin America Press. (2008). Hungry for justice. Retrieved from http://www.lapress.org/articles.asp?item=1&art=5478 on October 5, 2011.

Latour, B. (2004). Why has critique run out of steam? From matters of fact to matters of concern. *Critical Inquiry 30,* 225–248.

Leclerc-Madlala, S (1999) Demonising Women in the Era of AIDS: An Analysis of the Sociocultural Construction of HIV/AIDS in KwaZulu-Natal. Unpublished PhD Dissertation. Durban, Department of Anthropology, University of Natal.

Leclerc-Madlala, S. (2002). Youth, HIV/AIDS and the importance of sexual culture and context. *Social Dynamics.* Special Issue: *AIDS and Society, 28*(1), 20–41.

Lehrer, J. (2010). The truth wears off. *The New Yorker,* 13 December. Retrieved from http://www.newyorker.com/reporting/(2010)/12/13/101213fa_fact_lehrer#ixzz1JZw1fpYf on November 5, 2011.

Lenin, V. I. (1927). *Materialism and Empirio-Criticism.* New York: International Publishers.

Lesch, Anne Mosley. (1998). *The Sudan: Contested National Identities.* Bloomington, Indianapolis, and Oxford: Indiana University Press and James Currey.

Levin Institute, The. (2011). What is globalization? Retrieved from http://www.globalization101.org/What_is_Globalization.html on September 6 2011.

Levy, J. S. (1981). World system analysis: A great power framework. In W. R. Thompson (Ed.). *Contending Approaches to World System Analysis.* Beverly Hills: Sage, 183–202.

Lewis, B. (1993). The question of Orientalism. In B. Lewis, *Islam and the West.* New York: Oxford University Press, 99–118.

Ley indigena (Indigenous Law). (1993). Retrieved from http://www.uta.cl/masma/patri_edu/PDF/LeyIndigena.pdf on October 5 2009.

Ley Orgánica Constitutional de Enseñanza. (1990). Retrieved from http://www.leychile.cl/Navegar?idNorma=30330 on October 5, 2009.

Lyle, J. T. (1994). *Regenerative Design for Sustainable Development.* New York: John Wiley.

Loomba, A. (1998). *Colonialism/Postcolonialism*. London and New York: Routledge.

MacDonald, T. (1996). *Schooling the Revolution: An Analysis of Development in Cuban Education since 1959*. London: Praxis Press.

Maffie, J. (2009). "In the end, we have the Gatling gun, and they have not": Future prospects of indigenous knowledges. *Futures, 41*(1), 53–65.

Mail and Guardian. (2011a). Local polls: So far, so good. 18 May. Retrieved from http://demarcation.mg.co.za/local-polls-so-far-so-good/ on June 6, 2011.

Mail and Guardian. (2011b). Less "wishy washy" needed on renewable energy in SA. 16 November. Retrieved from http://mg.co.za/article/(2011)-11–16-less-wishy-washy-needed-on-renewable-energy-in-sa/ on December 3, 2011.

Mandela, N. (1994). Statement by President Nelson Mandela at the OAU Meeting of Heads of State and Government. 13 June. Retrieved from http://www.anc.org.za/show. php?id=4888 on October 25, 2011.

Manning, K. (2011). In Chile, protesting students tweak tweets to win global support. Threat Level. Retrieved from http://www.wired.com/threatlevel/(2011)/11/chile-students/ on January 27, 2012.

Mannoni, O. (1956). *Prospero and Caliban: The Psychology of Colonisation*. P. Powesland, Trans. London: Methuen.

Mansata, B. (2008). Why Cuba is the only nation to achieve sustainable development. Retrieved from http://www.bhoomimagazine.org/index.php?option=com_k2&view=item&id=12%3Awhy-cuba-is-the-only-nation-to-achieve-sustainable-development&Itemid=14&tmpl=component&print=1 on September 24, 2011.

Mapuche Forum (Coordination of Mapuche Organizations and Territorial Entities). (2004). In Opposition to Free Market Globalization and Neo Colonialism, We Say: No to APEC. Retrieved from http://www.mapuche-nation. org/english/main/apec/no-apec-01.htm on June 16, 2009.

Mapuche Health Network. (2011). Chile: Categorical Rejection by Mapuche Health Network Concerning Convention UPOV 91 or "Monsanto Law." Retrieved from http://indigenouspeoplesissues.com/index.php?option=com_content&view=article&id=10716:may-26 on December 12, 2011.

Marcuse, H. (1964). *One-Dimensional Man*. Boston: Beacon Press.

Martínez, R. (2005). Che Guevara and the Political Economy of Socialism. Retrieved from www.revolutionarydemocracy.org/rdv11n1/che.htm

Massey, D. (1994). *Space, Place, and Gender*. Oxford: Polity Press.

Mbeki, T. (1996). Statement on behalf of the African National Constitutional Assembly of the Republic of South Africa Constitutional Bill. Retrieved from http://www.newzimbabwe.com/pages/zuma20.18786.html on October 5 2011.

Mbeki, T. (1999). Speech at the Opening of the Biennial of the Association for the Development of Education in Africa (ADEA), Johannesburg, December 5–9. Retrieved from http://www. dfa. gov. za/docs/speeches/(1999)/mbek1206.htm on June 3, 2011.

Mbiti, J. (1969). *African Religions and Philosophy*. London: Heinemann.

McCarthy, C. (2006). *The Road*. New York: Vintage.

McLaren, P. L. (2000). *Che Guevara, Paulo Freire, and the Pedagogy of Revolution*. Lanham, MD: Rowman and Littlefield.

McLennan, G. (1998). The question of Eurocentrism: A comment on Immanuel Wallerstein. *New Left Review 231*, 153–158.

McEvoy-Levy, S. (2006). *Troublemakers or Peacemakers? Youth And Post-accord Peace Building*. Notre Dame, IN: University of Notre Dame Press.

Meadows, D. H., Meadows, D. L., Randers, J., and Behrens, W.W. III. (1972). *The Limits to Growth*. New York: Universe Books.

Meadows, D.H, Randers, J. and Meadows, D.L. (2004). *The Limits to Growth: The 30-Year Update*. Vermont: Chelsea Green Publishing.

Mehlinger, H. D. (Ed.). (1981). Social Studies around the World. In *UNESCO Handbook for the Teaching of Social Studies*. Beckenham: Croom Helm.

Meredith, P. (1998). Hybridity in the Third Space: Rethinking Bi-cultural Politics in Aotearoa/New Zealand. *Paper Presented at the Oru Rangahau Māori Research and Development Conference*, Massey University, 7–9 July. Retrieved from http://lianz.waikato.ac.nz/PAPERS/paul/hybridity.pdf on November 5, 2011.

Merton, R. K. (1973). The normative structure of science. In R. K. Merton (Ed.). *The Sociology of Science: Theoretical and Empirical Investigations*. Chicago: University of Chicago Press, 267–278.

Metz, H. C. (Ed.). (1991). *Sudan–A Country Study*. Washington, DC: Government Printing Office.

Meyer, J. W., Boli, J., Thomas, G. M., & Ramirez, F. O. (1997). World society and the nation-state. *American Journal of Sociology,103*(1), 144–181.

Mgbeoji, I. (2006). *Global Biopiracy: Patents, Plants, and Indigenous Knowledge*. Vancouver: University of British Columbia Press.

Mkabela, Q. (2005). Using the Afrocentric method in researching indigenous African culture. *The Qualitative Report*, *10*(1), 178–189.

MINEDUC. *Educación Intercultural Bilingüe* (EIB). n.d. Retrieved from http://www.mineduc.cl/index0.php?id_portal=28 on November 6 2010.

MINEDUC (2001a). Currículo Nacional. Marcos Curriculares (Parvularia, básica y media). Retrieved from http://www.curriculum-mineduc.cl/curriculum/marcos-curriculares/ on November 5, 2010.

MINEDUC (2001b). *Estudio y Comprensión de la Sociedad* (Social science). Retrieved from www.curriculum-mineduc.cl/docs/fichas/8b03_est_y_comp_de_la_soc.pdf on November 6, 2010.

MINEDUC (2004). Lenguaje y Comunicación, Octavo Año Basico/Nivel Basico 6: *Las multiples tradiciones culturales de Chile*. Retrieved from http://www.educarchile.cl/Userfiles/P0001%5CFile%5CLenguaje_y_Comunicacion8.pdf on October 3, 2009.

MINEDUC (2005). *Orientaciones para la Contextualización de Planes y Programas para la Educación Intercultural Bilingüe*. Retrieved from http://www.peib.cl/link.exe/Documentos/?procesar=1&texto=contextualizacion&ano=Todos&tipo=Todos &buscar=Buscar> on October 3, 2009.

MINEDUC. (2008). *General Educational Law*. Retrieved from http://www.mineduc.cl/biblio/resumen/(2008)06021703380.EJES%20CLAVES%20LGE.pdf on November 5, 2010.

MINEDUC. (2009). *Programas the Estudio. Lenguaje y Comunicación*. Retrieved from www.curriculum-mineduc.cl/docs/fichas/8b01_lenguaje_y_comunicacion.pdf on November 5, 2010.

Ministry of Education. (2001). *Development of Education: National Report of Cuba*. Havana: International Education Office.

Moodie, T. (2004). Re-evaluating the idea of indigenous knowledge: Implications of anti-dualism in African philosophy and theology. Paper presented at African Renewal, African Renaissance: New Perspectives on Africa's Past and Africa's Present, The African Studies Association of Australia and the Pacific (AFSAAP) Annual Conference, University of Western Australia, November 26–28.

Morrisey, L. F. (2010). Interview with G. Quilaqueo: Mapuche—A people fighting against plunder and marginalization. Retrieved from http://www.sidint.net/interview-with-gustavo-quilaqueo-Mapuche-a-people-fighting-against-plundering-and-marginalization/ on February 21, 2010.

Morrow, S., Maaba, B. & Pulumani, L. (2004) Education in exile: SOMAFCO, the ANC school in Tanzania, 1978 to 1992. Cape Town: HSRC Press.

Motaung, T. (2009). EES Week 3: Visible Land, Invisible People. Retrieved from http://www. unpo.org/article/9276 on September 17, 2011.

Msila, V. (2007). From apartheid education to the Revised National Curriculum Statement: Pedagogy for identity formation and nation building in South Africa. *Nordic Journal of African Studies*, 16(2), 146–160.

Muehlebach, A. (2003). What self in self-determination? Notes from the frontiers of transnational indigenous activism. *Identities: Global Studies in Culture and Power*, 10, 241–268.

Naess, A. (1973). The shallow and the deep, long-range ecology movement. *Inquiry*, 16, 95–100.

Nattrass, N. (2004). *The Moral Economy of AIDS*. New York: Cambridge University Press.

Newell, P., & Paterson, M. (2010). *Review of Climate Capitalism: Global Warming and the Transformation of the Global Economy*. Cambridge: Cambridge University Press.

Ngũgĩ wa Thiong'o. (1981). *Decolonizing the Mind: The Politics of Language in African Literature*. London and Portsmouth: James Currey and Heinemann.

Niamir-Fuller, M. (1998). The resilience of pastoral herding in Sahelian Africa. In F. Berkes, & C. Folke (Eds.). *Linking Social and Ecological Systems: Management, Practices, and Social Mechanisms for Building Resilience*. Cambridge: Cambridge University Press.

Nicol, A. (2002). *Save the Children (UK) South Sudan Programme*. London: Save the Children, UK.

Norwegian Education Trust Fund. (2002). *What Is the NETF?* Retrieved from http://www.worldbank.org/afr/netf/ on October 9, 2011.

Nsamenang, A. B. (2011). Toward a philosophy for Africa's education. In A. B. Nsamenang & T. M. S. Tchombe (Eds.). *Handbook of African Educational Theories and Practices: A Generative Teacher Education Curriculum*. Bamenda, Cameroon: Human Development Resource Centre (HDRC), 55–67.

Nsamenang, A. B., & Tchombe, T. M. S. (2011). Introduction: Generative pedagogy in the context of all cultures can contribute scientific knowledge of universal value. In A. B. Nsamenang & T. M. S. Tchombe (Eds.). *Handbook of African Educational Theories and Practices. A Generative Teacher Education Curriculum*. Bamenda, Cameroon: Human Development Resource Centre (HDRC), 5–21.

Ntuli, P. P. (2002). Indigenous knowledge systems the African renaissance. In C. A. Odora Hoppers (Ed.). *Indigenous Knowledge and the Integration of Knowledge Systems*. Claremont, Cape Town: New Africa Books, 53–66.

Nyerere, J. (1974.) Education and liberation. *Development Dialogue*, 2, 46–52.

Ocampo, L. M. (2004). A Brief History of Educational Inequality from Apartheid to the Present. Retrieved from http://www. stanford. edu/~jbaugh/saw/Lizet_Education_Inequity.html on September 7, 2011.

Odora Hoppers, C. A. (2002 a). Indigenous knowledge and the integration of knowledge systems. In C. A. Odora Hoppers (Ed.). *Indigenous Knowledge and the Integration of Knowledge Systems: Towards a Philosophy of Articulation*. Claremont, Cape Town: New Africa Books, 2–22.

Odora Hoppers, C. A. (2002b). (Ed.). *Indigenous Knowledge and the Integration of Knowledge Systems*. Claremont, Cape Town: New Africa Books.

Odora Hoppers, C. A., & Makhale-Mahlangu, P. (1998). *A Comparative Study of the Development, Integration and Protection of Indigenous Systems in the Third World. An Analytical Framework Document*. Pretoria:Human Sciences Research Council (HSRC).

Ogunnyi. M. B. (1988). Adapting Western science to traditional African culture. *International Journal of Science Education*, 10(1), 1–9.

Ogunnyi, M. B. (2003). Traditional cosmology and science education. In M. B. Ogunnyi & K. Rochford (Eds.). *The Pursuit of Excellence in Science and Mathematics Education*. Cape Town: University of Western Cape, 22–30.

Oreske, N., and Conway, E. M. M. (2011). *Merchants of Doubt: How a Handful of Scientists Obscured the Truth on Issues from Tobacco Smoke to Global Warming.* London: Bloomsbury.

Organisation for Economic Co-operation and Development (OECD). (2010). Gap between rich and poor in South Africa widens. Retrieved from http://mybroadband.co.za/vb/showthread. php/214936-Gap-between-rich-and-poor-in-South-Africa-widens on January 3, 2011.

Orimoogunje, O. C. (2009.)The social function of verbal arts in the Yoruba indigenous health care practices. Retrieved from http://www.articlesbase.com/alternative-medicine-articles/the-social-functions-of-verbal-arts-in-the-yorbindigenous-healthcare-practices-852676.html on January 6 2010.

Ortiz, P. R. (2007). *Intercultural Bilingual Education, Indigenous Knowledge and the Construction of Ethnic Identity: An Ethnography of a Mapuche School in Chile.* PhD thesis. Austin: The University of Texas at Austin, Faculty of Education.

Oyenak, C. (2006). *Multicultural Education in Support of Peace in the Sudan.* Oslo: HiO-report, No. 3.

Oyserman, D., and Wing-Sing Lee, S. (2007). Priming "culture": Culture as situated cognition. In S. Kitayama. and D. Cohen (Eds.). *Handbook of Cultural Psychology.* New York and London: Guildford Press, 255–283.

Palmer, A. R. (2000). Quasireplication and the contract of error: Lessons from six ratios heritabilities and fluctuating asymmetry. *Annual Review of Ecology and Systematics, 31,* 441–480.

Pattanyak, D. P. (1986). Educational use of mother tongue. In B. Spolsky (Ed.). *Languages and Education in Multilingual Settings.* Clevedon: Multilingual Matters Ltd., 5–15.

Pattberg, P. (2007). Conquest, domination, and control: Europe's mastery of nature in historic perspective. *Journal of Political Ecology, 14,* 1–9.

Paulston, R. G. (1973). Changes in Cuban education. In R. L. Cummings & D. A. Lemke (Eds.). *Educational Innovation in Latin America.* Methuchen, NJ: Scarecrow Press.

Pauw, B. A. (1975). *Christianity and Xhosa Tradition: Belief and Ritual among Xhosa-speaking Christians.* Cape Town and New York: Oxford University Press.

Peat, F. D. (1996). *Blackfoot Physics: A Journey into the Native American Universe.* London: Fourth Estate.

Peat, F. D. (1992). *Superstrings and the Theory of Everything.* London: Abacus.

Penn, M. (2008). *The Dynamic Debut of Raul Castro: Picking up the Broken Pieces beneath the Rubble of Fidel. Council on Hemispheric Affairs, November 4.* Retrieved from http://www.coha.org/(2008)/11/the-dynamic-debut-of-raul-castro-picking-up-the-broken-pieces-of-stormbattered-but-now-oil-rich-cuba-and-moving-ahead-with-mixed-prospects/ on October 10, 2011.

Peoples Assemblies Network. (2011). Chile Joins Year of Global Indignation. Retrieved from http://www.peoplesassemblies.org/(2011)/08/chile-joins-year-of-global-indignation/ on September 23, 2011.

Pérez, F. (director). (2003). *Suite Habana* [documentary film]. Wanda Vision S.A. and Instituto Cubano del Arte e Industrias Cinematogroficos (ICAIC).

Peterson, S. (2000). *Me Against My Brother: At War in Somalia, Sudan, and Rwanda.* London and New York: Routledge.

Pihl, J. (2001). Paradoxes of inclusion and exclusion in Norwegian educational reforms in the 1990s. *Nordisk Tidsskrift for Spesialpedagogikk. 1,* 14–33.

Pinto, R. J. (2003). *La formación del Estado y la nación, y el pueblo mapuche. De la inclusión a la exclusión.* Santiago de Chile: Ediciones de la Dirección de Bibliotecas, Archivos y Museos (DIBAM).

Postero, N. G. (2007). *Now We Are Citizens: Indigenous Politics Postmulticultural Bolivia.* Stanford, CA: Stanford University Press.

Powel, A. l & Frankenstein, M. (Eds.). *Ethnomathematics: Challenging Eurocentrism in Mathematics Education.* New York: SUNY Press.

Pnyv (2006). Mapuche people of Chile call for support against genetic tree mono-cultures. Retrieved from http://www.tt-beta.pnyv.org/index.php?id=449&L=14&tx_ttnews%5Btt_news%5D=849&tx_ttnews%5BbackPid%5D=448&cHash=5edc57d480 on June 21 2011.

Prakash, G. (1992). Postcolonial criticism and Indian historiography. *Social Text, 31*(32), 8–19.

Programa Orígenes. (2006). Retrieved from http://www.origenes.cl/images/descargas/Memoria/1.pdf on October 6 2010.

Prus, R. C. (1975). Resisting designations: An extension of attribution theory into a negotiated context. *Sociological Inquiry, 45*(1), 3–14.

Ramphal, A. (2005). Quality and Equality in Education: Gendered Politics of Institutional Change. Paper presented at Seminar in Dhaka, 31 January–1 February. Retrieved from http://www.ungei.org/resources/index_618.html on November 3 2011.

Ramphele, M. 1993. *A Bed Called Home: Life in the Migrant Labour Hostels of Cape Town.* Cape Town: David Philip; Edinburgh: Edinburgh University Press, in association with The International African Institute.

Randers, J. (2008). Global collapse—Fact or fiction? *Futures, 40,* 853–864.

Ranganathan. A. (2004). Using ICT to Place Indigenous Knowledge Systems at the Heart of Education for Sustainable Development. Retrieved from http://www.ceeindia.org/esf/download/paper47.pdf on June 6 2011.

Ranger, T. (1987). Religion, development, and African Christian identity. In K. Holst Petersen (Ed.). *Religion, Development, and African Identity.* Uppsala: Scandinavian Institute of African Studies, 29–54.

Rapkin, D. P. (1981). The inadequacy of a single logic: Integrating political and material approaches to the world system. In W. R. Thompson (Ed.). *Contending Approaches to World System Analysis.* Beverly Hills: Sage, 241–268.

Red Feather Institute. (2001). A Great Job: Cuba and Social Justice. Retrieved from http://uwacadweb.uwyo.edu/Red_Feather/CUBA/008report.html on June 5, 2009.

Rees, M. (2004). *Our Final Century: Will the Human Race Survive the Twenty-first Century?* London: Heinemann.

Reid-Henry, S. (2007). The contested spaces of Cuban development: Post-socialism, post-colonialism, and the geography of transition. *Geoforum, 38,* 445–455.

Renshon, S. (Ed.). (1993). *The Political Psychology of the Gulf War: Leaders, Publics, and the Process of Conflict.* Pittsburgh: University of Pittsburgh Press.

Rich, A. (1986). Invisibility in academe. In A. Rich. *Blood, Bread and Poetry: Selected Prose, 1979–1985.* London: Norton.

Richards, P. (2010). Of Indians and terrorists: How the state and local elites construct the Mapuche in neoliberal multicultural Chile. *Journal of Latin American Studies, 42,* 59–90.

Richter, M. (2003). Traditional Medicines and Traditional Healers in South Africa. Discussion paper prepared for the Treatment Action Campaign and AIDS Law Project. Johannesburg.

Rios, J and Crabtree, S. (2006). Urban Cubans Optimistic About Schools, Not About Work; Less than half say Cubans can get ahead by working hard. Retrieved from http://www.highbeam.com/doc/1G1-158854152.html on September 6, 2011.

Rivera, F., & Becker, J. R. (2007). Ethnomathematics in the global episteme: Quo vadis? In B. Atweh, M. Borba, A. Barton, N. Gough, C. Keitel, C. Vistro-Yu,

& R. Vithal (Eds.). *Internationalization and Globalization of Mathematics and Science Education*. Dordrecht, The Netherlands: Springer, 209–227.

Rose, P., & Greeley, M. (2006). Education in Fragile States: Capturing Lessons and Identifying Good Practice. Retrieved from http://www.ineesite.org/core_references/Education_in_Fragile_States.pdf on January 19, 2010.

Ross, A. (1996). Introduction. *Social Text 46/47*, 14(1 & 2), 1–13.

Ross, A. (2000). *Curriculum: Construction and Critique*. London and New York: Falmer.

Ross, L. (1977). The intuitive psychologist and his shortcomings: Distortions in the attribution process. In L. Berkowitz (Ed.). *Advances in Experimental Social Psychology*. Volume 10. New York: Academic Press, 173–240.

Roxborough, I. (1979). *Theories of Underdevelopment*. London: Macmillan.

Rubinstein, D. (2001). *Culture, Structure, and Agency: Toward a Truly Multidimensional Society*. London: Sage.

Said, E. W. (1979). *Orientalism*. New York: Vintage Books.

Said, E. W. (1984). *The World, the Text, and the Critic*. London: Faber and Faber.

Said, E. W. (1993). *Culture and Imperialism*. New York: Vintage Books.

Salam, A. H. A., & Waal, A. D. (Eds). (2001). *The Phoenix State: Civil Society and the Future of Sudan*. Lawrenceville, NJ: The Red Sea Press.

Salmond, A. (1985). Māori epistemologies. In J. Overing (Ed.). *Reason and Morality*. London: Tavistock Publications, 240–263.

Samoff, J., & Carrol, B. (2003). *From Manpower Planning to the Knowledge Era: World Bank Policies on Higher Education in Africa*. UNESCO Forum Occasional Paper Series Paper No. 2. Paris: UNESCO.

Saney, I. (2004). *Cuba: A Revolution in Motion*. London: Zed Books.

Santos, B. de Sousa. (Ed.). (2008). *Another Knowledge is Possible: Beyond Northern Epistemologies*. London: Verso.

Santos, B. de Sousa, Nunes, J.A., and Meneses, M.P. Introduction. Opening Up the Canon of Knowledge and Recognition of Difference. In Santos, B. de Sousa. (Ed.). (2008). *Another Knowledge is Possible: Beyond Northern Epistemologies*. London: Verso, ix- lxii.

Sarup, M. (1996). *Identity, Culture, and the Postmodern World*. Edinburgh: Edinburgh University Press.

Saunders, K. (Ed.). (2002). *Post-development Thought: Rethinking Modernity, Postcolonialism, and Representation*. London: Zed Books.

Save the Children. (2011). A Post-Independence Agenda for South Sudan. Retrieved from http://reliefweb.int/sites/reliefweb.int/files/resources/Full_Report_1746.pdf on January 4, 2012.

SciDev.net. (2011). Chile's flourishing market for indigenous medicine. Retrieved from http://www.scidev.net/po/features/medicina-indgena-em-alta-no-chile.html on January 26, 2012.

Semali, L., & Kincheloe J. (1999). Introduction: What is indigenous knowledge and why should we study it? In L. Semali & J. Kincheloe (Eds.). *What Is Indigenous Knowledge: Voices from the Academy*. London: Falmer, 3–57.

Shiva, V. (2007). Biodiversity, intellectual property rights, and globalization. In B. de Sousa Santos (Ed.). *Another Knowledge Is Possible: Beyond Northern Epistemologies*. London and New York: Verso, 272–288.

Sillitoe, P. (1998). The Development of Indigenous Knowledge. A New Applied Anthropology. *Current Anthropology, 39*(2), 223–235.

Sillitoe, P. (2000). Let them eat the cake.Indigenous knowledge, science, and the "poorest of the poor." *Anthropology Today, 16*(6), 3–7.

Simone, T. A. M. (1994). *In Whose Image? Political Islam and Urban Practices in Sudan*. Chicago and London: University of Chicago Press.

SIT Study Abroad. (2011). Chile: Public Health, Traditional Medicine, and Community Empowerment. Retrieved from http://www.sit.edu/studyabroad/ssa_cih.cfm on January 19, 2012.

Skeie, G. (1998). *En kulturbevisst religionspdagogikk.* PhD thesis. Trondheim: Norwegian University of Science and Technology.

Skocpol, T. (1982). Wallerstein's world capitalist system: A theoretical and historical critique. *American Journal of Sociology, 82*(5), 1075–1090.

Smith, G. H. (2000). Protecting and respecting indigenous knowledge. In M. Battiste, (Ed.). *Reclaiming Indigenous Voice and Vision.* Vancouver: University of British Columbia Press, 209–224.

Smith, A., & Vaux, T. (2003). *Conflict and International Development.* London: Department for International Development.

Smith, M. G. (1988). Pluralism, race, and ethnicity in selected African countries. In J. Rex & D. Mason (Eds.). *Theories of Race and Ethnic Relations.* Cambridge: Cambridge University Press, 187–226.

Sobe, N. W., & Timberlake, R. N. (2010). Staying the (post) socialist course: Global/local transformations and Cuban education. In I. Silova (Ed.). *Post-Socialism is not Dead: (Re) Reading the Global in Comparative Education.* International Perspectives on Education and Society, 14. Bingley, UK, Emerald, 351–367.

Sommers, M. (2005). *Islands of Education: Schooling, Civil War, and the Southern Sudanese.* Paris: UNESCO, IIEP.

Stiegler, U. (2008). From the assimilation to the acceptance of the other? Educational policy for indigenous people in Latin America and the "intercultural bilingual education" in Chile. *Revista electrónica teoría de la Educación: Educación y Cultura en la Sociedad de la Información, 9*(2), 52–76.

Syllabus For Primary Schools. (2002). Volume 2: *Primary 6–8.* Nairobi: New Sudan Curriculum Committee.

Tablata, C. (2003). *Che Guevara: Economics and Politics in the Transition to Socialism.* New York: Pathfinder.

Talbani, A. (1996). Pedagogy, power, and discourse: Transformation of Islamic education. *Comparative Education Review, 40*(1), 66–83.

Taylor, C. (1982). Rationality. In M. Hollis & S. Lukes (Eds.). *Rationality and Relativism.* Cambridge: MIT Press, 87–105.

Taylor, C. (1992). *Multiculturalism and the Politics of Recognition: An Essay by Charles Taylor.* Princeton, NJ: Princeton University Press.

Teffo, L. J., & Roux, A. P. J. (2000). Metaphysical thinking in Africa. In P. H. Coetzee & A. P. J. Roux (Eds.). *Philosophy in Africa.* Oxford: Oxford University Press, 292–305.

Teixeira-Poit, S., & Smith, K. I. (2008). Core and periphery relations: A case study of the Maya. *Journal of World-Systems Research, 14*(1), 22–49.

Thomas, E. (2010). *Against the Gathering Storm: Securing Sudan's Comprehensive Peace Agreement.* London: Chatham House.

Thompson, J. (1984). *Studies in the Theory of Ideology.* Cambridge: Polity Press.

Times Live. (2010). Nestle accused of SA bio-piracy. May 27. Retrieved from http://www.timeslive.co.za/business/article473765.ece/Nestle-accused-of-SA-bio-piracy on November 3, 2011.

Towards Sustainability. (2011). Resources for advancing a sustainable future. Retrieved from http://www.towards-sustainability.co.uk/ on November 6, 2011.

Tucker, V. (1999). The myth of development: A critique of Eurocentric discourse. In R. Munck & D. O'Hearn (Eds.). *Critical Development Theory.* London: Zed Books, 1–26.

Turnbull, D. (2007). *Masons, Tricksters and Cartographers: Studies in the History of Science, Technology, and Medicine.* London and New York: Routledge.

Turner, G (2008). *A Comparison of "The Limits to Growth" with Thirty Years of Reality*. Socio-Economics and the Environment in Discussion (SEED) Working Paper Series (2008–09)CSIRO (Commonwealth Scientific and Industrial Research Organization).

Tymoczko, T. (Ed.). 1986. *New Directions in the Philosophy of Mathematics*. Boston: Birkhauser.

UNEP. United Nations Environment Programme (2008). *Indigenous Knowledge in Disaster Management in Africa*. Nairobi, UNEP.

UNESCO. (1968). *The Use of the Vernacular Languages in Education Monographs on Fundamental Education VIII*. Paris: UNESCO.

UNESCO. (2002). *Education for Sustainability*. Retrieved from http://unesdoc.unesco.org/images/0012/001271/127100e.pdf on June 5 2008.

UNESCO. (2003). *Beginnings: Local & Indigenous Knowledge Systems (LINKS) Project*. Retrieved from http://portal.unesco.org/science/en/ev.php-URL_ID=4856&URL_DO=DO_TOPIC&URL_SECTION=201.html on August 6, 2009.

UNESCO. (2003–2004). *The EFA Global Monitoring Report . Gender and Education for All—The Leap to Equality*. Retrieved from http://www.unesco.org/new/en/education/themes/leading-the-international-agenda/efareport/reports/(2003)4-gender/ on January 14 2010.

UNESCO (2005 a). United Nations Decade of Education for Sustainable Development Retrieved from http://unesdoc.unesco.org/images/0014/001416/141629e.pdf on January 18 2009.

UNESCO. (2005b). *The EFA Global Monitoring Report (2005)*. Paris: UNESCO.

UNESCO. (2008). *Media as Partners in Education for Sustainable Development*. Retrieved from http://unesdoc.unesco.org/images/0015/001587/158787e.pdf on November 23 2010.

UNESCO. (2010). *Mobilizing Resources for International Development Cooperation in Education: What Innovative Mechanisms and Partnerships?* Retrieved from http://unesdoc.unesco.org/images/0019/001921/192179e.pdf on November 17, 2011.

UNESCO (2011a). *Global Monitoring Report. The Hidden Crisis: Armed Conflict and Education*. Retrieved from http://unesdoc.unesco.org/images/0019/001907/190743e.pdf on January 6 2012.

UNESCO. (2011b). *Building a Better Future: Education for an Independent South Sudan*. Retrieved from http://unesdoc.unesco.org/images/0019/001930/193052E.pdf on January 23 2012.

UNESCO (2011c). International Day of the World's Indigenous Peoples. Retrieved from http://www.unesco.org/new/en/natural-sciences/about-us/single-view/news/international_day_of_the_worlds_indigenous_peoples/ on January 3, 2012.

UNESCO/UNEP (2011). *Climate Change Starter's Guide Book*. Retrieved from http://unesdoc.unesco.org/images/0021/002111/211136e.pdf on November 3, 2011.

UNESCO Institute of Statistics. (2007). Chile. Retrieved from http://stats.uis.unesco.org/unesco/TableViewer/document.aspx?ReportId=121&IF_Language=eng&BR_Country=1520 on January 14, 2009.

UNESCO Institute of Statistics. (2009). Cuban Education. Retrieved from http://stats.uis.unesco.org/unesco/TableViewer/document.aspx?ReportId=121&IF_Language=eng&BR_Country=1920&BR_Region=40520 on November 3, 2010.

UNICEF. (2005). *Southern Sudan: Early Marriage Threatens Girls' Education*. Retrieved from http://www.unicef.org/infobycountry/sudan_28206.html on June 14, 2008.

UNICEF. (2006). *Teachers Go Back to School in Southern Sudan*. Retrieved from http://www.unicef.org/infobycountry/sudan_36089.html on June 14 2008.

UNICEF/AET. (2002). *School Baseline Assessment Report Southern Sudan.* May. Nairobi: UNICEF/AET.

Union for the Protection of New Varieties of Plants (UPOV). (1991). Retrieved from http://www.upov.int/portal/index.html.en on October 3, 2011.

United Nations. (1992). *The United Nations Conference on Environment & Development.* Retrieved from http://www.un.org/esa/sustdev/documents/agenda21/english/Agenda21.pdf on February 6, 2008.

United Nations. (2002a). *The Johannesburg Declaration on Sustainable Development.* Retrieved from http://trade.ec.europa.eu/doclib/docs/(2004)/april/tradoc_116827.pdf on February 6, 2008.

United Nations. (2002b). *Plan of Implementation. World Summit on Sustainable Development.* Retrieved from http://www.un.org/esa/sustdev/documents/WSSD_POI_PD/English/WSSD_PlanImpl.pdf on February 6, 2008.

United Nations. (2004). *The Concept of Indigenous Peoples.* Retrieved from https://docs.google.com/viewer?a=v&q=cache:9rD7tG63SQEJ:www.un.org/esa/socdev/unpfii/documents/workshop_data_background.doc+United+Nations.+(2004).+The+Concept+of+Indigenous+Peoples&hl=no&pid=bl&srcid=ADGEESicHBNzaPzbSAK9bSkH6ck_yawO_RZoQvTcWJOBeb2irOGJ8GDrd7-CdYxeG6PuKroWvg6PcvLWp8JIsWwEKHfCQTBMtLXxDXXjrTA1OVSo7-WApGoSO5UF4-W8vlVyFOQidrDDjN&sig=AHIEtbTMr-u7-T7Ph8q7_dyx7-JoNssM5Jg on April 3, 2009.

United Nations. (2010) "We can end poverty. 2015 Millennium Development Goals." Retrieved from http://www.un.org/millenniumgoals/education.shtml on January 5, 2011.

United Nations. (2010). *MDG Gap Task Force.* New York. Retrieved from http://www.un-ngls.org/spip.php?page=article_s&id_article=2977 on January 5, 2011.

United Nations Development Programme (UNDP). (2004).Human Development Report 2004: Cultural Liberty in Today's Diverse World. Retrieved from http://hdr.undp.org/reports/global/2004/pdf/hdr04_backmatter_1.pdf on June 15, 2011.

United Nations Development Programme (UNDP). (2011). *Sudan: Environment and Energy for Sustainable Development.* Retrieved from http://www.sd.undp.org/focus_environment.htm on December 2011.

United Nations Environment Programme (UNEP) (2007). *Sudan: Post-Conflict Environmental Assessment.* Nairobi, Kenya. Retrieved from http://postconflict.unep.ch/publications/sudan/00_fwd.pdf on May 6, 2009.

United Nations Environment Programme (UNEP). (2008). *Indigenous Knowledge in Disaster Management in Africa.* Nairobi, Kenya. Retrieved from http://www.unep.org/IK/PDF/IndigenousBooklet.pdf on April 3, 2008.

Van Noordwijk, M. 1984. *Ecology Textbook for the Sudan.* Khartoum: Khartoum University Press.

Van Rensburg, P. (2005). Acceptance Speech for the Right Livelihood Award. Retrieved from http://www.rightlivelihood.org/vanrensburg_pictures.html on December 3, 2011

Van Rooyen, M. J. (2010). *Experiences of Child Psychiatric Nurses: An Ecosystemic Study.* M. A. Thesis. University of South Africa.

Vasquez, G. R. (2010). Education from Inside Deep America. In L. Meyer & B. M. Alvarado (Eds.). *New World of Indigenous Resistance.* San Francisco: City Lights Books,277–283.

Ver Beek, K. A. (2000). Spirituality: A development taboo. *Development in Practice, 10*(1), 31–43.

Vivas, E. (2011). Anti-capitalism and environmentalism as a political alternative. *International Viewpoint, 439.* Retrieved from http://www.internationalviewpoint.org/spip.php?article2246 on December 20, 2011.

Walker, P. (2001). Journeys around the medicine wheel: A story of indigenous research in a Western university. *The Australian Journal of Indigenous Education, 29*(2), 18–21.

Wall, S. and Arden, H. 1990.*Wisdomkeepers. Meetings with Native American Spiritual Elders*. Beyond Words Publishing, Hillsboro

Wallerstein, I. (1989). *The Modern World-System III: The Second Era of Great Expansion of the Capitalist World Economy, 1730–1840*. New York: Academic Press.

Wallerstein, I. (1990). Culture as the ideological battleground of the modern world-system theory. *Culture and Society, 7*(2), 31–55.

Wallerstein, I. (1995). *Historical Capitalism, with Capitalist Civilization*. London: Verso.

Wallerstein, I. (1997). Eurocentrism and its avatars: The dilemmas of social science. *New Left Review, 226*, 93–107.

Wallerstein, I. (1999). *The End of the World as We Know It: Social Science for the Twenty-first Century*. Minneapolis: University of Minnesota Press.

Wallerstein, I. (2000a). From sociology to historical social science: Prospects and obstacles. *British Journal of Sociology, 51*(1), 25–35.

Wallerstein, I. (2000b). Globalization or the age of transition? A long-term view on the trajectory of the world-system. *International Sociology, 15*(2), 249–265.

Wallerstein, I. (2006). *European Universalism: The Rhetoric of Power*. New York: New Press.

Wallerstein, I. (2010). Structural crises. *New Left Review, 62*, 133–142.

Wane, N. N. (2006). Is decolonizing possible? In G. J. S Dei & A. Kempf (Eds.). *Anti-Colonialism and Education: The Politics of Resistance*. Rotterdam: Sense Publishers, 87–106.

Weber, M. (2001) *The Protestant Ethic and the Spirit of Capitalism*. Los Angeles: Roxbury. (Original publication 1905.)

White, H. (1987). *Tropics of Discourse: Essays in Cultural Criticism*. Baltimore, MD, and London: Johns Hopkins University Press.

White, L. (1974). *The Historical Roots of Our Ecological Crisis (with Discussion of St. Francis)*. Ecology and Religion in History. New York: Harper & Row.

Williams, E. (1996). Reading in Two Languages at Year Five in African Primary Schools. Retrieved from http://www.rdg.ac.uk/AcaDepts/cl/slals/reading2.htm on September 3, 2009.

Wolfensohn, J. (2001). A Great Job: Cuba and Social Justice. Red Feather Institute. Retrieved from http://uwacadweb.uwyo.edu/Red_Feather/CUBA/008report. html on June 7, 2007.

Wolff, H. E. (2006). Background and history—Language politics and planning in Africa. In H. Alidou, Y. S. Diallo, K. Heugh, H. E. Wolff, B. Brock-Utne, & A. Boly (Eds.).*Optimizing Learning and Education in Africa—The Language Factor. A Stock-taking Research on Mother Tongue and Bilingual Education in Sub-Saharan Africa*. Biennial Meeting. Gabon: ADEA, GTZ, and UNESCO, 26–55.

World Bank, The. (2008). *The Global Monitoring Report*. Retrieved from http://web.worldbank.org/WBSITE/EXTERNAL/EXTDEC/EXTGLOBALMONITOR/EXTGLOMONREP(2008)/0,menuPK:4738069_pagePK:64168427_piPK:64168435_theSiteP-_piPK:64168435_theSitePK:4738057,00.html on June 17, 2010.

World Bank, The. (2011,). *Education Strategy 2020*. Retrieved from http://web.worldbank.org/wbsite/external/topics/exteducation/0,,contentmdk:2 on November 6, 2011.

World Health Organization, The (WHO). (2011). *Traditional Medicine. Definitions*. Retrieved from http://www.google.com/search?hl=en&rls=com.

microsoft:no:IE-Address&q=related:www.who.int/medicines/areas/traditional/
definitions/en/index.html+WHO+traditional+medicine+for+diagnosis,+prevent
ion&tbo=1&sa=X&ei=PqfwTrP_COTX0QH4rsioAg&ved=0CCYQHzAA on
November 7, 2011.
World Trade Organization, The (WTO). (1994). TRIPS Agreement (the Trade-
Related Aspects of Intellectual Property Rights). Retrieved from http://www.
wto.org/english/tratop_e/trips_e/t_agm0_e.htm on April 6, 2010.
World Wildlife Fund. (2006). *Living Planet Report.* Gland: Switzerland.
World Wildlife Fund. (2010). *Living Planet Report.* Retrieved from http://www.
worldwildlife.org/who/financialinfo/2010AR/WWFBinaryitem18606.pdf on
February 12, 2011.
Wright, R. (2004). *A Short History of Progress.* Toronto: House of Anansi Press.
Yunkaporta, T. (2009). *Aboriginal Pedagogies at the cultural interface.* (PhD the-
sis). James Cook University. Retrieved from http://eprints.jcu.edu.au/10974/
3/03Portfolio.pdf on November 14, 2011.
ZDNet (2006).Google accused of biopiracy. Retrieved from http://www.zdnet.
co.uk/news/regulation/2006/03/29/google-accused-of-bio-piracy-39260264/
on November 3, 2010.
Zeleza, P. T. (2009). What happened to the African Renaissance? The challenges
of development in the twenty-First century. *Comparative Studies of South Asia,
Africa and the Middle East, 29*(2), 155–170.

Index